MARVEL VISIONARIES

MARVEL® VISIONARIES™: GIL KANE. Contains material originally published in magazine form as TALES TO ASTONIS TALES OF SUSPENSE #88-91; CAPTAIN MARVEL (Vol. 1) #17 and 23; DAREDEVIL (Vol. 1) #146; MARVEL PREMIERE #15; WHAT IF? (Vol. 1) #3 and #24; AMAZING SPIDER-MAN (Vol. 1) #99; MARVEL COMICS PRESENTS #116; M MARVEL WESTERN #44; KID COLT OUTLAW #161; WESTERN GUNFIGHTERS #31; and SUB-MARINER #44. First p August 2002. ISBN# 0-7851-0888-2. Published by MARVEL COMICS, a division of MARVEL ENTERTAINMENT GROU OFFICE OF PUBLICATION: 10 EAST 40th STREET, NEW YORK, NY 10016. Price $24.99 per copy in the U. $40.00 in Canada (GST# R127032852). Prir Canada. STAN LEE, Chairman Emeritus.

10 9 8 7 6 5 4 3 2 1

CREDITS

TALES TO ASTONISH #76
Writer: Stan Lee
Layouts: Jack Kirby
Pencils: Gil Kane
Inks: Mike Esposito
Letters: Art Simek
Color Restoration: Digital Chameleon

TALES OF SUSPENSE #88-89
Writer: Stan Lee
Illustrator: Gil Kane
Letters: Sam Rosen

TALES OF SUSPENSE #90-91
Writer: Stan Lee
Pencils: Gil Kane
Inks: Joe Sinnott
Letters: Art Simek

CAPTAIN MARVEL #17
Writer: Roy Thomas
Pencils: Gil Kane
Inks: Dan Adkins
Letters: Art Simek

AMAZING SPIDER-MAN #99
Writer: Stan Lee
Pencils: Gil Kane
Inks: Frank Giacoia
Letters: Art Simek
Color Restoration: Digital Chameleon

MARVEL PREMIERE #1
Writer: Roy Thomas
Pencils: Gil Kane
Inks: Dan Adkins
Letters: Sam Rosen

MARVEL PREMIERE #15
Writer: Roy Thomas
Pencils: Gil Kane
Inks: Dick Giordano
Letters: Gaspar Saladino
Colorist: Glynis Wein

WHAT IF? #3
Plot: Jim Shooter & Gil Kane
Script: Jim Shooter
Pencils: Gil Kane
Inks: Klaus Janson
Letters: Denise Wohl
Colorist: George Roussos

DAREDEVIL #146
Writer: Jim Shooter
Pencils: Gil Kane
Inks: Jim Mooney
Letters: Denise Wohl
Colorist: Don Warfield

WHAT IF? #24
Writer: Tony Isabella
Pencils: Gil Kane
Inks: Frank Giacoia
Letters: Tom Orzechowski
Colorist: Carl Gafford
Art Assists: Gafford, Poplaski,
Zalme & Albelo

MARVEL COMICS PRESENTS #116
Writer: Dan Slott
Illustrator: Gil Kane
Letters: Michael Higgins
Colorist: George Roussos

COVER COLORS:
Dan Kemp

COLOR CORRECTION:
Digital Chameleon, Patrick McGrath,
Miguel Villalobos & Jeof Vita

SPECIAL THANKS:
Tom Brevoort, David G. Hamilton,
Joe Heffernan, Dan Herman,
Ralph Macchio, Paul Shiple & Roy Thomas

EDITOR-IN-CHIEF:
Joe Quesada

PRESIDENT:
Bill Jemas

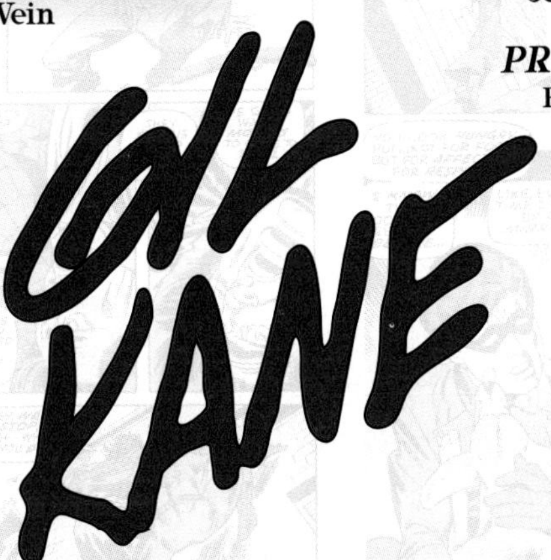

THE MARK OF KAN

By Roy Thomas

As a young man in the 1940s, Gil Kane had drawn a few stories here and there for Timely/Marvel Comics. But he spent the '50s and the first half of the '60s primarily at DC Comics, where he became the original artist of the Silver Age Green Lantern and Atom. Still, he was always restless — a wanderer at heart — and in the 1960s and '70s, he came into his own as an artist at Marvel. His work during that period — and since — has influenced Jim Starlin, Frank Miller and many another upcoming talent.

Like many other artists, of course, he penciled his first 1960s Marvel story over layouts by Jack Kirby, for inking by a third artist. And like others who also were drawing for DC in those days, he did it under a pseudonym — "Scott Edward," taken from the name of his son. For whatever reason, neither he nor writer/ editor Stan Lee was overjoyed with the Hulk story in *Tales to Astonish #76 (1966).* All the same, ere long, Gil drew a few covers for Marvel — and even four more Incredible Hulk episodes, this time doing full art.

It was while drawing Ol' Greenskin the second time around that he was tapped by Stan to illustrate Captain America, which "King" Kirby was too busy to continue. Gil both penciled and inked Cap in *Tales of Suspense #88-90* — but in #91, Stan had Gil's pencils embellished by Joltin' Joe Sinnott, then hitting his stride on *Fantastic Four* as Kirby's ultimate inker. This 1967 story arc marked Gil's last work for Marvel for a while, as he focused on producing his paperback opus *Blackhawk* — one of the first true graphic novels, which would debut the next year.

Circumstances kept bringing Gil back to comics in general, and to Marvel in particular. Though I was a writer and associate editor for Marvel, Gil's path and mine rarely had crossed. But one day in 1969, he waltzed into the Bullpen and told Stan he'd love to draw *Captain Marvel*, not exactly one of our most successful titles. Coincidentally, this was only a few days after I had revamped both Cap and his costume, and taken back the scripting reins. Gil loved my story, I loved his art (ably inked by Dan Adkins) ... and a lifelong friendship based on mutual respect and common interests was born. The original art for the *Captain Marvel #17* splash has hung in my foyer ever since. We stayed together only long enough to do five issues of *CM* — but it was a pure, unadulterated joy.

After that, he and I worked together whenever we got the chance. When I decided to launch a new feature that would be Marvel's answer to the phenomenal *Jesus Christ Superstar*, Gil was my first choice for artist; in *Marvel Premiere #1*, we developed "Warlock" — Adam Warlock, once Gil suggested giving him a first name. Again, we lined up Dan Adkins, always one of Gil's favorite inkers (besides himself) — even though after three "Warlock" stories, we got too busy elsewhere to continue our collaboratio always considered Captain Marvel and Wa among his personal favorites of projects he'd w on. Me, too.

Beyond a doubt, however, Gil's most important as ment at Marvel was *Amazing Spider-Man*. He pen the book off and on (mostly on) from 1970-73, inked and always overseen by his predecessor, Romita — whether the writer was Stan, Gerry Co or myself. "A Day in the Life of...," from #99, is a st alone story that spotlights the Lee-Kane team.

One night in 1974, I saw my first Kung Fu movie – the next morning, got Stan's OK to devel feature called "Iron Fist." Having decided only th would be a masked Kung Fu super hero wit insignia branded onto his chest, I approached G and together, we designed the hero and plotted his gin, which was beautifully inked by Dick Gior (For reasons I can't recall, Gil and I did only that Iron Fist installment, in *Marvel Premiere #15*, handed over our ideas to writer Len Wein, who on them from there.)

Though Gil never did as extended a run at Marv any hero as he did on *Amazing Spider-Man* nonetheless produced some formidable work w ever he felt challenged and stimulated. His 1977 o with scripter Jim Shooter in *What If #* considered a high point of that title's first series, he did a likewise memorable job on *Daredevil* also written by Shooter. And in *What If #24*, scripter Tony Isabella, Gil drew an alternate-w version of "The Death of Gwen Stacy," the artist's famous moment on *Amazing Spider-Man*.

If such were our task, we could fill a volume sev times thicker than this one with outstanding sto drawn by Gil Kane: those *Tales to Astonish* Hull his two best-selling issues of *Conan the Barba* (#17-18) ... "The Death of Gwen Stacy," of course.. illustrations for Kipling's Mowgli stories in *Ma Fanfare*... his excellent *Warlord of Mars* with M Wolfman and Rudy Nebres ... and during the 19 probably more action-packed, memorable Ma covers than ever were produced by any other ar before or since!

Fans and professionals the world over agree before his untimely death in January 2000, Gil lef mark both on Marvel and on the world of comic a

The Mark of Kane is a living monument left by a Marvel visionary.

Roy Thomas was a writer and editor for Marvel Comics from 80, and the company's editor-in-chief from 1972-74. Since mid-'80s, he has written numerous additional stories for Ma most recently The Ultron Imperative *with Kurt Busiek.*

THE INCREDIBLE HULK!
"I, AGAINST A WORLD!"
SUPPOSE YOU SAW THE HULK HURTLING TOWARDS THE WHITE HOUSE IN WASHINGTON, D.C.? WOULD YOU BELIEVE HE MERELY WANTED TO TELL THE PRESIDENT THAT RICK JONES NEEDS HIS HELP? OR, IN AN EFFORT TO SAFEGUARD THE CHIEF EXECUTIVE, WOULD YOU FIRE THE FANTASTIC T-GUN* AT HIM, AS THE TROOPS UNDER GENERAL ROSS' COMMAND DID, LITTLE DREAMING HE WOULD INSTANTLY VANISH, THEN REAPPEAR IN THE FAR DISTANT FUTURE!!
IT IS THE HULK--HE OF WHOM OUR ANCIENT LEGENDS TELL! BEWARE HIS BRUTAL POWER!
EVEN IN THE FUTURE I GOTTA FIGHT FOR MY LIFE AGAINST EVERYONE ELSE!
STAY BACK!! BACK!! YOU'RE JUST A PACK OF MEN--BUT ME, I'M THE HULK!
*T-GUN: EXPERIMENTAL DEVICE INVENTED BY BRUCE BANNER! SO NAMED BECAUSE ITS PURPOSE IS TO DISTORT LIGHT WAVES, AS A METHOD OF TIME TRAVEL!
LIVING PROOF THAT TEAMWORK PAYS OFF--!
SCRIPT.........STAN LEE
LAYOUT.......JACK KIRBY
PENCILLING....SCOTT EDWARD
INKING........MICKEY DEMEO
LETTERING.....ARTIE SIMEK
NO WONDER IT'S ANOTHER MARVEL MASTERWORK!
1

PROPELLED BY THE MOST INCREDIBLY POWERFUL ARMS OF ANY HUMAN, THE GIGANTIC BOULDER THUNDERS TO THE GROUND, SHATTERING WITH THE EXPLOSIVE FORCE OF A DOZEN MORTAR SHELLS--!

I'M THRU RUNNING! THRU BEING HOUNDED! NOBODY'S ATTACKING ME AGAIN-- NOBODY!!

WHOOM

PROTECT YOURSELVES! FORCE ALONE CANNOT STOP HIM! BUT WE HAVE OTHER MEANS!

E'S PREPARING TO
HARGE!! ONLY THE
ELTA MISSILE CAN
TOP HIM! FIRE!!

MISSILE STRAIGHT ON TARGET! IMPACT ASSURED!
NO MISSILE CAN HURT THE HULK!!
SSSSSSS

THEN, BEFORE THE SOUND OF THE GREEN GOLIATH'S THUNDEROUS CHALLENGE CAN DIE AWAY, HE WHO HAD BEEN BRUCE BANNER IS SWALLOWED UP BY THE SMOKE AND DEBRIS OF THE EXPLODING MISSILE!
KA-BOOM!

BUT, WHEN THE SMOKE CLEARS--WHEN THE CARNAGE BEGINS TO SUBSIDE--WHEN THE DEAFENING ECHO FADES INTO NOTHINGNESS--ONE FACT REMAINS--THOUGH SHAKEN AND STUNNED, THE HULK STILL STANDS!!
LOOK!! HOW CAN IT BE?? HE SURVIVED A DIRECT HIT! HE STILL LIVES!
NO MISSILE--CAN HURT--THE--HULK--!

TRULY THIS SURPASSES ALL REASON--ALL UNDERSTANDING!
SUCH A BEING IS FAR TOO WONDROUS TO BE DESTROYED! HE MUST BE CAPTURED! HE MUST BE STUDIED!
BRING YOU FORTH, THEN--THE CAPTIVATOR!
3

INSTANTLY, A STRANGE MACHINE LUMBERS TOWARDS THE HULK--OPERATED BY WIRELESS REMOTE CONTROL...
WHAT MAKES THEM THINK THIS THING CAN STOP ME??
I'LL RIP IT APART WITH MY BARE HANDS!
NOT SO, MIGHTY ONE! EVEN YOU CANNOT RESIST THE PRESSURE OF CONCENTRATED GRAVITY-- NOTHING THAT LIVES CAN!
DESPITE YOUR AWESO POWER, YOU ARE FAC THE SCIENTIFIC MARV OF THE 25TH CENTU --MARVELS YOU HAV NEVER DREAMED
THE HEAVY GRAVITY IS TAKING EFFECT! HE IS STIFFENING! WE HAVE WON!
HIS BRAIN, SUCH AS IT IS, CAN STILL THINK! HIS LIMBS CAN STILL FEEL! BUT HE IS POWERLESS TO MOVE!
IT CAN'T LAST FOREVER! SOONER OR LATER, I'LL SMASH THEM--!
QUICKLY! BEFORE THE EFFECTS WEAR OFF-- HE MUST BE SECURED!
WE'LL TAKE HIM TO TH FORTRESS-- WHILE W STILL CAN!
ONE OF THE PARADOXES OF TIME IS THE FACT THAT PAST, PRESENT, AND FUTURE EXIST SIMULTANEOUSL THUS, EVEN AS THE HULK IS ENCIRCLED, IF WE WERE TO TURN MANY HUNDRED YEARS INTO THE PAST, WE WOULD FIND-- ON THE WHITE HOUSE LAWN...
KEEP SEARCHING! THERE MUST BE A TRACE OF THE HULK SOME-WHERE!
THIS IS WHERE HE STOOD WHEN THE BLAST STRUCK HIM!
BUT HE'S GONE! AS THOUGH HE HAD NEVER EXISTED!
NO SIGN OF HULK! T-GUN MUST BE SOME SORT OF DISINTEGRATOR! OVER--!
NEGATIVE! IT IS KNOWN THAT BANNER WAS NOT WORKING ON DISINTEGRATOR! KEEP SEARCHING --BY ORDER OF GENERAL ROSS!
IF WE DON'T FIND THAT GREEN GARGOYLE, "THUNDERBOLT" ROSS'LL BE IN THE SOUP! THE CHIEF OF STAFF WILL HAVE HIS HIDE!

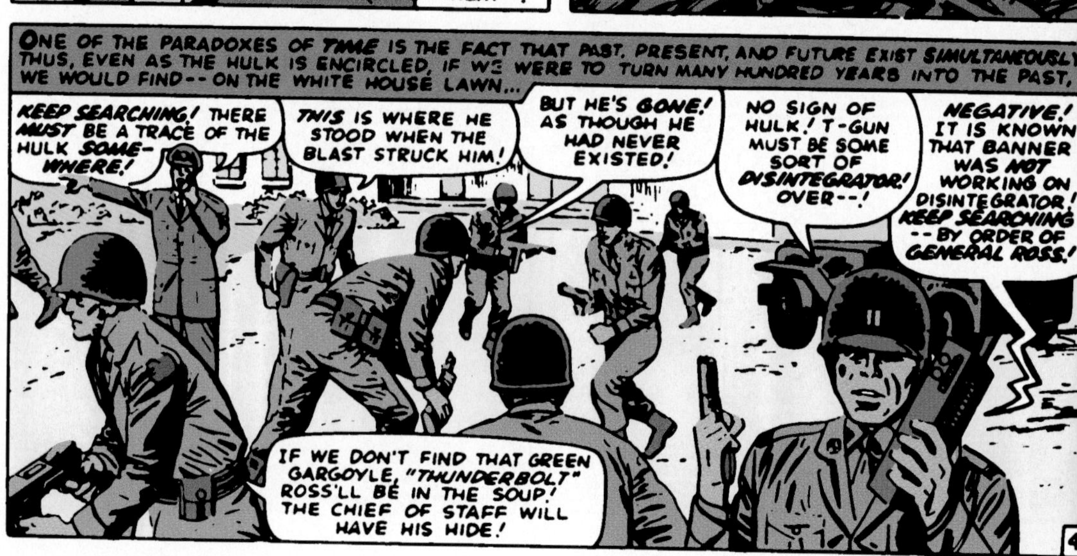

ENERAL, IF THE T-GUN OMIZED THE HULK, IT OULD HAVE DESTROYED ME OF THE TERRAIN EAR HIM, TOO-- BUT VERYTHING IS STILL INTACT!
I KNOW IT, TALBOT!! I'VE GOT EYES TO SEE WITH, HAVEN'T I? NOW STAND AT EASE, MAJOR, AND LET ME THINK!
UNTIL WE FIND OUT WHAT HAPPENED TO THE HULK, WE WON'T DARE USE THE T-GUN AGAIN!! GET EVERY AVAILABLE MAN, BUT BRING ME RESULTS, BLAST IT!
GENERAL, THE DEPUTY CHIEF OF STAFF IS ON HIS WAY TO SEE YOU, SIR!
OF ALL THE DOD-BLAMED, DING-BUSTED LUCK! WHAT IN SAM HILL AM I GOING TO TELL HIM??!!
TENNNN-HUT!!
AS YOU WERE, MEN! WHERE IS GENERAL ROSS??

GHT HERE, SIR! I ASN'T EXPECTING YOU SO SOON!
WHAT DIFFERENCE DOES THAT MAKE, GENERAL?? I HEARD THAT YOU LOST THE HULK! I WANT AN EXPLANATION, AND I WANT IT NOW!
YOU'LL HAVE TO GIVE ME MORE TIME, SIR!

MORE TIME??! YOU HAD THAT MUSCLE-BOUND FREAK RIGHT IN FRONT OF YOU! YOU WERE ARMED WITH OUR LATEST DEFENSIVE WEAPONRY! AND YOU BUNGLED THE JOB! AM I RIGHT, OR NOT??
NOW, HOLD ON, GENERAL! DON'T LET THAT ONE EXTRA STAR GO TO YOUR HEAD! THIS IS STILL MY ASSIGNMENT-- AND I'LL HANDLE IT MY WAY!

LL RIGHT, ROSS! WE WERE LASSMATES TOGETHER AT THE OINT-- AND YOUR DIVISION AS PULLED PLENTY OF HESTNUTS OUT OF THE FIRE OR THE PENTAGON TILL NOW! O I'LL GIVE YOU MORE TIME!
BUT HEAR THIS! THE HIGH COMMAND WANTS THE HULK-- OR WE WANT TO KNOW WHAT HAPPENED TO HIM! AND IF YOU CAN'T DELIVER, WE'LL GET SOME-ONE WHO CAN!
I READ YOU, SIR! THE HULK WILL BE FOUND!

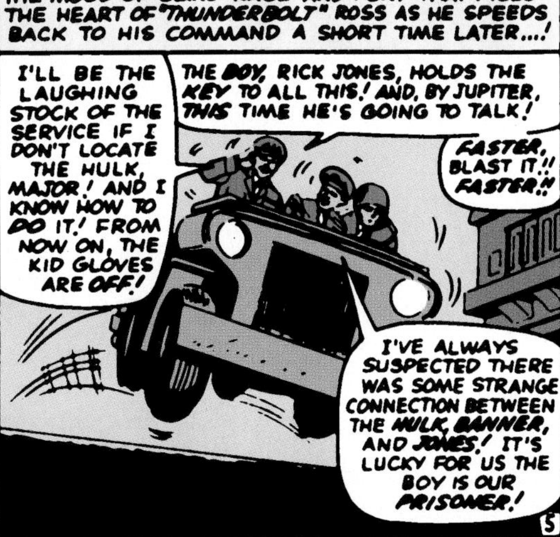

NO MERE WORDS OF OURS CAN FULLY DESCRIBE THE MOOD OF BLIND RAGE AND FURY THAT FILLS THE HEART OF "THUNDERBOLT" ROSS AS HE SPEEDS BACK TO HIS COMMAND A SHORT TIME LATER...!
I'LL BE THE LAUGHING STOCK OF THE SERVICE IF I DON'T LOCATE THE HULK, MAJOR! AND I KNOW HOW TO DO IT! FROM NOW ON, THE KID GLOVES ARE OFF!
THE BOY, RICK JONES, HOLDS THE KEY TO ALL THIS! AND, BY JUPITER, THIS TIME HE'S GOING TO TALK!
FASTER, BLAST IT!! FASTER!!
I'VE ALWAYS SUSPECTED THERE WAS SOME STRANGE CONNECTION BETWEEN THE HULK, BANNER, AND JONES! IT'S LUCKY FOR US THE BOY IS OUR PRISONER!
5

MEANWHILE, IN THE GRIM, OMINOUS WAR-TORN WORLD OF THE FAR *FUTURE*, THE STILL-MOTIONLESS *HULK* IS TRANSPORTED TO THE CITADEL OF HIS CAPTORS--

ONCE WE ENTER THE STONE FORTRESS, THE HULK WILL BE FOREVER WITHIN OUR POWER!

THAT'S WHAT *THEY* THINK! I FEEL THAT GRAVITY STUFF STARTIN' TO WEAKEN *NOW*!

THIS DUNGEON WAS CREATED TO WITHSTAND THE STRONGEST WEAPONS KNOWN TO MAN!
BUT, THE HULK IS NOT MERELY A WEAPON!! HIS STRENGTH EXCEEDS ANY POWER EVER KNOWN! AND HE IS GUIDED BY A HUMAN BRAIN!
ENOUGH TALK! FINISH THE JOB, AND LET US DEPART!

BUT, SECONDS AFTER THE MASSIVE CONCRETE DOOR SWINGS SHUT...
THEY DIDN'T EXPECT ME TO SNAP OUT OF IT SO FAST! BUT, I FOOLED 'EM!
SO THIS IS THE WORLD OF THE FUTURE! IT'S JUS A BIG NOTHIN'!! THEY ALL LOOK SCARED OF THEIR OW SHADOWS! I WONDER WHY.
AWW, WHAT DO I CARE?? I CAN LICK 'EM ALL! I'M THE HULK!! AND I GOT A LOT OF PAYIN' BACK T DO!

T BEFORE I TAKE IS PLACE APART, BETTER THINK-- UST LIKE BRUCE ANNER WOULDA DONE! I GOTTA GURE OUT HOW TO T BACK TO MY OWN TIME!
SOMETIMES THE CLOUDED BRAIN OF THE BESTIAL TITAN FORGETS THAT HE AND BRUCE BANNER ARE TRULY ONE AND THE SAME --FOR, LITTLE BY LITTLE, THE ORIGINAL NORMAL IDENTITY OF BANNER IS SUBMERGED BY THE STRONGER, MORE BRUTAL ESSENCE OF-- THE HULK!!

I'LL PLAY ALONG WITH 'EM FOR A WHILE--UNTIL I FIND OUT IF THEY HAVE SOME WAY FOR ME TO GET BACK AGAIN!
WITH ALL THE BIG SCIENTIFIC BRAINS AROUND HERE, THERE MAY BE SOME KINDA MACHINE, OR SOMETHING--!
AND, IF THERE IS, I'LL FIND IT-- IF I HAVETA TEAR THIS WHOLE WORLD APART--STONE BY STONE!!!

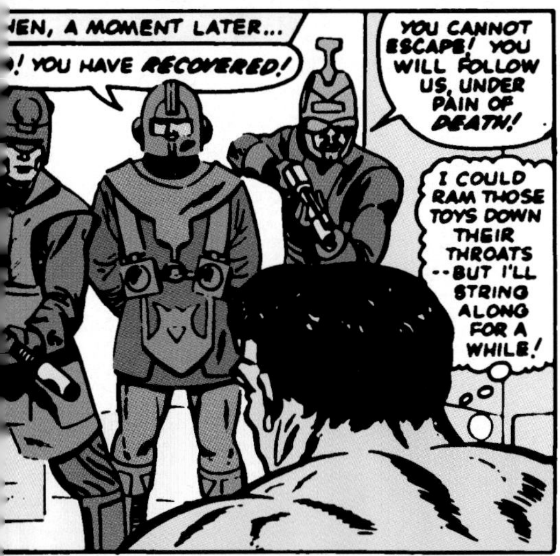
HEN, A MOMENT LATER...
! YOU HAVE RECOVERED!
YOU CANNOT ESCAPE! YOU WILL FOLLOW US, UNDER PAIN OF DEATH!
I COULD RAM THOSE TOYS DOWN THEIR THROATS --BUT I'LL STRING ALONG FOR A WHILE!

COME! KING ARRKAM IS NOT TO BE KEPT WAITING!
THEN MOVE-- BEFORE I STEP DOWN AND FLATTEN YA!

EED MY WORDS, LEGENDARY REATURE FROM THE DISTANT AST! DESPITE OUR GREAT CIENTIFIC KNOWLEDGE, OUR AGE IS IN DIRE PERIL!
THE EVIL ONE, WHOSE NAME ITSELF REPULSES US, THREATENS OUR LIBERTY, OUR CIVILIZATION, YEA--OUR VERY LIVES!
THAT'S YOUR PROBLEM! I GOT OTHER THINGS ON MY MIND!
HOLD YOUR TONGUE, BRUTE! YOU ARE ADDRESSING THE KING!
7

I KNOW WHAT YOU'RE LEADING UP TO!! YOU GOT SOME KINDA WAR ON YOUR HANDS, AND YOU WANT MY HELP! WELL, FORGET IT!
THE HULK DON'T CARE WHO'S THE GOOD GUYS OR THE BAD GUYS!!
STOP HIM! HE ADVANCES UPON HIS MAJESTY!

GET BACK, YOU FLEAS!! I HAD ENOUGH TALK!! I WANT OUT-- AND I WANT IT NOW!
IF YOU HAVE A MACHINE TO SEND ME BACK TO MY OWN TIME, USE IT ON ME. IF NOT, I'LL CAUSE MOR DAMAGE THAN A HUNDRE "EVIL ONES"!

KING ARRKAM YIELDS TO NO THREATS!! ATTACK HIM, MY LOYAL LEGIONS!!
DESPITE HIS SUPERHUMAN STRENGTH, YOU CAN OVER-WHELM HIM BY SHEER FORCE OF NUMBERS!!
YEAH? THAT'LL BE THE DAY!!

WE'LL RUSH HIM ALL AT ONCE!! HE CAN'T STOP ALL OF US!!
YOU STILL DON'T KNOW WHAT YOU'RE UP AGAINS HUH?? YOU STILL DON' KNOW THE POWER OF T HULK!!

THEN, MOVING WITH UNCANNY SPEED FOR ONE SO HUGE, THE GREEN BEHEMOTH SUDDENLY TEARS UP AN ENTIRE SECTION OF THE STONE FLOOR, WITH THE SUDDEN FORCE OF A THUNDERCLAP--!
YOU GOT A LOT TO LEARN ABOUT ME--!
AND HERE'S WHERE YOU'RE GONNA START--!!
SKRUNCH!

THIN SECONDS, THE RAGING RAMPAGER HAS ATTERED THE VANGUARD OF HIS FOES LIKE NPINS--!
HE OTHERS RE RUNNIN' AWAY!
WAIT! HERE ARE TWO YA FORGOT! I'LL TOSS 'EM AFTER YOU--!
RRAK!
THWAP!

BUT, THE SUPPLY OF FUTURISTIC WEAPONS WHICH CAN BE TURNED AGAINST THE HULK SEEMS VIRTUALLY INEXHAUSTIBLE...
PREPARE TO FIRE! POINT BLANK RANGE!
IF ANYTHING CAN STOP THAT ABORIGINE, THIS HIGH-INTENSITY PARALYZER HOWITZER WILL DO IT!
HURRY! NO TELLING WHAT HE'LL DO NEXT!

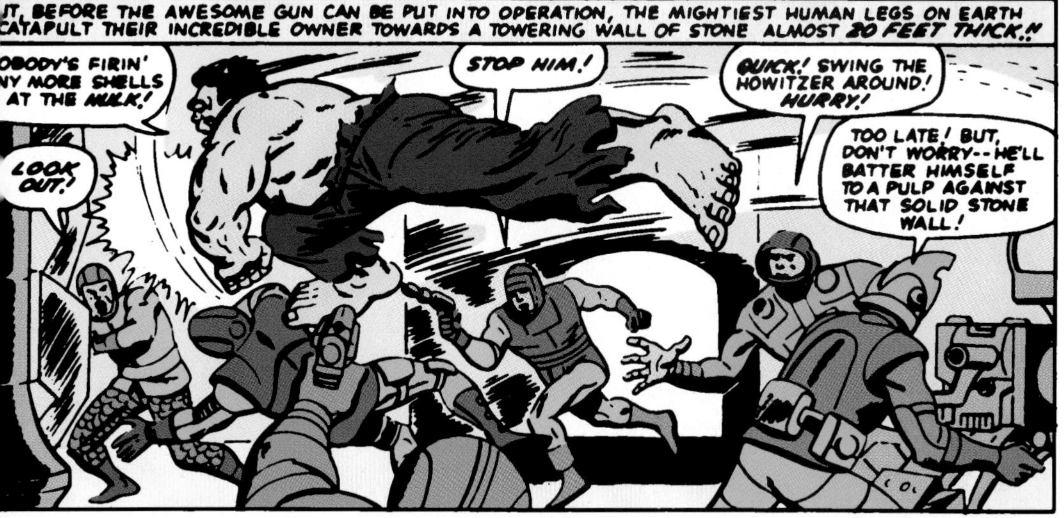
T, BEFORE THE AWESOME GUN CAN BE PUT INTO OPERATION, THE MIGHTIEST HUMAN LEGS ON EARTH CATAPULT THEIR INCREDIBLE OWNER TOWARDS A TOWERING WALL OF STONE ALMOST 20 FEET THICK!!
OBODY'S FIRIN' NY MORE SHELLS AT THE HULK!
LOOK OUT!
STOP HIM!
QUICK! SWING THE HOWITZER AROUND! HURRY!
TOO LATE! BUT, DON'T WORRY--HE'LL BATTER HIMSELF TO A PULP AGAINST THAT SOLID STONE WALL!

HEY THINK I'LL NOCK MYSELF UT WHEN I HIT!!
THAT'S WHY I ALWAYS HAVETA WIN!! NOBODY CAN BELIEVE HOW STRONG I REALLY AM!
CRASH!

THEN, WITH ONLY HIS BARE HANDS--WITH FINGERS STRONGER THAN STEEL GRAPPLING-HOOKS, THE GREEN-SKINNED BEHEMOTH LITERALLY TEARS THE WALL APART IN HIS FRANTIC SURGE TOWARDS FREEDOM--!
NOTHIN' CAN STOP THE HULK!! NOT NOW OR EVER!
SKRAK!
KRUNTCH!
THUMP!
9

THE PACE QUICKENS! THE PLOT THICKENS! A NEW WORLD OF WONDERMENT AWAITS YOU NEXT ISSUE! NO HIP HULK-LOVER CAN AFFORD TO MISS IT!

TALES OF SUSPENSE
featuring
IRON MAN AND CAPTAIN AMERICA
APPROVED BY THE COMICS CODE AUTHORITY
VEL
ICS
UP
88
APR
FEATURING:
POWER MAN!
THE SWORDSMAN!
And A MADLY MENACING
MYSTERY
VILLAIN!

STAN LEE PRESENTS: CAPTAIN AMERICA, LIVING LEGEND of WORLD WAR

ANAGED TO BREAK AWAY G ENOUGH TO BEAM THIS MESSAGE TO AVENGERS HQ!
YOU READ ME, COME TO A GULL ISLE, OFF THE STERN TIP OF NOVA SCOTIA!
URRY, CAP! THEY'RE OMING AGAIN! THEY'VE FOUND ME...!
L BE ERE, AD!
NOTHING THAT LIVES CAN STOP ME NOW!

JARVIS! ALERT THE AVENGERS! I'VE GOT TO LEAVE MY POST!
VERY GOOD, SIR! HAWKEYE IS YOUR ALTERNATE FOR THIS TOUR OF DUTY! I'LL CONTACT HIM AT ONCE!
WHERE SHALL I SAY YOU'VE GONE..?
TELL THEM I HAD TO--- NO! SAY NOTHING!
I'VE NEVER ABANDONED MY OFFICER-OF-THE-DAY POST BEFORE!
BUT, I'VE NEVER HAD SUCH CAUSE!
THEY'D JUST THINK--- I'M INSANE!

ONY STARK'S NEW SUPERSONIC RUISER IS THE FASTEST OF ALL OUR SHIPS!
IT'S LUCKY I GAVE IT A SHAKE-DOWN FLIGHT ONLY THIS MORNING! I'LL HAVE IT AIRBORNE WITHIN SECONDS!
USING ITS PROTOTYPE SOLAR CELLS FOR POWER, ANY POINT ON EARTH IS WITHIN ITS FLYING RANGE!
WHIRRRR

'VE FLOWN OVER EA GULL ISLE ANY TIMES--- BUT LWAYS THOUGHT IT AS JUST A BARREN, IFELESS CHUNK OF ROCK!
BUT, IF THAT'S WHERE BUCKY IS..!
NO! I MUSTN'T EVEN THINK IT! I MUSTN'T DARE ALLOW MYSELF TO HOPE!
SHOOOM!

BUT, THROUGH THE POWER OF OUR TIME-SPANNING IMAGINATION, LET US REACH SEA GULL ISLE MINUTES BEFORE THE STAR-SPANGLED AVENGER..AS WE SEE...
THIS IS THE PLACE --- BUT, THERE'S NOTHING THERE BELOW US!
WAIT! LOOK! THAT MOUNTAIN.. IT ISN'T A MOUNTAIN! IT'S MOVING--- LIKE A GIGANTIC, IMPOSSIBLE TRAP DOOR--!
SO...IT WASN'T A HOAX! THERE IS SOMEONE BELOW WHO OFFERED US A FORTUNE TO COME HERE!

BUT, WHO CAN IT BE CLEVER ENOUGH TO CAPTURE BOTH POWER MAN AND THE SWORDSMAN IN... LOOK!
ONCE YOU REALIZE THAT ALL THINGS ARE POSSIBLE, MY FRIEND... YOU WILL NEVER BE SHOCKED AGAIN!
BELOW US! IT-IT ISN'T POSSIBLE!
KKKAK
BUT, THE EQUIPMENT HERE... THE GIANT DYNAMOS... THE MACHINERY... ALL HIDDEN BENEATH A BARREN ISLAND... WHO COULD HAVE DONE IT?
THE SAME GENIUS WHO TRAPPED US WITHIN THIS PLASTIC BUBBLE... AND GUIDED IT HALF-WAY ACROSS THE CONTINENT... TO THIS VERY SPOT!
EVERYTHING BELOW IS CRACKLING WITH ENERGY! YOU CAN FEEL THE HUM... AND THE THROB OF RAW, HARNESSED FORCE ALL AROUND US!
NOW WE'RE ENTERING SOME KIND OF OVER-SIZED TUBE... WE'RE DROPPING DOWN... TO THE BOTTOM LEVEL!
RELAX, MY MIGHTY-MUSCLED FRIEND! IT WAS TO BE EXPECTED!
WHOEVER THE BRAIN BEHIND ALL THIS MAY BE... HE IS CERTAIN TO BE AWAITING US.. BELOW!

WE'VE LANDED! --AND LOOK!
THE PLASTIC BUBBLE WHICH WAS HOLDING US IS MELTING AWAY...!
NATURALLY! ITS ONLY PURPOSE WAS TO BRING US HERE...NOTHING MORE!
NOW WE'LL LEARN THE REAL REA-- WAIT!
LISTEN! THAT VOICE...FROM THE LOUDSPEAKER ABOVE--!
I BID YOU WELCOME! MY TRUE IDENTITY IS OF NO CONCERN TO YOU... BUT, SERVE ME WELL, AND YOU SHALL BE REWARDED BEYOND YOUR WILDEST DREAMS!
I HAVE BROUGHT YOU HERE TO DO THAT WHICH YOU DO BEST.. TO FIGHT A MIGHTY ENEMY!
NOT EVEN CAPTAIN AMERICA CAN STAND UP TO THE INVINCIBLE BLADE OF THE SWORDSMAN, OR TO POWER-MAN'S AWESOME, SUPER-HUMAN STRENGTH!

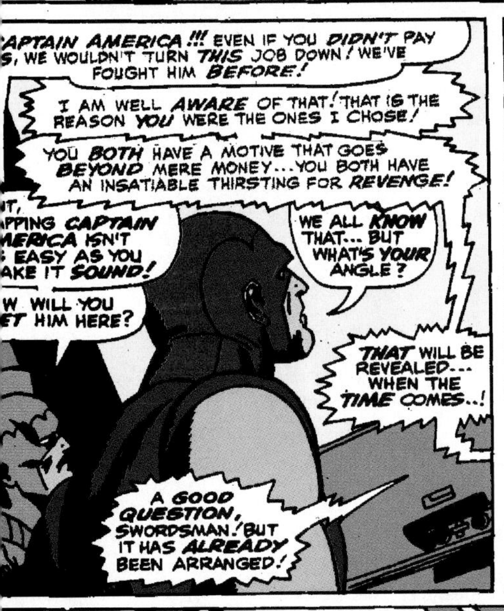
APTAIN AMERICA!!! EVEN IF YOU DIDN'T PAY S, WE WOULDN'T TURN THIS JOB DOWN! WE'VE FOUGHT HIM BEFORE!
I AM WELL AWARE OF THAT! THAT IS THE REASON YOU WERE THE ONES I CHOSE!
YOU BOTH HAVE A MOTIVE THAT GOES BEYOND MERE MONEY...YOU BOTH HAVE AN INSATIABLE THIRSTING FOR REVENGE!
IT, PPING CAPTAIN MERICA ISN'T S EASY AS YOU AKE IT SOUND!
W WILL YOU ET HIM HERE?
WE ALL KNOW THAT... BUT WHAT'S YOUR ANGLE?
THAT WILL BE REVEALED--- WHEN THE TIME COMES..!
A GOOD QUESTION, SWORDSMAN! BUT IT HAS ALREADY BEEN ARRANGED!

NOTICE THE AIR CRAFT WHICH EVEN NOW APPROACHES SEA GULL ISLE! ITS LONE OCCUPANT IS THE STAR-SPANGLED AVENGER... SEARCHING FOR HIS FORMER PARTNER---BUCKY!
BUT, BUCKY'S BEEN DEAD FOR YEARS! EVERYBODY KNOWS THAT!
WHO CARES ABOUT HIM... JUST SO LONG AS WE GET ANOTHER CRACK AT CAPTAIN AMERICA!
BUT, HOW COME WE WERE BROUGHT HERE TRAPPED IN A BUBBLE... AND HE ARRIVES UNDER HIS OWN STEAM?

SHALL NOT EMAIN "UNDER S OWN STEAM" CH LONGER! WATCH!
THAT NUTTY-LOOKIN' RAY GUN... WHAT'S IT DOING?
FIRING, OF COURSE! IT'S ABOUT TO CATCH AN AVENGER!
4.

SO THAT'S HOW THE PLASTIC BUBBLE IS CREATED! IT'S FORMED BY THE RAY GUN!
AS SOON AS THE BEAM REACHED ITS TARGET, IT SOLIDIFIED INTO A CIRCULAR SHAPE, SURROUNDING THAT ENTIRE AIRSHIP!
BUT... WHAT'S THE NEXT STEP?

AND, WITHIN THE NOW-CAPTIVE CRAFT, CAPTA AMERICA PONDERS THE SAME QUESTION...
THE SHIP'S CAUGHT WITHIN SOME STRANGE, ROUND PLASTIC GLOBE!
MY CONTROLS NO LONGER OPERATE!
WHOEVER IS WAITING DOWN BELOW WAS READY FOR AND I FLEW HEADLONG INT HIS TRAP!
BUT, I'D ENT A THOUSAN TRAPS... FO EVEN THE SLIMMES CHANCE O FINDING BUCK AGAIN

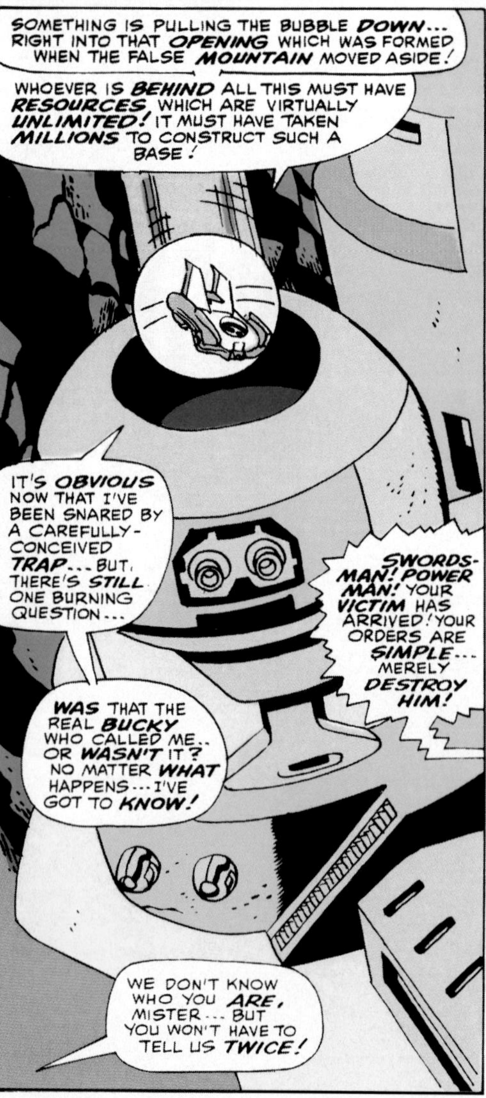

SOMETHING IS PULLING THE BUBBLE DOWN... RIGHT INTO THAT OPENING WHICH WAS FORMED WHEN THE FALSE MOUNTAIN MOVED ASIDE!
WHOEVER IS BEHIND ALL THIS MUST HAVE RESOURCES WHICH ARE VIRTUALLY UNLIMITED! IT MUST HAVE TAKEN MILLIONS TO CONSTRUCT SUCH A BASE!
IT'S OBVIOUS NOW THAT I'VE BEEN SNARED BY A CAREFULLY-CONCEIVED TRAP... BUT, THERE'S STILL ONE BURNING QUESTION...
WAS THAT THE REAL BUCKY WHO CALLED ME.. OR WASN'T IT? NO MATTER WHAT HAPPENS... I'VE GOT TO KNOW!
SWORDSMAN! POWER MAN! YOUR VICTIM HAS ARRIVED! YOUR ORDERS ARE SIMPLE... MERELY DESTROY HIM!
WE DON'T KNOW WHO YOU ARE, MISTER... BUT YOU WON'T HAVE TO TELL US TWICE!

HE'S LANDED! THE BUBBLE WILL BE FADING AWAY ANY SECOND, AND HE'LL BE FREE!
BUT, NOT FOR LONG, HE WON'T! AS SOON AS HE STEPS OUT OF THAT CONTRAPTION, HE'S GONNA BE MINE!
POWER MAN, YO A FOOL! HE BEA YOU IN THE PAS BECAUSE YOU D STOP TO USE Y HEAD
LET'S WORK A TEAM! YO CAN'T DEFEA CAPTAIN AME BY BRUTE STRENGTH ALONE!
THWUP!
REMEMBER THAT, BLADE-SLINGER! I GET 'IM FIRST!
ALL RIGHT, RUN, MUSCLE-BOUND MORON! I'LL CIRCLE AROUND THE OTHER WAY!

HERE HE COMES! NOW, I'LL JUST... UNNHHH!
RAK!
THE SWORDSMAN! IT CAN'T BE YOU WHO'S RESPONSIBLE FOR ALL THIS---!

...AND, I HAVEN'T TIME TO WASTE ON UNDER-LINGS!
PYONNG!
BLAST IT! HE PARRIED MY BLOW WITH HIS SWORD HILT!

ITHOUT THE OTHER AVENGERS R YOU TO FALL BACK ON, YOU LL NEVER ESCAPE MY FLASHING BLADE!
I'VE NO TIME FOR SMALL TALK, MISTER!
WHERE'S BUCKY?? IS HE HERE? HAVE YOU SEEN HIM??

ANSWER ME, YOU COSTUMED CREEP! WAS BUCKY HERE? WHERE IS HE? I'VE GOT TO KNOW---DO YOU HEAR? I'VE GOT TO KNOW!
THROP!
UNHHH--!

LL RIGHT, BIG AN! YOU'VE HAD IT!
NO MATTER HOW FAST... OR HOW CLEVER YOU ARE... YOU'LL NEVER ESCAPE FROM POWERMAN!
YOU TOO! I... SHOULD HAVE.. GUESSED!
6.

I ALWAYS SAID... THERE'S ONLY ONE THING THAT MATTERS... AND THAT'S POWER!
EVEN IF YOU HAD A MILLION SHIELDS, YOU COULDN'T SAVE YOURSELF FROM ME NOW!
DON'T NEED A MILLION!
ONE IS ALL IT TAKES TO CUSHION THE IMPACT OF HITTING THE WALL!
PKOWK!
KRRAZK

A LOT OF GOOD THAT'S GONNA DO YOU!
THE LONGER YOU KEEP FIGHTING BACK, THE MORE OF A BEATING YOU'LL TAKE... UNTIL YOU'RE DONE FOR!
THIS'LL TAKE SPLIT-SECOND TIMING! AS SOON AS HE'S IN POSITION... I'VE GOT TO MOVE! HIS OWN MOMENTUM WILL DO THE REST..!

NOW!
IT WORKED! BY DUCKING UNDER HIS LUNGE... AND PUNCHING IN THE DIRECTION OF HIS LEAP... I EMPLOY THE JUDO DEVICE OF FIGHTING HIM WITH HIS OWN FORCE!
HIS OWN STRENGTH SHOULD KNOCK HIM OUT MUCH SOONER THA I COULD HAVE DONE!

'LL KEEP
1 FOR A
ILE!
BUT, I'VE STILL GOT TO LEARN ABOUT BUCKY!
IT WAS HIS FACE ON THE SCREEN--- IT WAS HIS VOICE I HEARD! I KNOW IT! I COULDN'T MISTAKE A THING LIKE THAT!
THE SWORDSMAN! HE'LL KNOW! WHERE IS HE?
RIGHT HERE, MASKED MAN!
TAKE A REAL GOOD LOOK---
I'M PROBABLY THE LAST THING YOU'LL EVER SEE!
I FORGOT! HIS SWORD HAS ALL SORTS OF DEADLY DEVICES BUILT IN!
ZZZZZZZOKKK!
I'VE WAITED A LONG TIME FOR THIS GLORIOUS MOMENT, CAPTAIN AMERICA---
I'VE WAITED FAR TOO LONG FOR ME TO DENY MYSELF NOW!
YOU MUST BE DESTROYED! THERE'S NO OTHER WAY!
CLICK!
SPASS-ST!
THERE'S ONE WAY LEFT--!
WHAT IF I DECOY YOU INTO JUST THE STRIKING POSITION I WANT--- AND THEN DUCK?
ZAK!
YOUR SWORD'S BOLT WILL PASS HARMLESSLY OVER MY HEAD--- HITTING JUST THE SPOT I CHOSE --- BEHIND ME!

...THE MAIN ELECTRICAL CIRCUIT! I GAMBLED IT WOULD CAUSE A POWER FEEDBACK---SHOCKING YOU OUT OF ACTION!
ARGHHH..!
FIZZT
NOW...ALL THAT REMAINS IS TO FIND THE ONE BEHIND YOU...THE ONE WHO CREATED THIS DEADLY, DEMONIAC COMPLEX OF DESTRUCTION!

YOUR QUEST IS NEARLY AT AN END, CAPTAIN AMERICA!---I AM THE ONE YOU SEEK!
THEY WERE BUT BUMBLING CATSPAWS!
BUT, HAVE A CARE, AVENGER---FOR, ONLY I KNOW T SECRET OF YOUR YOUNG PARTNER'S RETURN!
IF I AM ATTACKED--IF ANY HARM SHOULD BEFAL ME---THEN THAT SECRET TOO SHALL PERISH!
SPEAK, THEN!
YOU HAD A REASON FOR LURING ME HERE! SPILL IT...WHILE YOU STILL CAN!
AHH...YOUR ANGER IS AWESOME TO BEHOLD...BUT, IT DOES NOT IMPRESS ME!

"FOR, I POSSESS POWER BEYOND YOUR IMAGINATION! IMAGINE THE SAME PLASTIC BUBBLE WITH WHICH YOU WERE CAPTURED... PICTURE IT A THOUSAND TIMES LARGER---FLOATING OVER ANY CITY ON EARTH..."

"SAFELY SHELTERED HERE, IN MY HIDDEN ISLE, HOW SIMPLE IT WILL BE FOR ME TO SET IT DOWN ON ANY SPOT I CHOOSE...BY MERELY UTILIZING MY REMOTE CONTROL APPARATUS..."

"AND, WHEN I RAISE IT ONCE AGAIN...THE CITY OF MY CHOICE SHALL BE HELPLESSLY IMPRISONE WITHIN---JUST AS YOU HAD BEEN
NOW, DO YOU PRESUME TO THREATEN ONE WHO CAN HOLD A CITY HOSTAGE??...ONE WHO SHALL SOON BE MASTER OF EARTH.

E TACKLED POWER-CRAZED MADMEN BEFORE!
'LL END UP THE SAME AS ALL THE OTHERS--!
NOW--- YOU'VE GOT FIVE SECONDS TO TELL THE TRUTH ABOUT BUCKY---!

SO! YOU CONSIDER ME MERELY A POWER-CRAZED MADMAN, DO YOU?
WATCH HOW QUICKLY I FORCE YOU TO CHANGE YOUR TUNE! FIRST--- I RENDER YOU TOTALLY HELPLESS--!
THE PLASTIC GLOBE!! IT'S ENGULFING ME AGAIN!!

CAN'T SCAPE! IT'S TOO FAST!!
HE--- SEEMS ABLE TO--- MAKE IT APPEAR-- OUT OF NOWHERE!
WHOOSH!

YOU WASTE YOUR TIME, CAPTAIN AMERICA! NOTHING CAN SHATTER MY LITTLE PLASTIC TRINKET--- UNLESS I SO DECIDE!
AND NOW--- BEFORE THE END COMES--- I SHALL CONFRONT YOU FACE-TO-FACE---
IT IS ONLY FITTING THAT I TELL YOU THE SECRET OF BUCKY --- BEFORE I DISPOSE OF YOU.. FOREVER!

E'S RIGHT! I CAN'T BREAK OUT! UT, AT LEAST I'LL SEE WHO MY CAPTOR IS---
IT MUST BE SOMEONE WHO HAS SOME REASON TO--- WHA--?!!
YOU!
I RATHER THOUGHT YOU WOULD BE SURPRISED!
FEAST YOUR EYES WELL UPON ME--- AS I SAVOR THIS TRIUMPHANT MOMENT--- FOR, I AM THE LAST SIGHT YOU WILL EVER AGAIN BEHOLD!!
NEXT ISSUE: "BACK FROM THE DEAD!"

Stan Lee PRESENTS: CAPTAIN AMERICA, LIVING LEGEND of WORLD WAR
"BACK FROM THE DEAD!"
THE RED SKULL! IT'S YOU! YOU'RE ALIVE!
OF COURSE, YOU WITLESS STAR-SPANGLED SIMPLETON!
I HAVE BEEN MERELY TOYING WITH YOU--PAYING YOU BACK IN KIND FOR THE FATE I NEARLY SUFFERED DUE TO YOUR BUMBLING INTERFERENCE!
LURED TO MYSTERIOUS SEA GULL ISLE BY A DESPERATE CALL FROM ONE WHO CLAIMED TO BE BUCKY BARNES, CAP'S FIGHTING PARTNER OF WORLD WAR II, THE GALLANT AVENGER SPEEDS TO THE SPOT, ONLY TO BE CHALLENGED BY POWER MAN AND THE SWASH-BUCKLING SWORDSMAN!
HOWEVER, OUR SHIELD-SLINGING SENTINEL SUCCEEDS IN DEFEATING THEM BOTH, ONLY TO COME FACE-TO-FACE WITH THE REAL MASTER OF MENACE WHO HAD PLANNED THE ENTIRE FATAL TRAP---!
AN AGONIZING, ACTION-PACKED EXTRAVAGANZA BY: SMILIN' STAN LEE and GREGARIOUS GIL KANE
LETTERED BY: SAM ROSEN || KIBITZED BY: IRVING FORBUSH
OH, BY THE WAY... "BACK FROM THE DEAD" DOESN'T MERELY PERTAIN TO THE RED SKULL HIMSELF! WHAT ELSE DO WE MEAN BY OUR TANTALIZING TITLE? HANG LOOSE, HERO--- SHOCK-TIME'S A' COMIN'---!

N I POSSESSED THE MATCHLESS
SMIC CUBE.. THOSE MANY MONTHS
O... I HAD THE ENTIRE WORLD IN THE
M OF MY HAND! *
THERE WAS NOTHING I COULD NOT ACCOMPLISH.. NO FOE I COULD NOT DEFEAT! THE UNEARTHLY POWER OF THE GLEAMING CUBE WAS MINE ALONE!
ON'T TAKE OUR WORD FOR IT,
EPTICAL ONE... IT'S ALL IN SUSPENSE
BI... JUST WHERE WE LEFT IT! .. SUPERCILIOUS STAN.

"BUT THEN, JUST WHEN I THOUGHT I HAD SCORED MY GREATEST VICTORY... WHEN I THOUGHT I HAD FINISHED YOU... FOREVER.. THE IMPOSSIBLE HAPPENED..!"
"THROUGH MY OWN MONUMENTAL CARE-LESSNESS, YOU TRANSFORMED MY TRIUMPH INTO A DISMAL, DISASTROUS DEFEAT!!

E IRREPLACEABLE CUBE WAS HURLED INTO THE SEA
LOW, AS I UNHESITATINGLY THREW MYSELF AFTER
E MOST PRICELESS, MOST OMNIPOWERFUL OBJECT
ALL THE WORLD!"

"BUT, IN MY BLIND, UNTHINKING PANIC, I FORGOT THAT I WAS WEARING A SUIT OF HEAVY ARMOR..ARMOR WHICH DRAGGED ME HELPLESSLY TO THE BOTTOM..."
"I KNEW I WAS DOOMED... AND YOU, TOO, LEFT THE SITE... GIVING ME UP FOR LOST--!"

BUT, SO FAR-REACHING WAS THE POWER OF THE CUBE,
AT ITS DISTANT RAYS STILL GAVE ME THE ENERGY I
EEDED TO REMAIN ALIVE WITHOUT OXYGEN..."

"AND, THOUGH THE SWIRLING SEA CARRIED IT EVER FURTHER FROM THE SPOT, STILL THE PULSATING IMPULSES BOLSTERED MY OWN STRENGTH UNTIL I WAS ABLE TO REACH THE SURFACE ONCE MORE!"
2.

"BY THE TIME I FINALLY REACHED SAFETY, YOU HAD LONG SINCE DEPARTED--- BUT MY BRAIN WAS ALREADY DEVISING A FITTING REVENGE UPON THE MAN WHO HAD COST ME MASTERY OF---THE WORLD!"
SEA GULL ISLE---ONE OF THE MANY VAST, SECRET INSTALLATIONS THE FUEHRER PROVIDED FOR ME IN THE DAYS WHEN WE THOUGHT THE REICH WOULD LIVE FOR A THOUSAND YEARS!
IT IS THERE... AMIDST MY GREATEST WEAPONS..THAT CAPTAIN AMERICA MUST MEET HIS DEATH!
AND NOW, SINCE I HAVE TRANSPORTED POWER MAN AND HIS SWORD-SWINGING ALLY AWAY FROM THIS ISLE, WE ARE FREE TO CONTINUE WITH OUR LETHAL LITTLE TABLEAU ---
THEN, WHEN YOU HAVE FINALLY MET THE FATE WHICH I HAVE PREORDAINED FOR YOU, I SHALL RESUME MY ETERNAL PLAN TO PUT ALL OF MANKIND UNDER THE MERCILESS RULE OF ITS MASTER...THE REDOUBTABLE RED SKULL!
NOTICE HOW MY UNCANNY PLASTIC BUBBLE TRANS-PORTS YOU WHEREVER I WISH IT TO!
IT IS JUST SUCH A DEVICE, MAGNIFIED MANY THOUSAND TIMES WHICH WILL BRING THE POWERS OF EARTH TO THEIR KNEES...
FOR I SHALL USE JUST SUCH AN UNSHATTERABLE BUBBLE TO IMPRISON ACTUAL CITIES, UNTIL A HELPLESS, TERROR-STRICKEN MANKIND BEGS THE RED SKULL FOR ITS OWN LIBERATION!
AND LIBERATE THEM I SHALL... ALTHOUGH IT WILL BE UPON MY TERMS ALONE!
HOWEVER, I FEAR MY SOLILOQUEY MAY PROVE TIRESOME TO YOU!
THEREFORE, LET US NOW RETURN TO THE MATTER AT HAND...NAMELY, THE FINAL EXECUTION OF CAPTAIN AMERICA!
NEEDLESS TO SAY THIS IS SO GRATIFYING AN EXPERIENCE.. SO LONG-AWAITED A VICTORY... THAT I DON'T WANT IT TO END TOO SOON.
THEREFORE, I TRUST YOU WILL FORGIVE ME IF I SEEM TO DELAY YOUR ULTIMATE DESTRUCTION JUST A LITTLE WHILE LONGER!
BY SIMPLY THROWING A SWITCH HE CAUSED A H OPENING TO APPEAR I THE FLOOR BENEATH
AND THE PLASTIC BUBBLE IS BRINGING ME DOWN TO THE BOTTOM AS THOUGH IT HAS A MIND OF ITS OWN!
A MAN OF ACTION SUCH AS YOURSELF SHOULD NOT BE SO RUDELY CONFINED!
THEREFORE, MY INSTINCTIVE SENSE OF CHARITY CAUSES ME TO SET YOU FREE!
THAK!
ALTHOUGH FREEDOM, ALAS, CAN BRING NEW DANGERS...AS YOU ARE NOW ABOUT TO LEARN!

SOUND OF A HEAVY
TAL DOOR--- SLIDING
PEN BEHIND ME!
NEW IT!
OTHER ONE
SKULL'S
ADLY PLAY-
NGS--- A
NT, ARMORED
OBOT!
CLANK!
SKASK!!
NOW FIGHT, YOU LIBERTY-LOVING FOOL!!
FIGHT FOR THE WORTHLESS, MISERABLE LIFE WHICH WILL SOON BE TAKEN FROM YOU.. FOREVER!
MATTER WHAT
PPENS..OR
W HOPELESS
SEEMS..I
ARE NOT
IVE UP!
HAH! YOUR SPEED IS AS DAZZLING AS EVER!
A PITY THAT IT SHALL SERVE YOU TO NO AVAIL!
FOR ALL I NEED DO IS INCREASE THE POWER OF MY ROBOT'S RAY!
NOT TILL I LEARN WHAT THE RED SKULL DOES KNOW ABOUT BUCKY BARNES!
N'T JUST
EMAIN HERE
LIKE A
SITTING
DUCK!
MY ONLY CHANCE IS TO DO THE UNEXPECTED--- I'VE GOT TO ATTACK--- BEFORE IT'S TOO LATE!
BTANNG!
NO USE! CAN'T GET PAST HIS BUILT-IN PROPELLER-LIKE DEFENSE!!
AND..HE KEEPS COMING CLOSER..!

HIS ARM--EXTENDING.. HURTLING LIKE A BATTERING RAM!
WHROOM!
HAD I BEEN A SPLIT-SECOND SLOWER... IT WOULD ALL BE OVER NOW!

BUT THEN, BEFORE THE ROBOT CAN MAKE ANOTHER MOVE, A FLASHING, SLASHING, GLISTENING STAR-SPANGLED SHIELD SLICES THROUGH THE DEADLY METAL ARM WITH THE SPEED OF THOUGHT..!
ZAK!

YOU CLUMSY MASKED BUNGLER!!
YOU DAMAGED SOMETHING THAT TOOK ME YEARS TO CREATE
FOR THAT, YOU'LL PA A PRICE THAT WILL GREATER THAN EVE
COME OFF IT, SKULL! WE BOTH KNOW YOU CAN ONLY KILL A FELLA ONCE!
STILL YOU DEFY ME!! STILL YOUR ACCURSED SPIRIT IS UNBROKEN!
WELL, NOT FOR LONG WILL IT REMAIN THAT WAY! NO--- NOT FOR LONG!!
THE ROBOT IS LEAVING! WHAT ELSE DOES THE SKULL HAVE WAITING IN STORE FOR ME??

HE DIDN'T LEAVE ME GUESSING FOR VERY LONG!!
A MINIATURE MISSILE COMING TOWARDS ME... PICKING UP SPEED AS IT GETS CLOSER!
SSSSS

SSSSSSSSSSS
I DUCKED IT JUST IN TIME, BUT...
HERE COMES ANOTHER! HOW LONG CAN I KEEP THIS UP?!

E'S JUST WING WITH ME NOW-- USING IT TO 'ROUND IN CLES, SO I ON'T KNOW HEN IT'LL ATTACK!
MY ONLY CHANCE IS TO STRIKE AT HIS ACHILLES HEEL--HIS MAD, UNHOLY PRIDE!
I'M DISAPPOINTED IN YOU, SKULL! I KNOW I'M TRAPPED --BUT I EXPECTED YOU TO COME UP WITH SOMETHING FAR CLEVERER, FAR WORTHIER OF THE RED SKULL!
ANY TWO-BIT PENNY-ANTE HOOD IN TOWN COULD HAVE DREAMED UP A CAPER LIKE THIS!
PERHAPS YOU'RE RIGHT, CAPTAIN AMERICA!
AND, SINCE YOU ARE DOOMED ANYWAY, I MIGHT AS WELL FOREGO THE REMAINDER OF THE PRELIMINARIES AND GET TO THE MAIN EVENT--!
SO FAR, SO GOOD! HE'S REMOVING THE MISSILE!
BUT NOW-- WHAT'S NEXT IN STORE?!!
PREPARE YOURSELF, AVENGER--PREPARE FOR THE GREATEST SHOCK OF ALL!
NOT ONLY ARE YOU ABOUT TO MEET YOUR WELL-DESERVED FINISH, BUT--
IT WILL BE AT THE HANDS OF--THE LAST ONE ON EARTH FROM WHOM YOU WOULD EXPECT SUCH A FATE--!
YOU!!
IT--IT JUST CAN'T BE!!
SURPRISED, CAPTAIN AMERICA? AHH, BUT THE GREATEST SURPRISE IS YET TO COME--!!

NO, CAP-- YOUR EYES AREN'T PLAYING TRICKS ON YOU!!
IT'S ME, ALL RIGHT!! I'M A LITTLE OLDER-- I'M A LITTLE BIGGER--AND STRONGER-- BUT I'M STILL--
BUCKY BARNES!
BUT--IT CAN'T BE! YOU'RE DEAD!! I SAW YOU DIE! IT ISN'T POSSIBLE--AFTER ALL THESE YEARS--!!
I FORGOT TO MENTION ONE OTHER THING-- I'M ALSO A LO SMARTER NOW
WHAT'S WRONG, CAP?? YOU SOUND DIS-APPOINTED! IS THAT IT?
I REALIZE NOW THAT YOU WERE JEALOUS OF --YOU ALWAYS ENVIED ME!! YOU WANTED THE LIMELIGHT--THE GLORY--ALL TO YOURSEL
THAT'S WHY YOU LET ME DIE!! THAT'S WHY YOU NEVER BOTHERED SEARCHING FOR ME--AFTER ALL THESE YEARS!! I KNOW THE TRUTH AT LAST!
NO, BUCKY --NO! YOU'RE MAD--!
YOU'VE GOT IT ALL WRONG, SON--!
THWOP!
IT WON'T WORK, MISTER! YOU'LL NEVER FAST-TALK ME INTO ANYTHING AGAIN!
BUCKY-- WAIT!! UHHH!
I'VE BEEN WAITING TOO LONG FOR MY CHANCE--TO PAY YOU BACK!

'VE GOT IT ALL BACKWARDS, I WAS NEVER JEALOUS YOU! WE WERE PARTNERS- EMEMBER? WE WERE EAM--A REAT EAM!
WHAT CHANGED YOU? WHAT MADE YOU SO BITTER--SO HOSTILE??
YOU--YOU'RE LOOKING AT ME--AS THOUGH WE'RE DEADLY ENEMIES!!

ZOK!
YOU BETTER BELIEVE IT, CAP!

M NOT THE HERO- ORSHIPPING EEN-AGER HO USED TO VE IN YOUR HADOW ANY MORE, BIG MAN!!
MAYBE YOU NEVER BOTHERED TO FIND ME-- BUT THE RED SKULL DID!!
HE SAVED MY LIFE-- TRAINED ME--TAUGHT ME ALL THE THINGS I HAD TO KNOW-- SHOWED ME WHAT A ROTTEN, CRUMMY DOUBLE-CROSSER YOU ALWAYS WERE!
SO THAT'S IT! YOU WERE BRAIN-WASHED BY THE RED-- UNHHH!

BRAIN- VASHED, MY FOOT!!
I JUST FINALLY LEARNED WHAT THE SCORE IS!
I LEARNED WHO MY FRIEND WAS--AND WHO MY REAL ENEMY WAS--!
I'M THE ONLY ONE WHO CAN BEAT YOU IN A STAND-UP FIGHT--
'CAUSE I KNOW ALL YOUR TRICKS, AND ALL YOUR DEFENSIVE TACTICS!
SO IT'S GOTTA BE ME WHO FINISHES YOU OFF--FOREVER!!

OKAY, KID-- YOU CALLED IT! THE GLOVES ARE OFF NOW!
YOU'RE NOT THE BUCKY BARNES I ONCE KNEW! YOU'RE A MANIACAL, HATE-FILLED KILLER--THANKS TO THE RED SKULL!

IF IT MAKES YOU FEEL BETTER, CALL ME WHAT YOU WANT TO--IT DOESN'T MATTER ANYWAY!

HAH! I THOUGHT YOU KNEW ALL MY OLD TRICKS?!!
HOW COME YOU DIDN'T REMEMBER THIS ONE, BRIGHT BOY?

YOU'RE AN OLD MAN BY NOW!! YOU CAN'T HOLD ME LIKE THAT!
THEN WHY DON'T YOU BREAK AWAY?
I WILL! I-- WILL--!

SURE! WHEN LIONS LEARN HOW TO MOO!
YOU'VE HAD IT, PAL!
L-LET ME UP--!
AS A MATTER OF FACT --I WILL!

--BECAUSE IT'LL GIVE ME A CHANCE TO END THIS FRACAS--ONCE AND FOR ALL!

WHIZZTTTTT!
BTAM!
IT ALMOST WORKED, SKULL-- BUT YOU MADE ONE MISTAKE-- YOU OVERDID IT!
I REALIZED --AT THE END --THAT IT COULDN'T BE THE REAL BUCKY BARNES!

IT LOOKS LIKE I WAS
INDEED A PITY, MY VALIANT VICTIM!
THE ROBOT WHOM I FASHIONED IN THE FORM OF YOUR LONG-DEAD PARTNER WOULD HAVE BEEN ONE OF MY GREATEST CREATIONS!

AND, HOW IT WOULD HAVE PLEASED ME IF YOU HAD GONE DOWN TO DEFEAT, THINKING YOUR OWN INSIPID PARTNER HAD FINALLY BETRAYED YOU!
BUT, NO MATTER! HERE, ON MY OWN FORTIFIED ISLAND, THE RED SKULL HOLDS ALL THE CARDS!
ALL I NEED DO IS CONSIGN YOU TO A DIFFERENT FATE! AND SO I SHALL!
YOU PUT UP A MOST DETERMINED STRUGGLE, CAPTAIN AMERICA! BUT I AM STILL THE VICTOR!

AND NOW, FAREWELL! MINE IS THE LAST FACE YOU SHALL EVER SEE--MY VOICE IS THE LAST YOU SHALL EVER HEAR!
RANCH!

THE WALLS-- STARTING TO MOVE--CLOSING IN ON ME!
NO PLACE TO RUN!! NO PLACE TO TURN!!
THIS MAY BE MY SWAN SONG, SKULL--BUT AT LEAST THE MEMORY OF BUCKY BARNES IS STILL UNSULLIED!
SO, EVEN THOUGH I DIE--YOU'VE FAILED ONCE MORE!
RRRRRRRRRRRRR
NEXT ISSUE:
"CAPTAIN AMERICA, TRAITOR!"

APPROVED BY THE COMICS CODE AUTHORITY
TALES OF SUSPENSE
featuring
CAPTAIN AMERICA AND IRON MAN
MARVEL COMICS GROUP
12¢ IND.
90 JUN
"...AND MEN SHALL CALL HIM TRAITOR!"
AN EPIC TO STAGGER YOUR SENSES!
THE MOST INCREDIBLE CRIME OF ALL TIME!

Stan Lee presents: CAPTAIN AMERICA, LIVING LEGEND of WORLD WAR II.™
"...AND MEN SHALL CALL HIM TRAITOR!"
AND NOW, FAREWELL!
MINE IS THE LAST FACE YOU SHALL EVER SEE!
MY VOICE IS THE LAST YOU SHALL EVER HEAR!
SURELY THE MOST UNNECESSARY WORDS EVER PENNED ARE THESE-- CONTINUED FROM LAST ISH!
THE WALLS-- MOVING-- CLOSING IN ON ME!!
DOES THIS MEAN-- THE RED SKULL WINS-- AT LAST?!!
SKRANCH
WRITTEN IN THE FIERY FLASH OF INSPIRATION BY: SMILIN' STAN LEE
PENCILLED IN THE FIRST BLUSH OF ENTHUSIASM BY: GARRULOUS GIL KANE
INKED IN THE DAZZLING GLOW OF JUBILATION BY: JOVIAL JOE SINNOTT
LETTERED IN THE LONELY GRIP OF LETHARGY BY: ADORABLE ARTIE SIMEK

NOW, AS THE END INEXORABLY APPROACHES--I'LL DEAL MY MOST SHATTERING BLOW--

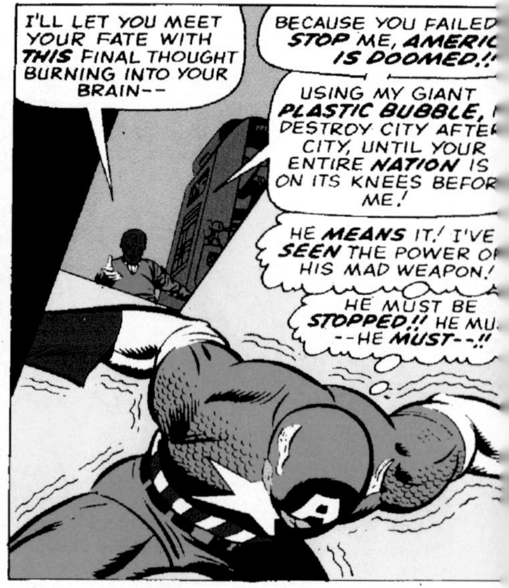
I'LL LET YOU MEET YOUR FATE WITH THIS FINAL THOUGHT BURNING INTO YOUR BRAIN--
BECAUSE YOU FAILED STOP ME, AMERIC IS DOOMED!!
USING MY GIANT PLASTIC BUBBLE, DESTROY CITY AFTER CITY, UNTIL YOUR ENTIRE NATION IS ON ITS KNEES BEFOR ME!
HE MEANS IT! I'VE SEEN THE POWER OF HIS MAD WEAPON!
HE MUST BE STOPPED!! HE MU --HE MUST--!!

TO MAKE CERTAIN YOU FIND NO LAST MINUTE MEANS OF SCALING THE SHEER WALLS, I'LL TAKE A FINAL PRECAUTION--!
THOSE LASER BEAMS WILL PROVE AN IMPENETRABLE BARRIER TO ANY MAN!
AND NOW, FAREWELL! A MAN OF MY SENSIBILITIES ABHORS THE SIGHT OF BLOODSHED!
CLICK!

HIS CONTROL PANEL!! HE'S DESERTED IT!
THAT MEANS THERE'S STILL CHANCE--IF I CAN BRING MY ARM BACK FAR ENOUGH--
EVERYTHING DEPENDS ON-- THIS ONE THROW--!

I DID IT! I SMASHED THE MECHANISM!

THE WALLS HAVE STOPPED--THE LASER BEAMS ARE GONE!
AND, THAT LOOSE WIRE--DANGLING FROM ABOVE-- MY TICKET OUT--!

YOU GLOATED TOO SOON, SKULL--.
THE FINAL CURTAIN HASN'T YET RUNG DOWN!

ALREADY REACHED THE SURFACE--VIA THAT GLASS-ENCLOSED PNEUMATIC LIFT--!
IF HE LEAVES THE ISLE--BEFORE I CAN REACH HIM--HE'LL STILL USE HIS DEADLY BUBBLE!!
I-I'M TOO LATE! HE'S ALREADY TAKING OFF!
IT TOOK TOO LONG FOR THE LIFT TO COME DOWN FOR ME--!
--BY TYING THE LOOSE WIRE TO THE INNER STRAP OF MY SHIELD--I'M STILL IN THE FIGHT!
NOW, IF I CAN JUST SWING CLEAR--BEFORE THE FALSE MOUNTAIN PEAK SNAPS SHUT AGAIN!
WHIRRRRR
HE'S GATHERING SPEED--STILL DOESN'T KNOW I'M HANGING ON BELOW HIM--!
I MADE IT!
BUT NOW--THE MOST DANGEROUS TASK STILL LIES AHEAD--!
3

I'VE GOT TO REACH THE SHIP-- CLIMBING HAND-OVER-HAND--BEFORE HE SEES ME!
BUT.. IT'S USELESS! THERE'S HIS FACE NOW--AT THE VIEW-PORT--LOOKING MY WAY!

CAPTAIN AMERICA STILL LIVES!
I CANNOT IMAGIN HOW HE ESCAPE BUT IT WILL DO NO GOOD.
KLAKK!

HE'S CHANGING COURSE-- INCREASING HIS SPEED--!
NOW--HE'S STARTING TO-- DIVE!!
HE'S HEADING FOR THE WATER-- AND I CAN'T--CLIMB UP IN TIME!

THANK YOU, MY STAR-SPANGLED VICTIM, FOR ALLOWING ME THE PLEASURE OF DEFEATING YOU TWICE!
SPLUNCH!
ALL I NEED DO IS REMAIN AT THIS ALTITUDE LONG ENOUGH FOR YOU TO DEFAULT --BY DROWNING!

I'VE BEATEN HIM BEFORE!! I'LL DO IT AGAIN-- SOMEHOW!
TOO MUCH AT ST --FOR ME--TO D THE GAUNTLET-N

BUT--ONE THING --HE CAN'T STOP ME--FROM DOING--
SO LONG AS-- MY STRENGTH --HOLDS OUT--!
I CAN STILL CLIMB...

I'VE GOT TO-- PULL MYSELF UP--ALONG THE WIRE--IGNORING THE PRESSURE--!!

I'M--GETTING IT!! JUST A LITTLE-- FURTHER--!
THERE'S--ONE THING--IN MY FAVOR--
HE CAN'T GET --ANY LOWER-- WITHOUT DAMAGING-- SHIP!!

I CAN BREATHE AGAIN!

HIS VIEW-PORT IS TOO HIGH-- THE SHIP'S TAIL SHIELD ME FROM HIS SIGHT!
SO FAR AS HE KNOWS, I'M STILL SUFFOCATING HELPLESSLY BELOW!

BUT, I'VE GOT TO REACH HIM BEFORE HE CAN LEARN HIS INTENDED VICTIM STILL LIVES--
AND, DOES MORE THAN JUST LIVE--

FOR NOW--ARMED ONCE AGAIN WITH MY SHIELD--
THE TIME HAS COME-- FOR CAPTAIN AMERICA TO--

--STRIKE BACK!!

I BROKE A PLEXIGLASS WINDOW ON THE OPPOSITE SIDE OF THE SHIP--
WITH LUCK, THE ROAR OF THE ENGINES PREVENTED THE SKULL FROM HEARING IT--
AND NOW--MY FINAL SWING--
5

MADE IT!
NOTHING WILL KEEP ME FROM THAT MURDEROUS MADMAN NOW!

WHILE, IN THE MAIN CONTROL ROOM OF THE STRANGELY SINISTER SKY CRAFT--
EVEN CAPTAIN AMERICA CANNOT HOLD HIS BREATH THIS LONG!
HE MUST BE DROWNED BY NOW!
WHICH MEANS I C TRANSFER SUPER-SO FLIGHT SPE --AND REA MY OBJECTI IN SECON
CLIK!

THERE IT IS-- NEW YORK CITY--
SLUMBERING INNOCENTLY --LITTLE DREAMING THE FANTASTIC FATE THAT AWAITS IT--!
NOW, AT THE PRESS OF A BUTTON, I ACTIVATE MY-ALL-ENCOMPASSING PLASTIC BUBBLE!!

WHEN IT ATTAINS MAXIMUM SIZE, IT IS CAPABLE OF ELECTRONICALLY ENVELOPING THE VERY HEART OF THE WORLD'S GREATEST METROPOLIS!
THEN, BY SETTING MY ANTI-GRAVITY IMPULSE WAVES TO FULL INTENSITY, I LIFT AN ENTIRE SQUARE MILE OF CITY AS EFFORTLESSLY AS A BUBBLE!
AFTER LENGTHY CONSULTATION AND SOUL-SEARCHING, THE EDITORIAL AND ADVISORY BOARD OF MIGHTY MARVEL HAVE UNANIMOUSLY AGREED NOT TO GIVE A DETAILED EXPLANATION OF HOW THE RED SKULL'S DEADLY PLASTIC BUBBLE OPERATES --JUST IN CASE THIS TOP-SECRET REVELATION SHOULD FALL INTO ENEMY HANDS! --SECURITY-CONSCIOUS STAN.

MILLIONS OF LIVES DWELL WITHIN THAT AREA--LIVES THAT THE RED SKULL NOW HOLDS IN THE PALM OF HIS HAND!
ALL I NEED DO IS CONVINCE WASHINGTON THAT I CAN SEIZE ANY SECTION OF ANY CITY AS EASILY AS THIS--
AND ANYTHING I MAY DEMAND WILL BE MINE FOR THE ASKING!

NOT A CHANCE, SKULL!
NOT WHILE CAPTAIN AMERICA STILL LIVES!
YOU AGAIN!!

DON'T TOUCH THAT SWITCH!!
HAH! YOU'RE TOO LATE!
SKLAKK!

HAVEN'T YOU REALIZED YET THAT YOUR OWN COURAGE AND STAMINA ARE USELESS AGAINST THE POWER AND THE WEAPONS OF THE MATCHLESS RED SKULL?!!
NO MATTER HOW MANY LIVES YOU SEEM TO POSSESS--
THE FINAL TRIUMPH SHALL ALWAYS BE--MINE!
THWUP!

IT WAS ONLY A 12-FOOT DROP--NOT ENOUGH TO INJURE ME!
WHY WOULD THE SKULL HAVE DONE IT--UNLESS--?
WHAT'S THAT--SNEAKING AROUND FROM BEHIND?

STEEL TENTACLES!!

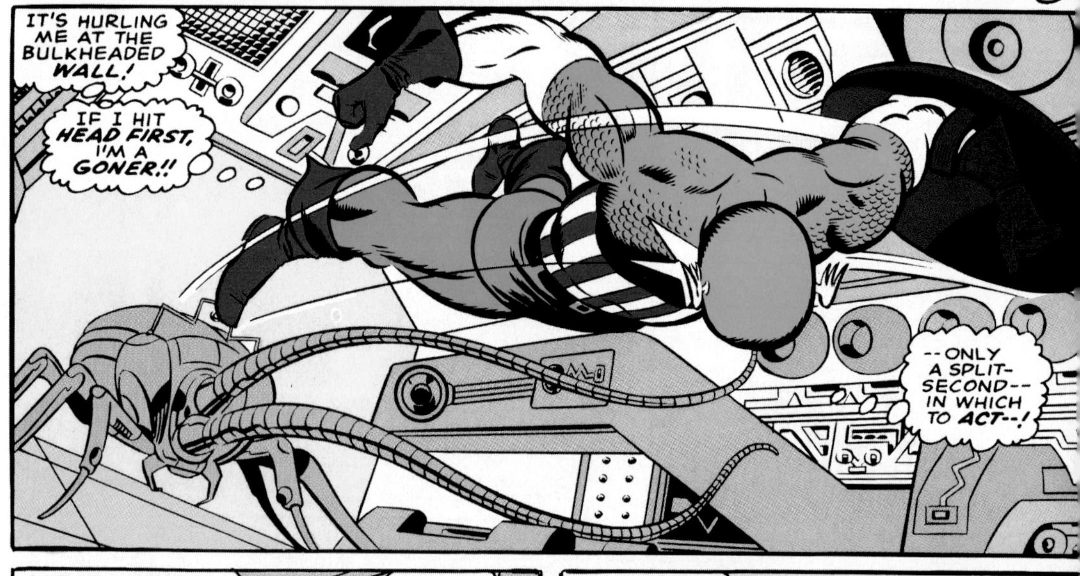
IT'S HURLING ME AT THE BULKHEADED WALL!
IF I HIT HEAD FIRST, I'M A GONER!!
--ONLY A SPLIT-SECOND--IN WHICH TO ACT--!

GOT TO MANAGE--A COMPLETE SOMERSAULT--IN MID-AIR--!
AND THEN--
THANNG!

A FAST BACK-FLIP--TO PUT ME ABOVE THE ATTACKING STEEL ROBOT!!
MADE IT!!

, IF I CAN
ST LEAP
P HIS BACK
FORE HE
AN SPIN
ROUND--!

SO LONG AS THE SKULL HAS CONTROL OF HIS PLASTIC BUBBLE WEAPON, I CAN'T AFFORD TO WASTE A SINGLE SECOND!

ONE EXTRA HEART-BEAT'S DELAY MAY MEAN THE DESTRUCTION OF AN ENTIRE CITY!!

BY SMASHING HIS ANTENNA, I'LL MAKE THIS MONSTROSITY BLIND--UNABLE TO GUIDE HIMSELF!

--WHICH MEANS IT'S FINALLY CAPTAIN AMERICA'S TURN--

SWAK!

--TO ATTACK!

AN USE THE
ILIENT STEEL
CK OF THE
NG BELOW
TO FURNISH
THE SPRING
I NEED--!

ANG

STAND AWAY FROM THOSE CONTROLS!!

AGAIN YOU RETURN!!

NOW, YOU LEAVE ME NO CHOICE--

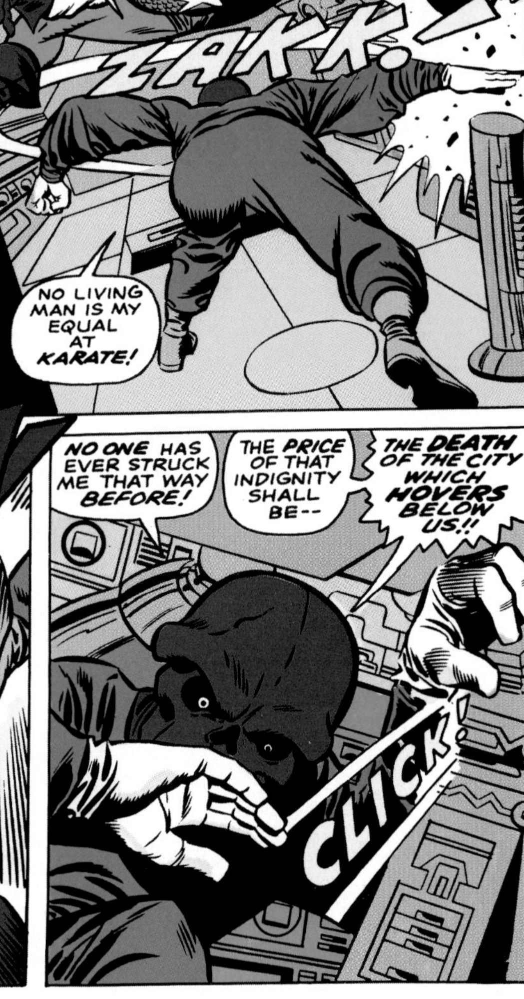

ET THOSE
WORDS
BE
YOUR
PITAPH!

BTAM!

NO! YOU'VE RELEASED THE SAFETY! IF YOU PRESS THAT BUTTON AGAIN--THE BUBBLE WILL BREAK--!
--AND MORE THAN A MILLION LIVES WILL PLUMMET TO THEIR DOOM!
NO WAY I CAN REACH HIM IN TIME! I DARE NOT EVEN TRY!!
YOU CAN'T!! YOU MUSTN'T!! NAME YOUR TERMS!! I-I'LL DO ANYTHING--!
YOUR WORD!! GIVE ME YOUR WORD--AS AN AVENGER--TO SERVE ME--FOR 24 HOURS!

I MUST!! I'VE NO OTHER CHOICE!
I--GIVE YOU--MY WORD!

HAH! NOW THE CITY INTERESTS ME NO LONGER!
IT HAS SERV
ITS PURPOSE
SINCE T
WORLD H
SEEN I
POWER--
RETUR
IT TO
NORM

NOW, I'LL DISSOLVE MY MAGNIFICENT BUBBLE--FOR IT IS TIME TO ASSIGN YOU YOUR FIRST TASK IN MY BEHALF!
I HAD TO PLEDGE MY WORD--I HAD TO! MY LIFE DOESN'T MATTER--BUT I HAD TO SAVE THE OTHERS--THE COUNTLESS INNOCENT VICTIMS!

STAND IN FRONT OF THAT TV LENS AS I BREAK INTO EVERY PROGRAM ON EARTH!
FOR, THE ENTIRE WORLD MUST LEARN OF MY TOTAL VICTORY!
ATTENTION, HELPLESS MANKIND
WHAT I HAVE DONE TO NEW YOR
CITY IS BUT A SAMPLE OF WHAT
THE RED SKULL CAN ACCOMPLIS
WITH THE HELP OF MY NEW PARTNER-IN-EVIL-- THE ONCE HEROIC CAPTAIN AMERICA!!
SPEAK, YOU STAR-SPANGLED SWINE!! SPEAK--SO THAT ALL MAY SEE THAT CAPTAIN AMERICA HAS FINALLY BETRAYED THOSE WHO HAVE TRUSTED HIM!
WHO IS YOUR MASTER NOW?? SPEAK!!

I SERVE--ONLY--THE RED SKULL!
IT CAN'T BE!! AND YET--!
WE SAW HIM--WITH OUR OWN EYES!
HE SAID IT! WE-WE HEARD HIM--!
CAPTAIN AMERICA HAS ACTUALLY--TURNED TRAITOR!
IF HE--AND THE RED SKULL HAVE JOINED FORCES--THEN NONE OF US--ARE SAFE!!

SO--THE WORLD HAS BEEN WARNED!
BUT STILL THEY CANNOT SUSPECT--THEY CANNOT COMPREHEND--THE FATE THAT AWAITS THEM--
WHEN WE DELIVE
MY FINAL BLOW--TOGETHER!
NEXT
"THE LAST
DEFEAT!

Stan Lee PRESENTS: CAPTAIN AMERICA, LIVING LEGEND of WORLD WAR II.™
"THE LAST DEFEAT!"
IN ORDER TO SAVE THE CITY OF NEW YORK FROM ANNIHILATION AT THE MERCILESS HANDS OF THE RED SKULL, CAPTAIN AMERICA HAS PLEDGED TO SERVE THE MASTER OF VILLAINY FOR 24 HOURS! HOWEVER, UNAWARE OF THE REASON FOR CAP'S HEART-RENDING DECISION, A SHOCKED CITIZENRY CAN FIND ONLY ONE WORD FOR THE TORTURED RED-WHITE-AND-BLUE AVENGER--
TRAITOR!
TRAITOR!!
TRAITOR!
TRAITOR!
TRAITOR!!
TRAITOR!
TRAITOR!
TRAITOR!!
TRAITOR!
TRAITOR!!
TRAITOR!
TRAITOR!
TRAITOR!!
A PRAISEWORTHY PRESENTATION, PAINSTAKINGLY PRODUCED BY...
STAN (THE MAN) LEE and GIL (SUGAR LIPS) KANE
INKED BY: JOE SINNOTT
LETTERED BY: AL KURZROK

AS A BREATHLESS WORLD WAITS, AND WONDERS, IN FEARFUL ANTICIPATION OF THE RED SKULL'S NEXT MURDEROUS MOVE, A STRANGELY FORBIDDING SKY CRAFT BLAZES ACROSS THE WIDE ATLANTIC--
WE ARE NOW WELL INTO THE 23RD HOUR!
I HAVE KEPT YOU IN SUSPENSE LONG ENOUGH!
THE TIME IS COME FOR YOU TO FULFILL YOUR PLEDGE TO ME! WE WILL DELAY NO LONGER!

WHAT AN INDESCRIBABLE TRIUMPH THIS IS FOR ME!
NOT ONLY HAVE I GIV YOU YOUR LAST DEF --BUT I HAVE CONVINC THE WORLD THAT CAPTAIN AMERICA A TRAITOR!
AND, YOU A HELPLESS T REDEEM YOURSEL
BECAUSE YOUR STUPI CODE OF ETHI YOU WILL N EVEN BREA A PROMISE ME!!
BUT REMEMBER, SKULL-- WITHIN A MATTER OF MINUTES, THE 24 HOURS WILL HAVE ENDED!
I'LL BE FREE TO ACT ONCE AGAIN.

FOOL! BEFORE THESE LAST FEW MINUTES HAVE TICKED BY-- I'LL HAVE WHAT I WANT--
AND YOU WILL BE DESTROYED-- FOREVER!
NOW-- YOU WILL ANSWER THIS MOST VITAL QUESTION--
WHAT IS THE LOCATION OF THE XPT-1-- THE WORLD'S NEWEST ATOMIC SUBMARINE?!!
SPEAK!! YOU ARE PLEDGED TO ANSWER ME!!

THE XPT-1 IS CAPABLE OF CARRYING MORE POLARIS MISSILES THAN ANY SHIP AFLOAT!!
YOU CAN'T -- YOU MUSTN'T GET YOUR HANDS ON IT!
REMEMBER YOUR OATH!! YOU MUST TELL ME!!
IT-- IS CRUISING --IN THE NORT ATLANTIC--!
"I KNOW THAT YOU, AND THE OTHER ACCURSED AVENGERS, RECEIVE COMPLETE BRIEFINGS ON AMERICA'S GLOBAL DEFENSE POSTURE!"
-- CRUISING SPE IS 200 KNOTS, A THE PRESCRIB COURSE FOR H FIRST TOUR O DUTY SHAL BE--
"NOW, WITH 60 SECONDS OF YOUR PLEDGE TIME REMAINING, YOU MUST ANSWER ME--!"

I KNOW THAT, YOU STAR-SPANGLED SWINE!
I WANT THE EXACT LATITUDE AND LONGITUDE FROM YOU!
WHAT MAKES YOU THINK I WOULD KNOW?
STOP STALLING! YOU'RE DEALING WITH THE RED SKULL!!

AVE - OTHER DICE--!
AT THIS TIME, THE XPT-1 SHOULD BE IN THE AREA OF 50° LONGITUDE AND 45° LATITUDE!
HAH! THAT'S ALL I HAVE TO KNOW!
Y FINAL COMMAND YOU IS-- SEAT YOUR- ELF IN THAT ELECTRONIC CHAIR--QUICKLY!!
MY TRIUMPH IS NOW ABOUT TO BE UTTERLY AND TOTALLY COMPLETE!

HAH! GOOD-- GOOD! MY AUTOMATIC CEREBRAL LIE DETECTOR INFORMS ME THAT YOU HAVE DIVULGED THE TRUTH!
AND NOW, THE 24 HOURS ARE OVER! YOU ARE FREED OF YOUR PLEDGE!
CLACK!!
CLICK!
BUT, YOU'LL NEVER BE TRULY FREE AGAIN! FIRST, I STRAP YOU SECURELY WITHIN THAT CHAIR, AND THEN...
SKLATCH!

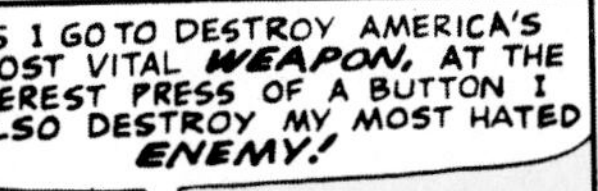
S I GO TO DESTROY AMERICA'S OST VITAL WEAPON, AT THE ERE ST PRESS OF A BUTTON I LSO DESTROY MY MOST HATED ENEMY!

ND, AS YOU GO TO EET YOUR DOOM, I LEAVE YOU WITH THIS INAL MESSAGE---!

IT WAS YOU YOURSELF WHO GAVE ME THE INFORMATION TO LAUNCH MY ATTACK UPON THE BASTION OF FREEDOM!
SO, WITH THAT IRONIC THOUGHT BURNING IN YOUR BRAIN, I BID YOU A LAST FAREWELL!!
THE CHAIR IS ON TRACKS!! HE'S SENDING IT HURTLING BACK-- TOWARDS WHAT?!!
ZOOM!

I'VE GOT TO BREAK FREE! BUT--THE STRAPS ARE SPECIALLY-TREATED BANDS OF UNBREAKABLE PLASTIC!
STILL, I MUSTN'T GIVE UP! --MUSTN'T PANIC!! THERE'S GOT TO BE A WAY--!! NO MATTER WHAT HAPPENS --MUST KEEP MY WITS ABOUT ME!
SHOOOSH
I'VE STOPPED! THAT MACHINE ABOVE--IT'S STARTING TO GENERATE HEAT!
NOW I UNDERSTAND! IT'S A HE RAY--GETTING HOTTER BY TH SECOND! IF I REMAIN HERE AN LONGER--I'M FINISHED!
BUT, THERE'S ALWAYS AN ESCAP IF A MAN KEEPS HIS NE I'VE GOT TO THINK- GOT TO- WAIT! I HAVE IT!
MY SHIELD!! IF CAN JUST FLEX M MUSCLES ENOUGH MOVE IT A FRACTI OF AN INCH--IT WILL CATCH THE RAYS OF BEAM--AT JUST T RIGHT ANGLE--
THERE! I'M GETTING IT!
SKREEEEEE
KRASK!
PERFECT! I MANAGED TO KICK THE HEATING ELEMENT-- SHATTERING IT!
NOW--A FAST BACK-FLIP, AND THEN--!
FTAK!
BY FOCUSING THE FIERY RAYS ON MY RESTRAINING STRAPS, MY SHIELD ENABLED ME TO BURN THEM OFF! ---I'M FREE AGAIN!
BUT, WAIT! THE SHIP!! IT'S STOPPED!
THE SKUL MUST HAV FOUND OUR SUB!
TOO RISKY TO TRY TO REACH HIM AGAIN--TOO MANY BOOBY TRAPS UP HERE!
MY FIRST DUTY IS TO WARN THE SUB--!
WE'RE NOT TOO HIGH OVER THE WATER! IF I CAN JUST GET UP ENOUGH STEAM--!
--TO BATTER MY WAY THRU THE WINDOW, BEHIND MY PROTECTIVE SHIELD--!
CRASH
I DID IT! NOTHING WILL STOP ME NOW!

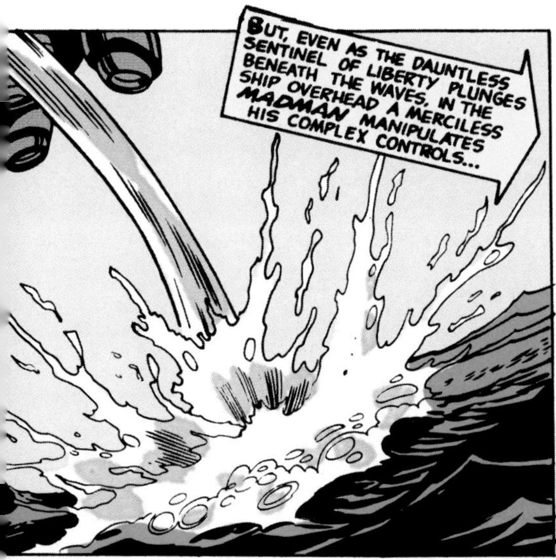
BUT, EVEN AS THE DAUNTLESS SENTINEL OF LIBERTY PLUNGES BENEATH THE WAVES, IN THE SHIP OVERHEAD A MERCILESS MADMAN MANIPULATES HIS COMPLEX CONTROLS...

MY FIRST TASK IS TO PUT THE ENTIRE CREW OF THE XPT-I UNDER MY HYPNOTIC CONTROL-- THRU THE USE OF MY SUBLIMINAL SONAR WAVES--!
ZAP!

NOW, ALL I NEED DO IS TRAIN MY CYBERNETIC SONAR ACTIVATOR AT THE SEA BELOW-- AND LET THE WAVES EXPAND--!

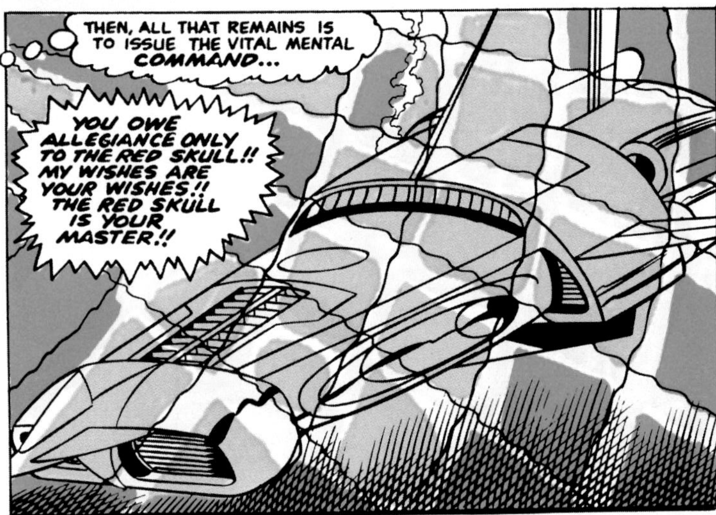
THEN, ALL THAT REMAINS IS TO ISSUE THE VITAL MENTAL COMMAND...
YOU OWE ALLEGIANCE ONLY TO THE RED SKULL!! MY WISHES ARE YOUR WISHES!! THE RED SKULL IS YOUR MASTER!!

AND NOW, YOU WILL SURFACE!! BRING THE XPT-I TO THE SURFACE!! YOU MUST OBEY!!

AND NOW, YOU WILL SURFACE!! BRING THE XPT-I TO THE SURFACE!! YOU MUST OBEY!!

NOW HEAR THIS! ATTENTION ALL HANDS! THIS IS THE CAPTAIN SPEAKING!
PREPARE TO SURFACE!

THE SOUND OF THROBBING ENGINES-- JUST AHEAD OF ME -- GETTING LOUDER!
IT'S THE SUB-- STARTING TO SURFACE! I'VE GOT TO REACH IT BEFORE THE SKULL DOES!
THE HATCH IS OPENING! IF I CAN JUST MAKE IT IN TIME--!
I MUST! I MUST!!
FROM HERE ON IN, EVERY SECOND COUNTS -- EVERY MOVE I MAKE CAN SPELL THE DIFFERENCE BETWEEN LIFE AND DEATH!
I'VE NO TIME TO EXPLAIN! YOU'VE GOT TO REACH MAXIMUM DEPTH -- AT ONCE!!
DON'T JUST STAND THERE, MAN!! THE RED SKULL IS ABOUT TO ATTACK!
THE RED SKULL -- IS --OUR MASTER!
LISTEN TO ME!! THIS IS NO TIME FOR CLOWNING! DON'T YOU --WAIT A MINUTE!!
THOSE STARING EYES!! THAT TRANCE-LIKE EXPRESSION! YOU MEANT WHAT YOU SAID!!
THE RED SKULL IS-- OUR MASTER!
HE TRIES TO TURN US AGAINST THE MASTER!! HE IS OUR ENEMY!
THEN-- I'M TOO LATE!! HE'S FOUND A WAY-- TO HYPNOTIZE YOU!! ALL OF YOU!
SEIZE HIM!
YOU MUSTN'T FIGHT ME!! YOU DON'T KNOW WHAT YOU'RE DOING -!!
IT'S NO USE!! YOU'RE NOT READING ME!!
I'VE GOT TO BREAK FREE!! EVEN IF IT MEANS BATTLING MY OWN COUNTRY-MEN THE SKULL MUST BE STOPPED!
GET BACK!! BACK, I SAY!! I DON'T WANT TO HURT YOU--!

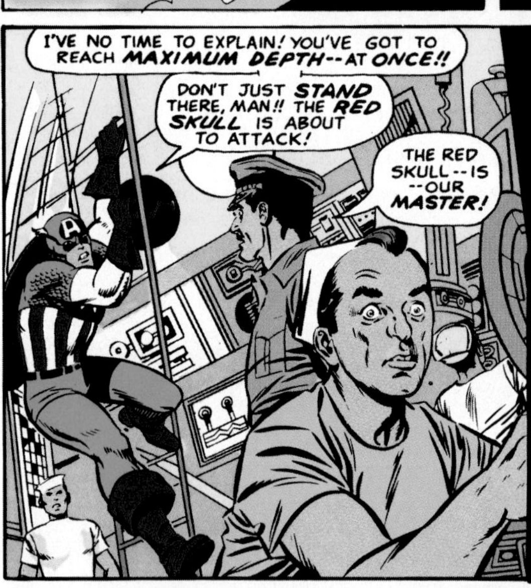

I SAID... BACK!

GOT TO REACH THE CONTROL ROOM-- NO MATTER WHAT!!
LUCKILY, THEY CAN'T THINK AS CLEARLY--OR MOVE AS FAST IN THEIR DAZED CONDITION!

HE IS THE MASTER'S ENEMY!
WE HAVE TO STOP--- UNHH!
MISTER, NOTHING'S GONNA STOP ME NOW!! AND I MEAN NOTHING!

I'LL GET HIM! I'LL--
UNPFFF!
HAVE TO MOVE FASTER!! --REINFORCEMENTS ON THE WAY!!

THERE HE GOES!! --STOP 'IM!!
THERE'S WHAT I WANT-- JUST AHEAD!!
NOW, IF MY LUCK'LL HOLD OUT-- JUST A MINUTE LONGER--!
THUMP THUD!
7

ONLY ONE GUARD TO GET PAST! I'M PRACTICALLY HOME FREE!

NO HARD FEELINGS, LAD-- I'M JUST TRYING TO HELP YOU ALL IN SPITE OF YOURSELVES!
WHOOOOF

THIS IS WHAT I WANT!
BY ADJUSTING THE REACTOR'S ENERGY OUTPUT, I SHOULD BE ABLE TO CANCEL OUT THE SKULL'S HYPNOTIC CONTROL!!
THERE! THIS SHOULD BRING THE CREW BACK TO NORMAL AGAIN!
CLAK!

BUT, THAT WAS ONLY HALF THE PROBLEM! THE OTHER ADJUSTMENT I MADE WILL SERVE TO--UH OH! LOOKS LIKE I'VE GOT COMPANY AGAIN!
IT'S CAPTAIN AMERICA!! HOW'D YOU GET ABOARD THIS SHIP??
SAY! WAIT A MINUTE!! ACCORDING TO THE NEWS BROADCASTS, YOU'VE TURNED TRAITOR!
WELL, AT LEAST I FREED THEM FROM THE SKULL'S HYPNOTIC EFFECT!
NOW I GET IT! YOU'RE TRYIN' TO SABOTAGE US--!!

BUT NOW, THEY'LL BE HARDER THAN EVER TO HOLD BACK!
LOOK! YOU'VE GOT IT ALL WRONG! I'M HERE TO HELP YOU! YOU'RE IN DESPERATE DANGER--!
BELAY IT, MATE! YOU'RE NOT PULLIN' THE WOOL OVER OUR EYES!
C'MON-- LET'S RUSH 'IM!

MEANWHILE, UNAWARE OF WHAT HAS TRANSPIRED BELOW, THE RED SKULL BARKS HIS FINAL COMMAND--
THIS IS YOUR MASTER-- THE RED SKULL!! NOW HEAR THIS--!
YOU MUST ABANDON SHIP!! EVERY ONE OF YOU-- ABANDON SHIP!
8

FIRST, I DESTROYED CAPTAIN AMERICA, WHO GAVE HIS LIFE IN A VAIN EFFORT TO SAVE YOU--
AND NEXT, THE XPT-1 SHALL BE MINE!
CAP WAS TELLIN' THE TRUTH!
NOW LISTEN! HERE'S WHAT WE'VE GOT TO DO--!

MINUTES LATER, THE ENTIRE CREW OF THE XPT-1 SILENTLY LEAVES THE SURFACED SHIP... AS THEY EXPRESSIONLESSLY MARCH INTO THE RED SKULL'S NOW-FLOATING CRAFT--;

WE CAN'T AFFORD TO HAVE HIM CATCH ON-- OR HIS NEXT HYPNOTIC ATTACK WOULD BE TWICE AS POWERFUL!

THEN, FINALLY-- AFTER THE LAST CREWAN HAS CROWDED INSIDE, THE MASTER VILLAIN'S SKY-SHIP BEGINS TO RISE-- LEAVING A SOLITARY FIGURE STANDING TRIUMPHANTLY UPON THE DECK OF THE NOW-ABANDONED XPT-1....
I'VE DONE IT! I'VE ACCOMPLISHED THE SEEMINGLY IMPOSSIBLE!
FIRST, I DESTROYED MY GREATEST ENEMY!! AND THEN--
SINGLE-HANDEDLY, I'VE CAPTURED THE MIGHTIEST FIGHTING MACHINE OF ALL!
WITH THIS NUCLEAR-POWERED, MULTI-MISSILE DREADNAUGHT UNDER MY CONTROL, NO FORCE ON EARTH CAN STAND AGAINST ME!

BUT NOW, I HAVE FAR MORE MONUMENTAL MATTERS TO CONSIDER--!
I MUST DECIDE WHICH UNSUSPECTING TARGET WILL BE THE FIRST TO FEEL MY IRRESISTIBLE MISSILE ATTACK!

FOR, ONLY BY COMPLETELY DECIMATING AN ENTIRE METROPOLIS CAN I MAKE THE WORLD REALIZE THAT IT MUST OBEY MY EVERY WHIM!
WITHIN A FEW SHORT HOURS, ALL OF EARTH SHALL GROVEL BENEATH THE HEEL OF THE MIGHTY RED SKULL!

BUT THEN, SECONDS LATER--
SKULL! THIS IS CAPTAIN AMERICA!
YOU ARE IN DEADLY DANGER! YOU HAVE 60 SECONDS TO LEAVE THE XPT-1!
ABANDON THE SHIP NOW! WE WILL PICK YOU UP! HURRY!
HE STILL LIVES!! MY WORST ENEMY STILL LIVES!!
IT CAN'T BE! IT CAN'T!! HE MUST NOT DEFEAT ME AGAIN!! NOT AGAIN!!

YOU DIDN'T REALIZE-- XPT-1 IS AN EXPERIMENTAL SHIP! HAVING SERVED ITS PURPOSE, IT WAS ON ITS FINAL VOYAGE -- TO BE DESTROYED!
I MERELY CHANG THE TIMING DEVICE! YOU HAVE ONLY 45 SECONDS WE'RE WAITING SKULL--!
NO! NO! I STILL HAVE A CHANCE!
IF I CAN REACH TH TIMING DEVIC BEFORE ZE SECOND--

SKULL! WE CAN'T WAIT ANY LONGER! WHERE ARE YOU?
I'LL REACH IT!! THE WORLD WILL YET BE MINE!
IT IS MY DESTINY TO RULE! I MUST BE TRUE-- TO MY DESTINY--!

BUT, ALAS, NO MAN EVER TRULY KNOWS-- HIS REAL DESTINY--

IT LOOKS LIKE THE END OF THE RED SKULL--AT LAST!
THE SKIPPER'S ALREADY ON THE RADIO, GIVING A REPORT OF WHAT'S HAPPENED, CAP!
YOU'LL BE MORE OF A HERO THAN EVER WHEN YOU GET ASHORE!
A HERO--??

I'M NO MORE A HERO THAN ANY MAN WHO FIGHTS FOR JUSTICE, AND FREEDOM, AND BROTHERHOOD!
SO LONG AS WE CHERISH LIBERTY --SO LONG AS THE BITTER WEED OF TYRANNY CAN NEVER TAKE ROOT UPON OUR SHORES --THEN ALL OF US ARE HEROES--
AND, THE DREAM WHICH IS AMERICA WILL LONG ENDURE!

APPROVED BY THE COMICS CODE AUTHORITY

THE SENSATIONAL NEW

CAPTAIN MARVEL

TM

UNCHAINED!

PT.
VEL
17
OCT

RVEL
ICS
OUP

ANE
KINS

HEAR ME, CAPTAIN MARVEL!

HEAR THE WORDS OF THE **INTELLIGENCE SUPREME,** OMNISCIENT **OVERMIND** OF THE FAR-DISTANT **KRE** **GALAXY!** IT WAS THE SINISTER SIREN CALL OF **VENGEANCE** THAT LURED YOU BACK TO EARTH... A RAVEN THIRST FOR THE SWEET NECTAR OF **JUSTICE** THAT PROVED YOUR UNDOING! YOU RISKED ALL FOR REVENGE UPON THE MURDEROUS **YON-ROGG... AND YOU HAVE PAID THE PRICE--!!**

YET, THAT PRI WAS NOT MER DEATH, BUT SOMETHING MORE TRAGIC MORE MONSTROUS FOR, A DIRE ACCIDENT HA HURLED YO FOR ALL TIM INTO THE DRE ANTI-COSMO KNOWN AS THE NEGATIV ZONE!!
STAN LEE EDITOR · ROY THOMAS WRITER · GIL KANE ARTIST
DAN ADKINS, EMBELLISHER
ARTIE SIMEK, LETTERER
IS THERE, THEN NO HOPE FOR M
IS THERE WAY TO ESC THIS DAR MADDENIN VOID?
AY, MAR-VELL, THERE IS A WAY... A WAY YOU SHALL FIND...
"AND A CHILD SHALL LEAD YOU!"

OOK, MAN OF THE KREE, THRU MY MIND'S FAR-ROVING EYE... YOU SEE THE COSTUMED TH WHO RACES THE WIND THRU FILTH-SWEPT BACKSTREETS...?
YES...(FOR, I READ YOUR THOUGHTS!)...RICK JONES IS YOUNG, MAR-VELL! BUT HOW OLD WERE YOU, WHEN YOU BECAME THE YOUNGEST OFFICER IN THE INTER-GALACTIC FLEET...?
WHAT IS THE AGE... AND WHAT IS THE SOUL-FELT EMOTION... THAT ARE THE HALLMARKS OF MANHOOD...?
HI YA, POOCH!
YOU LOOK HUNGRY, UP... NOT FOR FOOD, UT FOR AFFECTION... FOR RESPECT!
KNOW THAT OOK... I'VE EEN IT EFORE...
LIKE, EVERY TIME I PASS BY A MIRROR!
HOW DO YOU MEASURE ANGUISH, STAR-MAN? IS YOUR GRIEF-IN-EXILE ANY GREATER THAN THIS BOY'S, AS HE CRIES TO THE SHROUDED HEAVENS--
WHY ARE YOU HIDING FROM ME, CAP?
WHY??
WOULD HIS GRIEF BE LESSENED IF HE SENSED THAT THE MAN WHO SHUNS HIM IS NOT THE TRUE CAPTAIN AMERICA--
--BUT A MIRACULOUSLY-TRANSFORMED RED SKULL--PERHAPS THE MOST EVIL ENTITY OF ALL??
2

YET, THAT IS NEITHER HIS TO KNOW... NOR OURS TO REVEAL...AT LEAST, NOT TILL EVENTS HAVE RUN THEIR APPOINTED COURSE...!
WELL...I GOT THINGS TO DO!
S'LONG, POOCH!
ONE WAY
...I FEEL LIKE ONE OF HYDRA'S GOONS, STAKING OUT CAP'S HOTEL LIKE THIS!
BUT, HE'S LEFT WORD THAT NOBODY GETS IN TO SEE HIM...
NOT EVE THE GUY WHO'S SUPPOSE TO BE HIS PARTNER
HEY! WHO'S THAT DOWN THERE--?
IT'S--CAP!
HERE'S WHERE I GET TO THE BOTTOM OF THIS BIG HAIRY MYSTERY--
--FOR ONCE AND FOR ALL!
HEY, CAP--WAIT UP!
IT'S ME--RICK!
I GOTTA TALK TO YOU...!
EH?
YOUR PETTY CONCER DO NO MATTE TO M BOY.
ONLY CAPTA AMERICA MATTERS-
--AND, CAPTAIN AMERICA NEEDS NO ONE!!
SKAK!
CAN YOU FEEL IT, MAR-VELL, EVEN ACRO THE TRACKLESS VOI OF HYPER-SPACE? CAN YOU FEEL--NO THE BLOW, BUT TH STINGING PAIN OF--REJECTION.
OHHH

VOR THAT BLOW,
N OF THE KREE...
, ITS FLEETING
ACT MAY HAVE
N THE HAMMER-
D STROKE WHICH
RALDS YOUR
EDOM...!
ONE WAY
SPEED LIMIT 20 MPH
THAT TEARS IT!!
GHT
WELL
AKE
NG MY
TUME!
I EARNED IT!
AHH...GOOD AFTERNOON, MASTER RICK!
I TRUST THAT, BY NOW, YOU'VE LOCATED YOUR MENTOR...!?
YOU MEAN CAPTAIN EGO?
THAT STAR-SPANGLED SWELLHEAD CAN GO CHOKE ON HIS OWN MEDALS!
BULL! WHO AM I TRYIN' TO CON?
IF I'D REALLY MADE THE GRADE AS CAP'S SIDEKICK...
HE'D NEVER HAVE GIVEN ME THE BIG BRUSH-OFF!
I'M CUTTIN' OUT!
VELL, SEE YA, JARVIS... IT'S BEEN GRINS!
DON'T LOOK ON IT AS LOSING AN AVENGER...BUT GAINING A GUEST ROOM!
UT, MASTER
RICK...WHAT
ABOUT THE
AVENGERS?
WHAT
HALL I
AY TO
HEM...?
JUST TELL 'EM RICK JONES SAID GOOD-BYE...
...AND THEN MAIL ME BOTH THE TEARS THEY SHED...!
4

NUTS! WHERE DO I GET OFF PLAYING THE HARD-KNOCKS KID?
ME... WHO'S HAD ENOUGH BREAKS FOR TEN WOULD-BE HEROES!
"WASN'T I ON TAP WHEN BRUCE BANNER FIRST TURNED INTO THE BLOCK-BUSTIN' HULK? WASN'T IT OL' RICK THAT THE DOC DEPEND ON TO KEEP HIM UNDER CONTROL? HAH... MIGHT JUST AS WELL AFTER A RHINO WITH A CAN OF FLIT!"
"MAYBE REALLY FOUND OWN LE WHEN I LORDIN' OVER A BUNCH RADIO H CALLED TEEN BRIGAD
"YEAH THAT WAS MORE MY SPEE
"BUT NO... THAT WASN'T GOOD ENO FOR THE ONE AN ONLY RICK JONE I WOULDN'T QUI TILL I WAS UP THERE WITH T BIG KIDS... TIL COULD COM RUNNING W I HEARD T CRY--"

VENGERS ASSEMBLE!
IT WASN'T LONG, THOUGH, BEFORE I SPLIT THAT SCENE... NOT THAT THERE WAS ANY REASON WHY THE AVENGERS SHOULD HAVE NOTICED..."
'CAUSE THE HULK WAS IN HOT WATER AGAIN...AND I TOLD MYSELF HE NEEDED ME...AT LEAST, I DID UNTIL THE DAY HE TURNED ON ME... AND NEARLY TOTALED ME!"
"THAT WAS WHERE CAP CAME IN...CAP, WHO TRIED TO TURN A RUNNY-NOSED NOTHING INTO A FIRST-CLASS COSTUMED HERO!"
ONE WAY
BUT, THAT WAS MORE THAN EVEN HE COULD MANAGE!
YEAH, YOU'VE HAD YOUR BIG BREAK, JUNIOR...
...AND YOU BLEW IT!
6

SO HERE YOU ARE... A NOBODY, GOING NOWHERE...
...WITH AN AVENGERS I.D. TO SPEED YOU ON YOUR WAY!
NO BRASS RING EVER GUARANTEED MORE FREE RIDES...
...IF YOU'D USE IT!
WHICH YOU WON'T!
Rick Jones
AVENGER
FROM NOW ON, JONES...
WHETHER YOU HITCH IT OR WHETHER YOU HOOF IT...
YOU'RE STRICTLY YOUR OWN BOY!
WOOSH
...THOUG AFTER HOUR AND O TIRE THUM
HOLD THA TRUC SLOW DOW
COULD BE THE JONES LUCK IS STARTING TO TURN...!
...SURE THING, KID!
WHER YA HEADI
WHEN I GET THERE, FRIEND...
YOU'LL BE THE FIRST TO KNOW!
NOW, MAR-VELL... THE TIME HAS CO DO YOU FEEL IT... DO YOU KNOW WH YOU MUS DO...?
"YES... I KNO I KNOW..."

ATER, PAL!
AND DON'T TAKE ANY WOODEN **DIESELS!**
YOU'RE A **CRAZY KID,** GETTIN' OFF IN THE MIDDLE OF **NOWHERE!**
BUT, IF THAT'S HOW YOU GET YOUR KICKS, IT'S **YOUR** FUNERAL!
EAH... MY UNERAL!
ONLY THING IS, I DON'T KNOW **WHY** I SUDDENLY ASKED HIM TO PULL OVER!
AYBE I COULD **GURE** IT, IF GOT RID OF **XCEDRIN EADACHE NO. 101!**
THEN AGAIN, MAYBE I'M WHAT HE **SAID...**
JUST A CRAZY, MIXED-UP **KID...!**
UH OH! LOOKS LIKE MORE THAN A **SUMMER BREEZE** BREWIN'!
BETTER HEAD FOR **SHELTER,** RICK OL' BUDDY...
..IF HERE **IS** ANY!
THOSE **BOULDERS** UP THERE OUGHT TO--
HEY! I'M NOT **ALONE** UP HERE-- THERE'S SOMEBODY **UP AHEAD--!**
NO-- IT **CAN'T** BE!
BUT-- IT **IS--!!**
8

IT'S--
CAP!
AND YET--
IS IT?
THE FIGURE'S
GLOWING...
SAYING
NOTHING...
JUST
GESTURING...
...AND NOW...
IT'S
TURNING TO
FLEE!
NO!
WHOEVER, OR
WHATEVER
YOU ARE...
YOU'RE NOT
RUNNING
OUT ON
ME...!
I
WON'T
LET
YOU!!

--I MIGHT WELL TRY CKLING HADOW!
NO MATTER HOW FAST I RUN--YOU STAY THE SAME DISTANCE AHEAD OF ME!
WHO ARE YOU? WHERE ARE YOU LEADING ME?
AND, ABOVE ALL--
WHY??
SHRIEK YOUR QUESTIONS TO THE WIND, RICK JONES--THEY SHALL HAVE NO ANSWERS--
--UNTIL YOU OVERTAKE THE FLEETING FORM WHICH RACES BEFORE YOU, LIKE SOME ELUSIVE MEMORY--!
10

I MUST BE OUTTA MY TREE HOUSE!
WHY ELSE WOULD I KEEP RUNNING OVER HILL AND DALE LIKE A MADMAN?
HE'S AS FAR AHEAD OF ME AS EVER!
BUT, I CAN'T GIVE UP NOW!
I CAN'T-- AND I WON'T!
I MAY BE A SUPERHE WASH-O ...BUT I'M QUITTE
AND, IT LOOKS LIKE CLEAN LIVING PAYS OFF AGAIN!
"CAP"--OR WHOEVER-- IS RUNNING INTO THAT CAVE!
IT MA BE SO KIND O TRA
BUT WHAT THE HEY-- NOBODY LIVES FOREVER-

THAT'S IT, RICK JONES... PLUNGE RIGHT IN... INTO THE DARKNESS WHICH SEIZES YOU LIKE A LIVING VISE! FOLLOW THE GLOWING WILL-O'-THE-WISP THAT LEADS YOU DOWN, DOWNWARD INTO THE MURKY BLACK...
...UNTIL ABRUPTLY, AROUND ONE CRAGGY BEND...
FAN-TASTIC!
I'VE BEEN IN MAD SCIENTISTS' LABS BEFORE --BUT THIS TAKES THE TEST TUBE!
WEIRD MACHINERY... WEIRDER LIGHTING... AND STATUES OF THINGS THAT NEVER WALKED THIS PL
COMPARED TO THIS SET-UP, DOC BANNER AND THE AVENGERS ARE JUST PLAYIN' WITH TINKER TOYS!
BUT-- WHERE'S MY SHY, RETIRING SHIELD-SLINGER?
THERE HE IS-- STANDING IN THAT ARCHED DOORWAY --BECKONING ME TO FOLLOW HIM!
I'VE GOT A FEELING WE'RE GETTIN' DOWN TO THE NITTY-GRITTY!
WELL, I'VE COME THIS FAR...
12

...NO SENSE TURNING BACK NOW!
WHA--?? CAP'S DOING A FADE-OUT ON ME--!
HE'S GONE!!
BUT--HE WAS POINTING AT THESE FAR-OUT--BRACELETS!
IS IT JUST MY OVER-WORKED IMAGINATION--
OR ARE THOSE THINGS THROBBING WITH LIGHT--LIKE THEY'RE ALIVE?
CAN'T RESIST TRYING 'EM ON--AND THEY FIT!
I'D HAVE SWORN THEY WERE TOO BIG FOR ME--!
"THEY WERE TOO LARGE, EARTHLING... UNTIL YOU DONNED THEM!"
"DO NOT BE AFRAID, SON, OF THE IMAGE YOU SEE BEFORE YOU... OR THE WORDS YOU HEAR...!"
BITE YOUR TONGUE, SHADOW-MAN!
YOU'RE TALKING TO A GUY WHO WAS ALMOST AN AVENGER!
I DON'T SCARE EASY!
"THEN, DO AS I SAY... AND SLAM YOUR WRIS TOGETHER.. WITH ALL TH FORCE YO CAN MUSTER!!"
SURE! WHY NOT?
WE AIM TO PLEASE...!

TANG
FAN-TASTIC!
SOMETHING'S--HAPPENING TO ME--LIKE I WAS CHANGING--
--LIKE I WASN'T RICK JONES ANY MORE--BUT--
--CAPTAIN MARVEL!!
I'M FREE OF THE NEGATIVE ZONE!
FREE!
14

"NOW--WAIT JUST A MINUTE, MASKED MAN!"
"MAYBE YOU'RE FREE, BUT WHAT ABOUT ME-- RICK JONES?"
"I FEEL-- WEIGHTLESS-- ALL ZONKED OUT--LIKE I'M IN BETWEEN A DOZEN DIFFERENT PLACES! WHERE AM I??
YOU ARE IN--
--THE NEGA-TIVE ZONE!
BUT FEAR NOT, YOU WON'T STAY THERE FOREVER--
--AS I WOULD HAVE DONE--
--IF NOT FOR THESE MILLENNIA OLD NEGA-BANDS
THEY ARE THE ONLY RECORDED ANTIDOTE TO THE KIND OF RADIATION THAT BLASTED ME INTO THE ANTI-COSMOS!
BUT, THOU THEY H BEE FOR BIDDEN
AND SO THEY HAVE, MAR-VELL--BECAUSE OF THE POWERS THEY CONFER UPON THEIR WEARER!
ALL THE MORE REASON WHY I SHOULD POSSESS THEM--
--RATHER THAN YOU!
YON-ROGG!!
YES, FOOL! YON-ROGG, YOUR ARCH-ENEMY!
YO RO WHOM HA TRAC ACROS UNIVER
YON-RO WHO CAUSE YOUR BELOVE DEAT
STALK HIM, MAR-VELL...S YOUR HUMAN PREY AS YO ONCE DID THE MISSHAPE CARNIVORGS OF FAR DIS-TANT BETELGEUSE!
CIRCLE...FEINT...THRUST AS YOU HAVE DONE AGAIN THE MARAUDING AAKON THE EMPIRE-CRAZED SKRU
YON-ROGG HESITATES-- DELAYS HIS FIRE...FOR, SUR HE SENSES THAT HIS FIRS BLAST MUST BE A TELLIN ONE...OR HE SHALL NEVER LIVE TO FIRE ANOTHER!
CIRCLE, AND SEARCH FOR A OPENING...THE SLIGHTES CARELESSNESS ON THE PA OF HIM YOU HATE!
NOW, MAR-VELL--NOW

I WAS--TOO SLOW!
--STILL STIFF--FROM DRIFTING IN THE NEGATIVE ZONE--!
AND NOW, MAR-VELL, YOUR FOE KNOWS THE MEANING OF FEAR...KNOWS THAT HE FACES NOT A MERE MAN OF THE KREE...BUT SOMETHING FAR, FAR MORE...!
WE SHALL SEE HOW YOU FARE WHEN THESE BOULDERS BAR YOUR PATH!
WHAT YOUR EYES BEHOLD, ASSASSIN--
WILL YOUR MIND BELIEVE?
BY THE GREAT PAMA!
ET--YOU RVIVED A ROTONIC BURST!
NO ONE HAS EVER DONE THAT BEFORE!
NO ONE!
ACCURSED FATES!
I FOLLOWED THE BOY--MY INSTRUMENTS SHOWING THAT HE WAS UNDER MAR-VELL'S MENTAL DOMINION!
HE LED ME HERE--TO THE LONG-LOST KREE OUTPOST I SOUGHT!
AND NOW I MUST FLEE--LIKE SOME EARTH-SPAWNED CUR!
16

BUT, IF THE LEGENDARY NEGA-BANDS STILL ELUDE MY GRASP--
PERHAPS REVENGE SHALL NOT!
YON-ROGG CRUISER LIFTIN OFF!
FOR AL MY SPEE --I CANN REACH I IN TIME
VAROOOOMM
AND YET, WHAT DO I TRULY KNOW OF MY SPEED--OR ANY OTHER OF MY FORMER POWERS?
FOR, I NOW POSSESS NO POWERS--BUT THOSE WHICH THE NEGA-BANDS BESTOW UPON ME!
I WONDER IF--
I CAN FLY!!
BUT, THE CRUISER EVEN NOW APPROACHES ESCAPE VELOCITY!
I MUST OVERTAK IT WITHIN MOMENTS-
--OR MY CHANCE IS LOST!!

--YOU CLOSE N FOR THE KILL, EH, MAR-VELL?
ETTER FOR OU THAT YOU AD REMAINED ON KREE-LAR!
FOR, YOU HAVE LOST YOUR HEART TO THIS PRIMITIVE PLANET!
AND NOW, IT SHALL HAVE YOUR LIFE, AS WELL--!
AROL!
CAROL ANVERS!
IF YON-ROGG CAPTURED HER--IT CAN ONLY HAVE BEEN TO GET AT ME!
SHE MUST NOT DIE--EVEN IF THAT FIEND ESCAPES!
WAIT! SHE--ISN'T BREATHING--!
SHE'S--TICKING!!
SHE ISN'T CAROL--NOT EVEN HUMAN!
SHE'S A BOMB--A BOMB SET TO EXPLOOOOO
18

THE SHEER IMPACT --WOULD HAVE TURNED ANOTHER MAN--TO SHREDDED ATOMS!
YET-- I LIVE-- I LIVE!
BUT--MY WRIST-BANDS NO LONGER KEEP ME ALOFT!
I'M FALLING-- PLUNGING TO MY DEATH-- UNLESS--
YES!
THE INSTANT THAT I TURNED MY THOUGHTS TO SOARING--
--I COULD FLY ONCE MORE!!
THAT, THEN, IS THE ALL-BUT-FORGOTTEN POWER OF THESE BANDS...
...TO TRANSFORM MENTAL ENERGY INTO PHYSICAL
JUST AS THEY ALSO EXCHANGED MY NEGATIVE ATOMS...
...WITH THE POSITIVE ONES OF THE YOUNG EARTH-LING!
YET, ALL MY POWERS COULD NOT GAIN ME THE VENGEANCE I CRAVE...!
"NEVER MIND TH WEEPIN AND GNASHIN OF TEET SILVER TOP..."

THIS IS THAT 'YOUNG EARTHLING' TALKIN'-- REMEMBER ME?"
"BUT WHEN DO I GET OUT OF HERE--IF I DO?"
"I'VE ENJOYED THE RINGSIDE SEAT AND ALL..."
T WAS EVER MY TENT ROB OU OF OUR FE TO VE MY WN--
--EVEN IF THAT WERE WITHIN MY POWER!
--WHICH IT ISN'T!
KTHNG!
BROTHER RICK IS BACK IN TOWN!
FAAAN-TASTIC!
SOMETHING HAPPENED TO ME WHEN WE TWO...TRADED ATOMS!
SOMETHING LIKE...A MERGING!
HE'S PART OF ME NOW--LIKE I AM OF HIM!
I EVEN SHARE MAR-VELL'S DESIRE... FOR REVENGE!
AND SOMEHOW, I KNOW I'M GONNA FIND YON-ROGG FOR HIM...
...IF IT TAKES ME THE REST OF MY LIFE...!
"AND, IT JUST MIGHT, RICK JONES... IT JUST MIGHT..."
"...UNLESS HE FINDS YOU FIRST!!"

SPIDER-MAN
15¢
99
AUG
02457
the AMAZING SPIDER-MAN
MARVEL COMICS GROUP
PANIC IN THE PRISON!

THE AMAZING SPIDER-MAN!
A DAY IN THE LIFE OF...
FEATURING: PANIC IN THE PRISON!
THIS ONE YOU DON'T DARE MISS!
ALSO FEATURING: SPIDEY ON T.V.!
BY:
TAN LEE AUTHOR
GIL KANE PENCILLER
FRANK GIACOIA INKER
ARTIE SIMEK LETTERER
609Z

PETER PARKER AND GWEN STACY HAVE FOUND EACH OTHER AGAIN--

AND, AS FAR AS THEY'RE CONCERNED, NO ONE ELSE EXISTS IN THE ENTIRE WORLD.
EVEN THOUGH SHE HASN'T MENTIONED HIM--SHE SEEMS TO HAVE LOST HER BITTERNESS OVER --SPIDER-MAN
AND FOR ONCE, I'M GO MAKE LIKE THE WEB SPINNER WAS NEVER BORN! I'M NOT GONN LET HIM COME BETWE US AGAIN

HAPPY, GWENDY?
CAN'T YOU TELL, MAN O' MINE?
I FEEL LIKE I'M FLOATING-- NOT EVEN TOUCHING THE GROUND
VOT

YOU KNOW, HONEY-- A GAL LIKE YOU CAN BE--HABIT-FORMING

ARE YOU TRYING TO TELL ME SOMETHING, MR. PARKER?

YOU KNOW IT, LADY
HOTEL
BAR

AND YOU ALSO KNOW--WHAT I'M TRYING TO ASK
WHAT I WANNA KNOW IS--HOW WILL YOU FEEL AFTER I ASK IT?

HAT DO
U THIN--
OH!
I THINK YOU TALK TOO MUCH

SINCE IT'S NOT POLITE TO LOOK IN ON SUCH PERSONAL STUFF, AND SINCE THIS REALLY ISN'T A LOVE STORY MAG, LET'S SKIP AHEAD A FEW MINUTES, WHERE WE FIND--
I'LL PICK YOU UP TONIGHT, GWENDY
I'LL BE COUNTING THE SECONDS

KAY, PARKER--YOU'RE NALLY GETTING YOUR RSONAL LIFE TOGETHER--
AND THIS TIME, YOU'RE NOT GONNA BLOW IT
ACME

BUT, THE FIRST THING I'VE GOTTA DO BEFORE I POP THE QUESTION, IS--MAKE SURE I CAN SUPPORT A WIFE
AND THAT MEANS-- A JOB

I CAN'T GO BACK TO MR. OSBORN--'CAUSE I'M AFRAID TO RISK HIS TURNING INTO THE GOBLIN AGAIN*
SO IT LOOKS LIKE I'VE GOTTA HEAD FOR THE DAILY BUGLE NOW
*READERS OF OUR PREVIOUS ISSUES'LL KNOW WHAT WE MEAN. THE OTHERS CAN TAKE OUR WORD FOR IT! --STAN.

NYWAY, I'VE MODIFIED MY ECRET LITTLE IDEY CAMERA-- RNED IT INTO A REAL SUB-MINI
AND I'VE BEEN ANXIOUS TO GET A CHANCE TO GIVE IT A TRYOUT

MR. ROBERTSON! CAN I TALK TO YOU FOR A MINUTE?
THOSE DULCET, BELL-LIKE TONES--
THEY CAN ONLY BELONG TO--

PETER PARKER! BEEN LOOKIN' FOR YOU, SON
THERE'S A JOB WAITING
THERE IS?
3

LEMME JUST CHECK IT OUT WITH JAMESON

IS THAT PRISON ASSIGNMENT STILL UP FOR GRABS, JJ?
YEAH! ALL OUR TOP CAMERAMEN ARE EITHER SICK OR IN THE FIELD

I'M TRYING TO GET HOLD OF A GOOD FREE-LANCER NOW, BUT--
SAVE YOUR DIME, JONAH. YOUR WORRIES ARE OVER
PETER PARKER JUST DROPPED IN

PARKER, HUH? I WONDERED WHERE THAT KID HAD BEEN?
WELL, HE'S BETTER THAN NOBODY
COME OFF IT, MAN! HE'S GOOD AS THEY COME-- AND YOU KNOW IT
YEAH, BUT I DON'T WANNA TELL HIM

AWRIGHT! THERE'S A RIOT AT THE CITY PEN-- THEY'RE HOLDING THE WARDEN HOSTAGE
I NEED PICTURES! SO GET GOING
FIRST, LET'S TALK MONEY

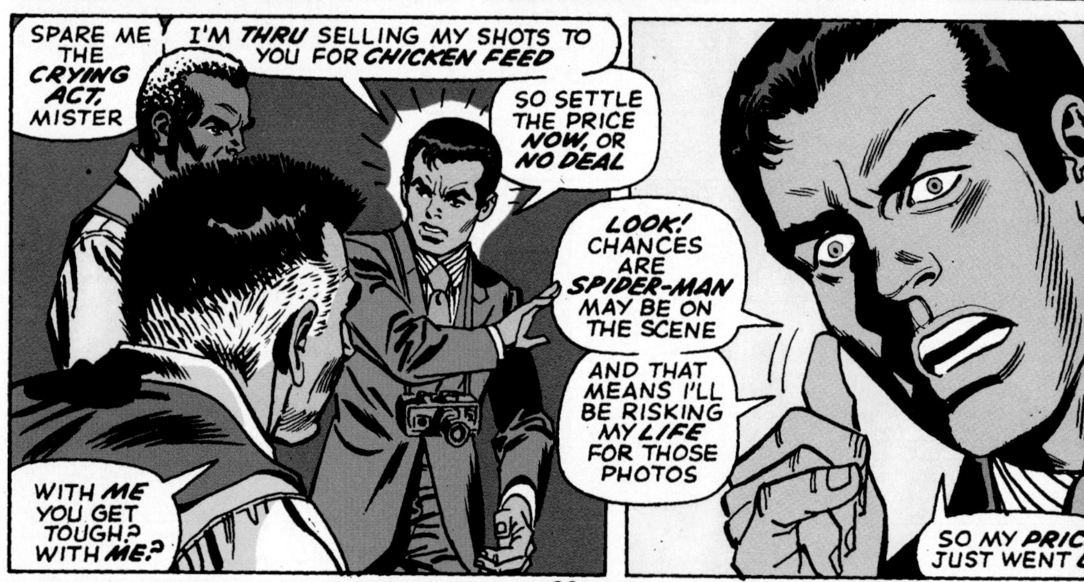
SPARE ME THE CRYING ACT, MISTER
I'M THRU SELLING MY SHOTS TO YOU FOR CHICKEN FEED
SO SETTLE THE PRICE NOW, OR NO DEAL
WITH ME YOU GET TOUGH? WITH ME?
LOOK! CHANCES ARE SPIDER-MAN MAY BE ON THE SCENE
AND THAT MEANS I'LL BE RISKING MY LIFE FOR THOSE PHOTOS

'RE PRESSURING
, 'CAUSE YOU'VE
OT ME OVER A
ARREL! YOU
NOW I NEED
THOSE PIX--
AND THAT'S NOT ALL! I WANNA BE A SPARE-TIME STAFF PHOTOGRAPHER--
AND THAT MEANS A SALARY

WHAT IF I SAY NO?
GO GET THE PIX YOURSELF

YOU'RE BLUFFING
I AM? TRY ME
YOU-- YOU-- YOU--

KAY--
U WIN!
O FOR
SHOTS
USE
AND YOU GOT YOURSELF A PART-TIME JOB
I'LL WORK OUT THE DETAILS WITH YOU LATER, PETE!
NOW GO GET THOSE PIX
OH, WOW! WILL I?!!
I CAN'T BELIEVE IT!

I DID IT! I DID IT
I FINALLY CAME OUT AHEAD OF THE OLD SKINFLINT
I WOULDN'T HAVE HAD THE NERVE-- IF NOT FOR GWEN

MY LUCK'S
FINALLY
HANGED!
M FLYIN'
NOW
LONG AS I HAVE GWENDY-- NOTHING CAN STOP ME

MY SUB-MINI'S ALL LOADED, AND READY TO GO
I'LL BRING 'EM BACK SHOTS THAT NO ONE ELSE COULD POSSIBLY GET

NO ONE, THAT IS--
--EXCEPT SPIDER-MAN
5

OF COURSE, IF THERE *IS* A RIOT AT THE CITY JAIL--
DON'T SMOKE

EVERY *OTH* NEWS PHOT IN *TOWN* W BE ON TH SCENE

BUT THEY'LL BE ON THE *OUTSIDE*-- LOOKING IN
NOTHING KEE *ME* FROM WHERE IT' *HAPPENIN*
THAT'S THE ONE *ADVANTAGE* OF BEING *SPIDER-MAN*--

JUST AS I THOUGHT! *POLICE CORDONS*-- ALL AROUND THE BUILDING
AND FAR BE IT FROM *ME* TO BREAK THRU A POLICE LINE--

NOT WHEN I CAN GO *ABOVE*

HEY! A COUPLE OF *CONS*--GUARDING TH *ROOF*

OD THING TURPO
D US TA KEEP
ATCH UP HERE
--IN CASE ANY WHIRLYBIRDS TRY'N LAND THE FUZZ ABOVE US
YEAH-- TURPO THINKS'A EVERY-THING

HERE'S ONE THING HE DIDN'T THINK OF!
MMPFF!

N'T WORRY
BOUT YOUR
UDDY--HE
WON'T BE
LONELY

NOW TALK! WHAT'S IT ALL ABOUT?
WE--WE'RE RIOTIN' TO BE TREATED LIKE HUMAN BEIN'S

THEY KEEP US CAGED LIKE ANIMALS
WE GOTTA WAIT MONTHS TO COME TO TRIAL

E JUST
VANT
OUR
GHTS--
HAT'S
ALL
AND TURPO SAID HE'D GET 'EM FOR US

HEY, WAIT! STOP! WH--WHAT'RE YOU DOIN'?
SETTING A RECORD! I'LL BE THE FIRST GUY EVER TO BREAK INTO JAIL
7

NOW, YOU STAY THERE AND THINK NICE THOUGHTS--
WHILE I GO FIND OUR FRIEND TURPO
AND, SINCE I'M NOT APT TO WIN ANY POPULARITY PRIZES IN A PLACE LIKE THIS--
THE LESS ANY-ONE SEES OF ME, THE BETTER
ANY WORD FROM TURPO YET?
NO! HE'S STILL IN WITH THE WARDEN
THE WARDEN BETTER COME ACROSS--OR ELSE
SO THAT'S THE SIZE OF IT, HUH?
LOOKS LIKE I'D BETTER GET TO THE WARDEN--BUT FAST
THOSE CONS IN THERE ARE PLAYING FOR KEEPS
THE ONE I SPOKE TO WAS LEVELLING WITH ME
HE REALLY MEANT IT ABOUT THOSE GRIPES
BUT--WHERE DOES THE BLAME LIE?
DO AS WE TELL YA, MAN
YOU CAN'T GET AWAY WITH THIS, TURPO
YOU'RE SELLING THOSE CO DOWN TH RIVER

SKIP THE SOB STORY, MAN--IF YA WANNA STAY HEALTHY
THEY DO THE RIOTIN'--AND TURPO'S GONNA ESCAPE! WHAT'S WRONG WITH THAT?

SO THAT'S WHAT IT'S ALL ABOUT
TURPO'S JUST USING THE RIOT AS A COVER FOR HIS OWN ESCAPE
I CALL THAT DIRTY POOL

EY, TURPO! WHAT OUT OUR LIST OF GRIEVANCES?
TAKE 'EM TO THE CHAPLAIN, SUCKER

THEN--YOU NEVER DID CARE ABOUT THE CONDITIONS IN HERE! YOU USED US--SO YOU COULD GET OUT
THAT'S WHAT I LIKE--A REAL SMART CON
YOU ROTTEN--

UH UH! NO NAMES
I DON'T CARE WHO I GOTTA VENTILATE TO GIT OUTTA HERE

AFTER WE'RE GONE, YOU GUYS CAN DEMONSTRATE ALL YA WANNA

YEAH! WE DON'T WANNA BUST UP YER PARTY

I JUST WANNA THANK YA FER BEIN' OUR PIGEONS

9

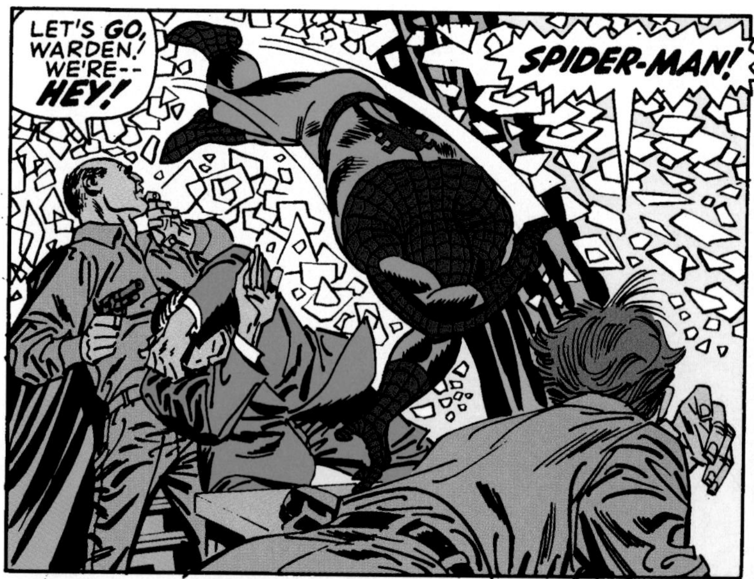
LET'S GO, WARDEN! WE'RE-- HEY!
SPIDER-MAN!

GUN 'IM DOWN, YOU GUYS
DON'T L 'IM ST US

TURPO, YOU'RE LIVING IN A FOOL'S PARADISE
YOU'VE ALREADY BEEN STOPPED

THIS WRAPS UP YOUR RIOT, WARDEN
NOT QUITE! THERE ARE TWO MORE OF TURPO'S MEN, OUTSIDE THE DOOR-- TO KEEP THE OTHERS FROM LEARNING HE'S BETRAYED THEM

THAT'S ALL I WANTED TO KNOW

OLD IT,
U GUYS
THERE'S SOMETHING YOU SHOULD KNOW
TURPO ORGANIZED YOUR RIOT--BUT HE DIDN'T CARE ABOUT CONDITIONS IN HERE
HE TRIED TO ESCAPE--USING THE WARDEN AS A HOSTAGE--WHILE YOU ALL COVERED FOR HIM
WHY SHOULD WE BELIEVE YOU?
CAUSE I'M
LLIN' YA TO! THE MAN'S TALKIN' STRAIGHT, HEAR?
BUT TURPO DON'T MEAN NOTHIN'! THERE'S SOMETHING MORE IMPORTANT--
THE WARDEN AGREES WITH MOST'A OUR GRIPES! HE SAID HE'LL TRY'N HELP US
YEAH? BUT WHAT'LL THEY DO TO US--ON ACCOUNT'A THE RIOT?
YOU DROP YOUR WEAPONS--RETURN TO OUR CELLS--I'LL REQUEST AMNESTY FOR EVERY LAST ONE OF YOU
E MEANS IT! NOW
'S UP TO THE CONS
THE WARDEN'S ALWAYS BEEN A RIGHT JOE! WATTA WE GOT TO LOSE?
OKAY! IT'S A DEAL, MAN
AND I'LL STUDY YOUR GRIEVANCE LIST

IT'S OVER! AND MY LITTLE SUB-MINI WAS JUST A'CLICKIN' AWAY
C'MON, YOU GUYS! WE'RE HEADIN' BACK
HEY! DID SEE THE WEB-SPINN DO HIS THING?

SECONDS LATER--
THE RIOT IS ENDED-- FOR NOW! BUT, IF WE DON'T GET THE MONEY WE NEED-- THE REFORMS WE NEED-- THESE PRISONS ARE GONNA EXPLODE
YOU TELL 'EM, WARDEN
AND YOU CAN QUOTE ME

AND NOW, I'D BETTER START-- UH OH!
SPIDER-MAN!

WHO CAN THAT BE?
WELL, THERE'S ONE WAY TO FIND OUT--

AM I GLAD I SAW YOU
HOW COME
IT'S A LUCKY BREAK--FOR BOTH OF US

YOU'RE JUST WHAT I NEED! I'VE NEVER HAD A GUEST LIKE YOU ON MY TV SHOW
COME ON IN, WILLYA?

JUST
RD WHAT
PPENED
AT THE
RISON
IT WAS
ON A
RADIO
NEWS
BULLETIN
DON'T TELL
ME! I WAS
THERE

I KNOW! THINK WHAT A SCOOP IT'LL BE FOR ME TO HAVE YOU ON MY SHOW-- THE VERY SAME NIGHT
I'M ALL SHOOK-UP

'LL BE GREAT
BLIC RELATIONS
OR YOU! PEOPLE
MIGHT START
LOVING YOU
CAN'T LIVE ON LOVE! WHAT'LL IT PAY?
HOW CAN YOU TALK ABOUT MONEY WHEN I'M OFFERING YOU FAME--GLAMOR?
YOU COULD BE ANOTHER ZSA ZSA GABOR
NO DOUGH, NO SHOW
ALL RIGHT-- I'LL PAY YOU THE USUAL RATE
IT'S A DEAL

UNNO WHAT THE
SUAL RATE IS--
BUT HOW BAD
CAN IT BE?
THINGS ARE GOING SO WELL, I'M GETTING NERVOUS
BE BACK BEFORE MIDNIGHT

I'D BETTER GET MY PICTURES OVER TO THE BUGLE NOW
AND JAMESON BETTER NOT WELCH ON HIS DEAL

ONCE I GET MY HANDS ON THE CASH HE PROMISED ME--
I'LL SHOW GWENDY THE BEST TIME SHE'S EVER HAD
IT'LL BE GREAT TO TREAT THAT LIVING DOLL THE WAY SHE DESERVES

I'LL RUSH THE NEGATIVES RIGHT DOWN TO THE BUGLE'S PHOTO LAB--
THEY OUGHTTA BE READY INSIDE THE HOUR

AND SO--
WE HEARD ABOUT IT ON THE RADIO, PARKER
EVERY-ONE WAS THERE--EXCEPT YOU
DON'T BELIEVE EVERY-THING YOU HEAR
I WAS THERE, ALSO

BUT I HADDA STAY HIDDEN--IN ORDER TO GET THESE PIX
YOU MEAN-- YOU GOT THEM?

HE GOT THEM, ALL RIGHT

I DON'T GET IT! THERE WERE TWO DOZEN PRO'S THERE--
AND, AS USUAL, PARKER GOT THE JUMP ON THEM ALL
DUNNO HOW YOU DID IT, SON--BUT GOOD WORK
THANKS, MR. ROBERTSON
I SURE HOPE HE DOESN'T KNOW

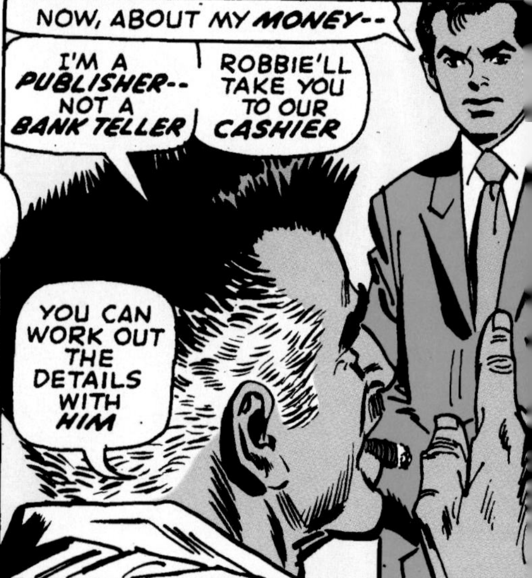
NOW, ABOUT MY MONEY--
I'M A PUBLISHER-- NOT A BANK TELLER
ROBBIE'LL TAKE YOU TO OUR CASHIER
YOU CAN WORK OUT THE DETAILS WITH HIM

E YOU LATER, JJ
REATS! WAYS REATS
IS HE EVER IN A GOOD MOOD?
SURE! HE'S GOTTA SLEEP SOMETIME

NOW THAT YOU'RE ON SALARY, REMEMBER-- PAY-DAY IS FRIDAY
SO DROP BY AFTER THREE --TO PICK UP YOUR CHECK
WE--DON'T GET PAID --TILL FRIDAY?

OH NO! I'M SEEING GWEN TONIGHT
HOW WILL I MANAGE TO TAKE HER OUT?

IOW 'VE TTA AKE AT TV HOW
AND I BETTER HOPE THEY'LL PAY ME-- RIGHT ON THE SPOT

I REALIZE I'M NOT A BIG NAME, HOLLYWOOD STAR
BUT I'M A LOT HARDER TO GET THAN THEY ARE
THAT GEM OF WISDOM OUGHTTA BE WORTH SOMETHING-- TO SOMEONE

SURE HOPE A GONNA BE ON TIME

THIS IS ONE APPOINTMENT I DON'T WANNA MISS

--'CAUSE IF I DON'T GET SOME GREEN-BACKS SOON-- FORGET IT!
16

YOUR OFFER STILL HOLD?
SPIDER-MAN! I WAS BEGINNING TO THINK YOU WOULDN'T SHOW
IT'S A GOOD THING I HUNG AROUND-- WAITING TILL THE LAST MINUTE

C'MON-- YOU'RE JUST IN TIME! THEY'RE ABOUT TO START THE TAPING NOW

I'LL GIVE YOU YOUR INTRO-- AND THEN I'LL TELL YOU HOW I WANT YOU TO ENTER--
FORGET IT! THAT'S NOT ONE OF MY HANG-UPS
AND, IF YOU GET STAGE-FRIGHT--

AND NOW--
HOLD IT

I'VE GOT A SURPR
FOR YOU THAT'S JU
TOO BIG TO KEE

AND SO, BEFORE WE GET INTO THE REGULAR PORTION OF OUR SHOW--
FASTEN YOUR SEATBELTS, 'CAUSE HERE COMES--

YOUR FRIENDLY, NEIGHBORHOOD SPIDER-MAN
NO. 1

A BAD ENTRANCE
UT WHAT DO YOU
FOR AN ENCORE?
TOO BAD I FORGOT MY GUITAR

HOW DO WE KNOW HE'S THE REAL SPIDER-MAN? ANY-ONE CAN WEAR A MASK
DID YOU HEAR THAT?
I HEARD IT

ET'S SEE OW MANY POSTERS CAN DO IS LITTLE STUNT
AND, IF WALKING UP THE WALL ISN'T ENOUGH--

THEY CAN ALWAYS TRY COMING DOWN AGAIN--ON THEIR OWN SPECIAL WEBBING
AND, IF ANY MORE PROOF IS NEEDED--

NO! NO! ENOUGH! THAT'S ENOUGH
YOU MADE YOUR POINT!

HAT SE CAN OU DO, PIDEY?
PLENTY
BUT FIRST, I'VE SOME-THING TO SAY

NOW THAT I'VE A CAPTIVE AUDIENCE, I WANNA TALK ABOUT SOME OTHER CAPTIVES--
I MEAN THE PRISONERS WHO ARE LOCKED-UP IN OUR UNDERSTAFFED, OVER-AGE, OVER-CROWDED JAILS
18

I'M TALKING ABOUT CONDITIONS WHERE YOUNG, FIRST-OFFENDERS ARE PUT IN THE SAME CELLS WITH HARDENED CRIMINALS--
--ABOUT AN ANTI-QUATED SYSTEM THAT MAKES PRISONS BREEDING GROUNDS FOR CRIME

I'M TALKING ABOUT MEN WHO STAY LOCKED-UP FOR MONTHS, WAITING FOR TRIAL--'CAUSE THERE AREN'T ENOUGH JUDGES--NOT ENOUGH COURTS--

CRIME--AND JUSTICE--ARE EVERYONE'S PROBLEM! AND IT'S A PROBLEM THAT MUST BE SOLVED BEFORE IT'S TOO LATE

SORRY ABOUT YOUR SHOW--BUT THERE'S STILL A WARRANT OUT FOR HIM
POLICE
HURRY! HE SEES US
OKAY, BOYS--CLOSE IN
QUICK! PUT ON THE SOAP COMMERCIAL

NUTS! THAT'S WHAT I GET FOR TALKING TOO MUCH
I SHOULD HAVE FIGURED THE COPS WOULD HAVE TO CLOSE IN

ANOTHER FEW SECONDS AND THEY'D HAVE HAD ME
ONIGHT
PUBLIC
NVITED

I WONDER IF THERE'LL EVER BE A WAY FOR ME TO CLEAR MYSELF OF--
OH NO! I JUST REMEMBERED SOMETHING
I TOOK OFF--BEFORE HE COULD PAY ME

--I CAN'T
LAY ANY
ONGER
S TIME
CHANGE
ND CALL
GWEN

BUT THIS TIME I'M NOT MAKING THE SAME OLD BRAINLESS MISTAKE
I'M NOT GONNA BLOW THE BIT, JUST 'CAUSE I'M SHORT OF CASH

I'LL JUST LEVEL WITH HER--TELL HER I'M BROKE
G. STACY
NO MORE PLAYING GAMES! NO MORE TRYING TO COVER THINGS

TER! I JUST
NEW YOU
ULDN'T BE
LATE
BUT--WHY DO YOU LOOK SO DOWN-CAST?
3A

I'M JUST DISAPPOINTED, HONEY! I WANTED TO--TAKE YOU TO THE BEST PLACE IN TOWN TONIGHT--GIVE YOU THE MOON! BUT--
PETER PARKER, YOU'RE AN IDIOT

WHAT DO YOU MEAN?
I'D NO INTEN-TION OF GOING OUT! I SPENT ALL AFTER-NOON COOKING DINNER FOR US
WE'RE STAYING RIGHT HERE

THIS IS ONE TIME I'M HAVING YOU ALL TO MYSELF
PARKER, YOU MAY HAVE BEEN A LOSER BEFORE--
BUT IT LOOKS LIKE YOU FINALLY DID SOMETHING RIGHT

NEXT:
THE SENSATIONAL 100TH ANNIVERSARY ISSUE YOU'VE BEEN WAITING FOR!
featuring:
"THE SUMMING UP!"
PLUS--
THE MOST-SHOCKING UNEXPECTED ENDING SPIDEY HAS EVER HAD!!

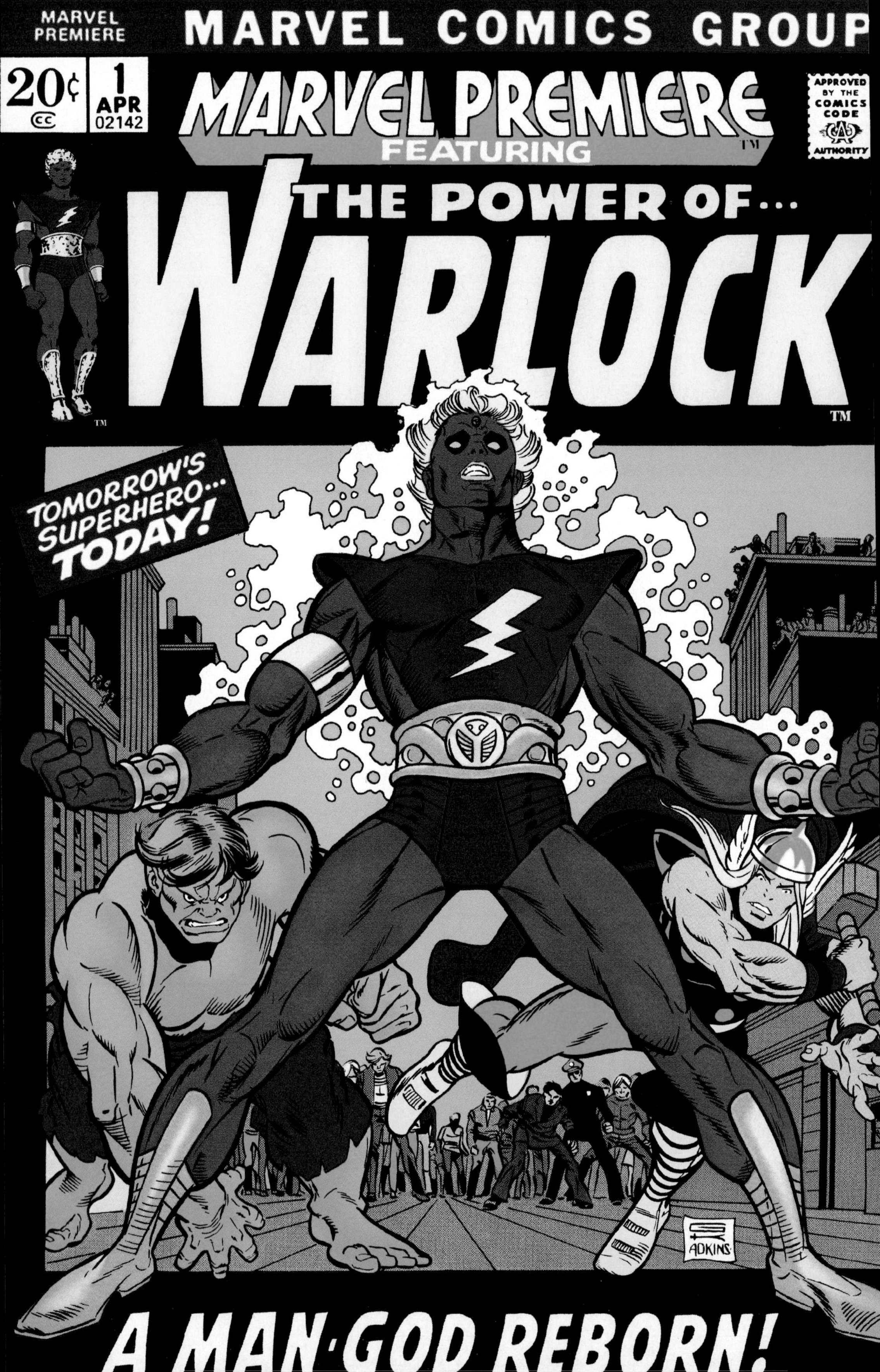

MARVEL PREMIERE
MARVEL COMICS GROUP
20¢
CC
1
APR
02142
MARVEL PREMIERE
FEATURING
TM
APPROVED BY THE COMICS CODE CA AUTHORITY
THE POWER OF...
WARLOCK
TM
TM
TOMORROW'S SUPERHERO... TODAY!
ADKINS
A MAN-GOD REBORN!

STAN LEE PRESENTS... THE BIRTHING OF AN IMPORTANT NEW SERIES, CONCEIVED AND EXECUTED BY:
ROY THOMAS WRITER and GIL KANE ARTIST
DAN ADKINS, EMBELLISHER
SAM ROSEN LETTERER
EATURING: AWESOME, EASHED POWER THE BEING KNOWN ONLY AS...
HIM
AND MEN SHALL CALL HIM...
WARLOCK!
NOW, LET THE WONDERMENT BEGIN--!

AT FIRST: A SPECK OF LIGHT AND DUST. AN ASTEROID, PERHAPS. ONE MORE CHUNK OF LIFELESS ROCK, DRIFTING AIMLESSLY IN FROM DEEP SPACE...
...AND PAST THE BLOOD-SCARRED FACE OF MARS, THAT ONCE WAS ALSO GOD OF WAR.

NEXT: IT ROLLS LIKE A POCK-MARKED MARBLE ACROSS THE BLACK HEAVENS, NEARLY BRUSHING THE MANY-CRATERED MOON.

NOW: IT SETTLES COMFORTABLY, EFFORTLESSLY, INTO AN ORBIT AROUND THE EARTH, AND WE GET A MUCH CLOSER LOOK AT IT...

...AND INTO IT...

...AND IT REALLY ISN'T JUST AN ASTEROID, AFTER ALL.

...UNLESS ALL ASTEROIDS CONCEAL (BENEATH THEIR STONE-COLD SKINS) A HUNDRED COILED MILES OF CORRIDORS... MACHINES WHICH HUM AND SOFTLY WHINE... AND NOTHING SHOWING OUTSIDE TO SUGGEST WHAT LIES WITHIN...

...SAVE A SMALL, DEFIANT ANTENNA WHICH JUTS PROUDLY INTO THE DARKNESS...AND TURNS... AND TURNS... AND TURNS...

HILE, INSIDE THE GENTLY PULSING
LANETOID, AN ARMORED WITNESS
URVEYS THAT WHICH THE SPINNING
NTENNA REVEALS...
...AND HE SIGHS.
OMMENCING:
ELECTRONIC
RNALS OF THE
EVOLUTIONARY...
PE ONE, TRACK
...THE STORY OF
OJECT ALPHA.
MONTHS I
TRAVERSED THE
S OF SPACE, TO
ONCE MORE THE
SS-12 GLOBE
WN AS SOL-III.
THE PLANET EARTH... MY HOMEWORLD.
AND NOW, IT IS FITTING THAT I DICTATE THESE MEMOIRS, TO BE RECORDED AND STORED ON MINIA-TURIZED TAPES EVEN AS I SPEAK THEM.
FOR, I'LL DO THIS DAY WHAT NO MAN BORN OF WOMAN HAS EVER BEFORE DREAMED OF DOING...
...OR LOSE MY IMMORTAL SOUL IN THE TRYING!
BUT, I RACE AHEAD OF MYSELF, IN MY PERIPATETIC MUSINGS.
IT IS AT THE BEGINNING THAT I MUST START.
PAINFUL THOUGH THE MEMORIES BE, ALL MUST BE RECORDED...
...THAT OTHERS MAY PROFIT FROM MY MISTAKES.
AND THERE WERE MISTAKES, WERE THERE NOT, MY FRIEND?
YOU WERE NOT CONTENT, THAT HALF-DECADE AGO, TO HAVE CREATED A RACE OF NEW-MEN...
...PARTLY ANIMAL, PARTLY HUMAN... AND SOMEHOW MORE THAN EITHER.
, YOU WERE
T CONTENT.
U HAD TO
SH HARDER...
RTHER...!*
ALL THESE YEARS... ALL THESE CHANGES AND NEVER A FAILURE!
YET, NEVER BEFORE HAVE I ATTEMPTED TO TRANSFORM A SUBJECT WOLF.
AH... ALREADY HIS BODY ACHIEVES TEMPORAL MOTION... HIS VERY GENES ARE SHIFTING, ALTERING...
*AS GLIMPSED IN THE NOW-CLASSIC THOR #134-135.--STAN.
3

"BUT, I HAD RECKONED WITHOUT THE INHERENT SAVAGERY OF THE WOLF--- AND, WHEN A FATEFUL ACCIDENT HURLED THE EXPERIMENT BEYOND MY CONTROL---
"---THE MAN-BEAST WAS BORN---!
I LIVE!
I FEEL!
"HATRED-- YES--- THE EMOTION WHICH SHACKLES MAN TO THE ANIMAL WITHIN HIM---
"HATRED WHICH EXTENDED TO ALL THAT LIVED---
"--AND WHICH LED THE MONSTER TO ATTACK BOTH MYSELF --AND THE ONE CALLED THOR.
"YET, EVEN MANIACAL HATRED PROVED INSUFFICIENT---
BKAM
"-- TO STAND BEFORE THE WRATH OF THE SON OF ODIN.
"BOTH THE MAN-BEAST AND HIS ARMY OF EVIL NEW-MEN WERE DEFEATED---
"--- SENT STREAKING TOWARD THE DISTANT DROMISANA GALAXY--- AND ETERNAL EXILE.
STILL, I SAW CLEARLY THAT EVEN MY LOYAL NEW-MEN POSED AN EVENTUAL THREAT TO HUMANKIND.
THUS, UNABLE TO BEAR TH THOUGHT O DESTROYING THEM, I TRAN PORTED US A TO A FAR-OF PLANET-
---WHERE M GRAVEST FEA CAME TRUE, A MY CREATION SOON REVERTE TO THEIR BESTI HERITAGE.

HEN THEY TURNED AGAINST ME, I FELT I GAINED AN ALLY WHEN I CAPTURED THE EN-SKINNED HULK*-- ONLY TO FIND---
CE NER! DO YOU ART THUS?
WHY DO YOU NOT CHANGE BACK TO THE HULK??
I-- I CAN'T.
NOT JUST-- ON A WHIM--!
*TALES TO ASTONISH #94-96. --STAN.
MY NEW-MEN! THEY'VE BROKEN IN!
THEN, I STAND OR DIE-- ALONE.
HE'LL BE KILLED.
AND I-- I CAN'T HELP HIM--
--BUT THE HULK CAN!
NOTHING CAN STOP HULK.
NOT NEW MEN-- NOT OLD MEN--
NOTHING!
THE HULK APPEARED-- TOO LATE.
I'M DYING. THERE'S ONLY TIME-- FOR ONE LAST, DESPERATE GAMBLE.
MUST REMOVE MY MASK--- MY SHATTERED ARMOR---
THIS CHAMBER WAS ESIGNED TO TURN A UMAN BEING--- BRUCE BANNER---
INTO WHAT AN WILL BE--- THE END OF MILLION NTURIES EVOLUTION.
NOW, WITH ONLY SECONDS TO LIVE, I'LL COMPLETE THAT EXPERIMENT--- UPON MYSELF.
FEELING WEAK. IF I'M EVER TO ACT, IT MUST BE--
5.

--NOW!

"THE NEW-MEN WERE SCATTERED LIKE CHAFF---AND, WHEN THE BLAST WAS OVER---

"---I WAS---CHANGED!
I AM THE ULTIMATE---THE BE-ALL AND END-ALL OF HUMAN EVOLUTION.
IMMORTAL AS I NOW AM, I HAVE NO REASON TO EXIST ON THIS PLANE.
"THEN, BEFORE THE UNCOMPRE-HENDING EYES OF THE BRUTISH BEHEMOTH---

"---I VANISHED!
I MUST NOW BECOME ONE---
--WITH THE ETERNAL COSMOS!
AND SO I DID.
YET, IN TIME, THE LONELINESS OF INFINITY PREYED UPON THE SPARK OF HUMANITY WHICH SMOLDERED WITHIN ME---
---DRIVING ME TO THE BRINK OF MADNESS!

MASTER! I BESEECH YOU---PROCEED TO LEVEL 10, POSTHASTE!
SIR RAAM!? HOW DARE YOU INTERRUPT ME WHILE I---
A LIGHT-YEAR OF PARDONS, MASTER. I MERELY---
NO, OLD FRIEND. IT IS RATHER I WHO SHOULD BEG FORGIVENESS OF YOU.
YOU WERE EVER MY MOST FAITHFUL RETAINER, EVEN BEFORE I BROUGHT YOU BACK FROM THE THRESHHOLD OF DEATH.
I KNOW YOU WOULD HARDLY INTRUDE UPON MY RAMBLINGS LIGHTLY.
LOCK 10 IT IS---AT ONCE!

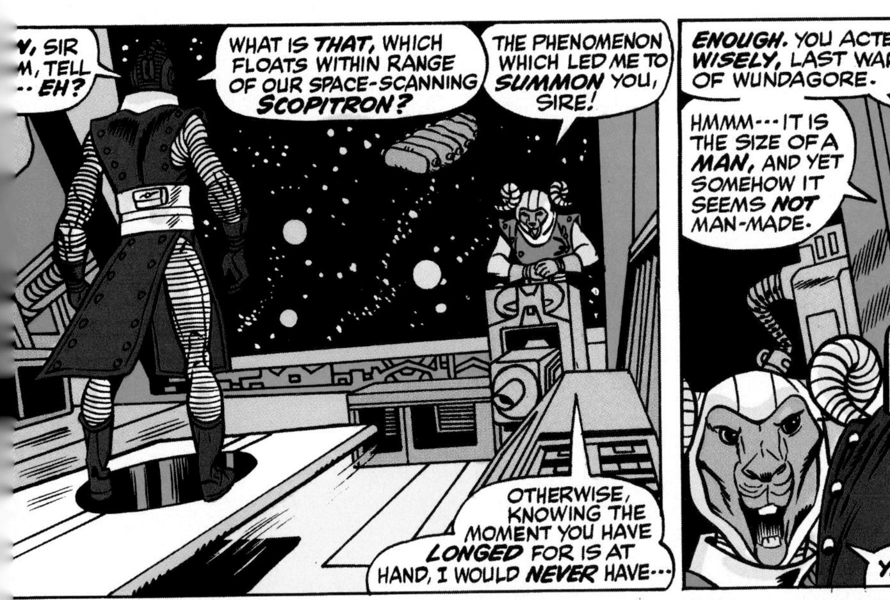
SIR
TELL
--EH?
WHAT IS THAT, WHICH FLOATS WITHIN RANGE OF OUR SPACE-SCANNING SCOPITRON?
THE PHENOMENON WHICH LED ME TO SUMMON YOU, SIRE!
OTHERWISE, KNOWING THE MOMENT YOU HAVE LONGED FOR IS AT HAND, I WOULD NEVER HAVE---
ENOUGH. YOU ACTED WISELY, LAST WARRIOR OF WUNDAGORE.
HMMM---IT IS THE SIZE OF A MAN, AND YET SOMEHOW IT SEEMS NOT MAN-MADE.
MAGNIFY THE IMAGE, UNTIL IT FILLS THE SCREEN.
YES, SIRE.

STILL CAN
LL LITTLE
OUT IT.
AND YET---BECAUSE
T MAY AFFECT MY
MISSION IN SOME WAY---
YES. YOU MUST BRING IT INTO THE LOCK.
IT SHALL BE DONE AS YOU COMMAND.

A FLICK OF THE HORNED NEW-MAN'S
GLOVED FINGER, AND THE GRAVITY
OF THE ARTIFICIAL PLANETOID IS
NCREASED---SLOWLY, SURELY---
---JUST ENOUGH TO PULL THE UNCANNY OBJECT GENTLY TOWARD IT...
---ONTO THE MAGNETIC LANDING-LIP WHICH DARTS OUT LIKE A GLEAMING TONGUE---

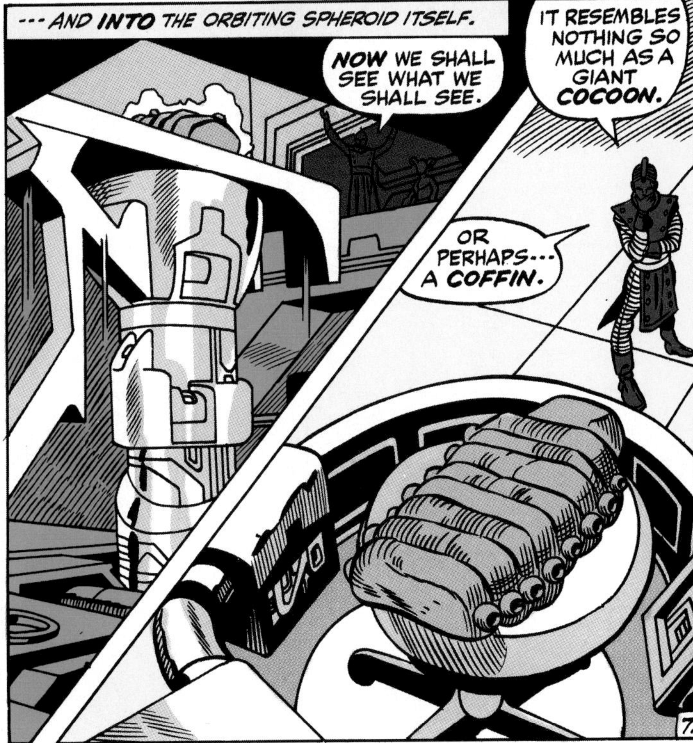
---AND INTO THE ORBITING SPHEROID ITSELF.
NOW WE SHALL SEE WHAT WE SHALL SEE.
IT RESEMBLES NOTHING SO MUCH AS A GIANT COCOON.
OR PERHAPS---A COFFIN.
7.

GO NOW, SIR RAAM, AND GUIDE THE SHIP TO POSITION TWO--THE FAR SIDE OF THE SUN--
WHEN YOU ARE READY, MASTER---
--WHILE I SEEK TO UNRAVEL THIS NEW MYSTERY.
--I SHALL BE READY!
TAGAR---
EACH OF
ALL OF
GONE.
ONLY
REMAINS
ALL THE
WHO
NO!
I MUST CONCENTRATE ---UPON THE TASK AT HAND.

FOR, I SENSE A LIVING BEING BENEATH THAT ENVELOPING SHROUD---
ALREADY, THE PSYCHE-PROBES ARE IN PLACE. GOOD.

---AND I, WHO SPENT MY LIFE PURSUING KNOWLEDGE, AND ABSOLUTE TRUTH---
--CANNOT PASS LIGHTLY BY ONE ENIGMA, WHILE EN ROUTE TO ANOTHER.
I MUST KNOW WHAT LIES WITHIN THAT--- COCOON.
AHH---AN IMAGE FORMS, PROJECTED ONTO THE MEGA-VIZ.
BUT-- AN IMAGE WHICH WOULD BLIND A MORTAL EYE!
THE GOLD-HUED DREAM OF HUMAN PERFECTION--- FEATURES CARVED FROM SOME DIVINE MODEL!
THE ONE WITHIN IS LIKE THE ULTIMATE, ULTRA-HUMAN NEW-MAN I ALWAYS DESIRED TO CREATE---
--THE ONE I WOULD HAVE MADE THE SON I NEVER HAD.
SON? I AM NO MAN'S SON--- NOR A WOMAN'S
I AM ONLY-- WHAT I AM.
YOU CAN HEAR ME?
YOU CAN SPEAK TO ME--- WITH THOUGHTS WHICH FILL THE MIND'S EAR WITH LIQUID MUSIC?

EN TELL ME WHO
U ARE, AND WHENCE
OU CAME HERE.
I WOULD
KNOW YOUR
NAME.
-HAVE
NAME.
HAVE
ER BEEN
LLED ANY
NG BUT
"HIM"!
MORE! I MUST
KNOW MORE.

AND, BECAUSE
I SENSE POWER
WITHIN YOU---AND
NOBILITY, SUCH
AS I WAS CREATED
TO STRIVE
TOWARD---
I SHALL TELL
YOU OF MY
BIRTH-- AND
OF MY RE-
BIRTH---
---AND WHY
I CHOSE
INSTEAD UN-
BIRTH AND
OBLIVION.

"I WAS FORMED WITHIN A COCOON SUCH AS THIS, ON A REMOTE ISLE ON EARTH---
"---THE ADVANCED GENETIC
CREATION OF EVIL MEN WHO
OPPOSED THE FABLED
FANTASTIC FOUR---
* AS CHRONICLED IN
F.F. #66-67.--STAN.

"YET, IN ALMOST THE SAME
MOMENT WHICH SAW MY
FIRST AWAKENING---
"---I SLEW THE EVIL
ONES---WHO WELL
DESERVED KILLING.

"STILL, I COULD NOT
BEAR THE THOUGHT
OF WHAT I HAD DONE
---AND SO, USING
THE VERY POWERS
WHICH THEY HAD
HAD GIVEN ME---
"---I FLED THE EARTH,
TO SEEK MY DESTINY
AMONG UNNUMBERED
STARS."

THEN YOU'VE NOT
RETURNED TO
EARTH SINCE
THAT TIME?
ONCE---
AND ONCE
ONLY.
IT PROVED
MORE THAN
ENOUGH.
9.

A JUXTAPOSITION OF UNHAPPY FATES BROUGHT MY LIFE-PRESERVING COCOON TO REST A SECOND TIME UPON THE PLANET OF MY UNIQUE BIRTH---
---WHERE, BECAUSE I WAS LONELY, I SOUGHT A WORTHY MATE---
---AND CAME INTO SOUL-SHATTERING CONFLICT WITH VENGEFUL THOR---GOD OF THE ROLLING THUNDER AND EMBODIMENT OF WORLD-DESTROYING POWER!

"AH, A **MIGHTY** BATTLE, THAT---!
"--BUT ONE WHICH I SWIFTLY SENSED I COULD NEVER HOPE TO **WIN**!

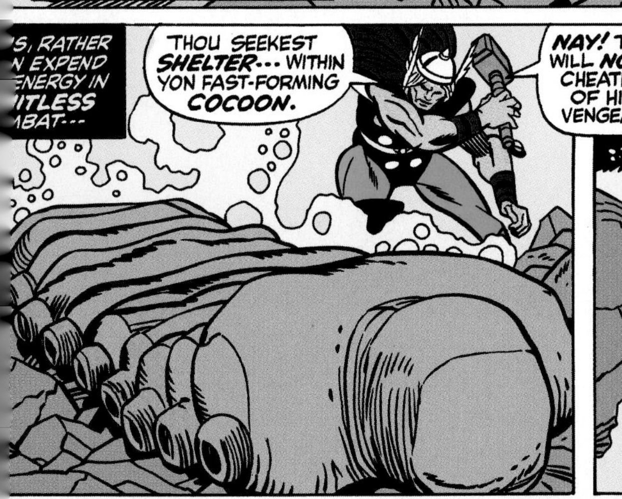
S, RATHER
N EXPEND
ENERGY IN
ITLESS
MBAT---
THOU SEEKEST **SHELTER**--- WITHIN YON FAST-FORMING **COCOON**.
NAY! THOR WILL **NOT** BE CHEATED OF HIS VENGEANCE!

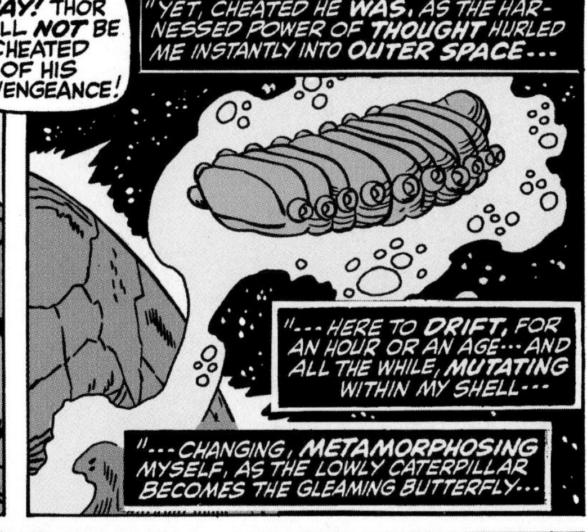
"YET, CHEATED HE **WAS**, AS THE HARNESSED POWER OF **THOUGHT** HURLED ME INSTANTLY INTO **OUTER SPACE**---
"---HERE TO **DRIFT**, FOR AN HOUR OR AN AGE---AND ALL THE WHILE, **MUTATING** WITHIN MY SHELL---
"---CHANGING, **METAMORPHOSING** MYSELF, AS THE LOWLY CATERPILLAR BECOMES THE GLEAMING BUTTERFLY---

---BUT NOW, I
OLEMNLY REQUEST
AT YOU **RESTORE**
E TO THE VOID
EYOND, FOR MY
ME OF EMERGENCE
HAS NOT YET
COME.
IT SHALL BE **DONE**.
THE **HIGH EVOLUTIONARY** HAS NO WISH TO THWART ONE WHO MAY BE AS **IMMORTAL** AS HIMSELF...
---THE MORE SO, SINCE YOU SEEM TO POSE NO THREAT TO **PROJECT ALPHA**.

PROJECT ALPHA? YOU **INTEREST** ME.
THEN, I WOULD BE PROUD TO **SHARE** MY PLAN WITH YOU.
UNLIKE YOURSELF, I ONCE WAS **HUMAN**--- **THEN** BECAME LIKE UNTO A GOD.
STILL, WHAT USE TO BE A **GOD**, WITHOUT A **WORLD** TO BE MY **SHRINE**?

THAT IS WHY MY SERVANT **RAAM** SECURED FOR ME THIS BALL OF ONCE-MOLTEN **ROCK** FROM THE EARTH WE'VE NOW LEFT BEHIND--
---FROM WHICH I'LL MAKE A **NEW** EARTH, IN MIRROR-IMAGE OF THE **OLD**.
11.

A NEW EARTH? BUT WHY, MAN-GOD?
MY OWN CONTACT WITH HUMANKIND HAS BEEN MOST LIMITED, I KNOW---
YET, THEY SEEMED TO ME TO BE MOST MEAN, BASE, AND MISERABLE CREATURES.
THERE IS---TRUTH IN WHAT YOU SAY.
AND, IN BLEAKER MOMENTS, I A PLAGUED WITH DOUBTS---WITH NAGGING UNCERTAINTIES---
---IN PURSUIT OF AN DREAM---A MADMAN'S FA

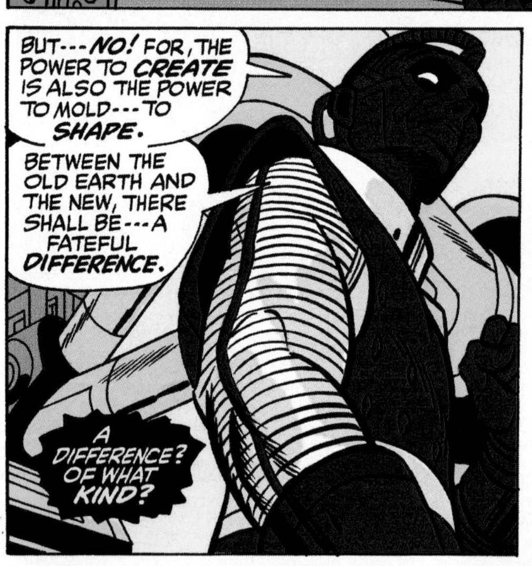
BUT---NO! FOR, THE POWER TO CREATE IS ALSO THE POWER TO MOLD---TO SHAPE.
BETWEEN THE OLD EARTH AND THE NEW, THERE SHALL BE---A FATEFUL DIFFERENCE.
A DIFFERENCE? OF WHAT KIND?

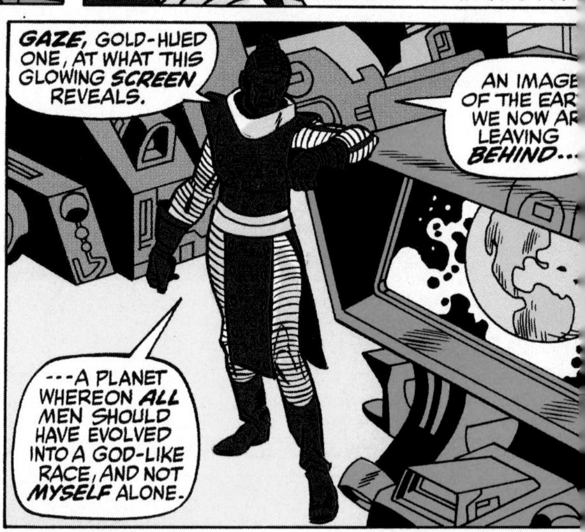
GAZE, GOLD-HUED ONE, AT WHAT THIS GLOWING SCREEN REVEALS.
AN IMAGE OF THE EAR WE NOW AR LEAVING BEHIND---
---A PLANET WHEREON ALL MEN SHOULD HAVE EVOLVED INTO A GOD-LIKE RACE, AND NOT MYSELF ALONE.

"BUT, THERE IS EVIL ABROAD IN THAT WORLD---AN INSTINCT OF HUMAN AGGRESSION WHICH LEADS TO ABUSE OF OFFICE BY THOSE IN POWER---
OFF THE PIGS!
UP THE ESTAB-LISHMENT
"---AND MINDLESS, DESTRUCTIVE REVOLT BY THOSE DENIED POWER.

"IT IS A WORLD WHICH FIGHTS ONE WAR IN ORDER TO END ALL WARS---THEN FIGHTS ANOTHER--AND STILL ANOTHER---

"---A WORLD FAR BETTER AT COUNTING BODIES, THAN AT COUNTING COSTS---!

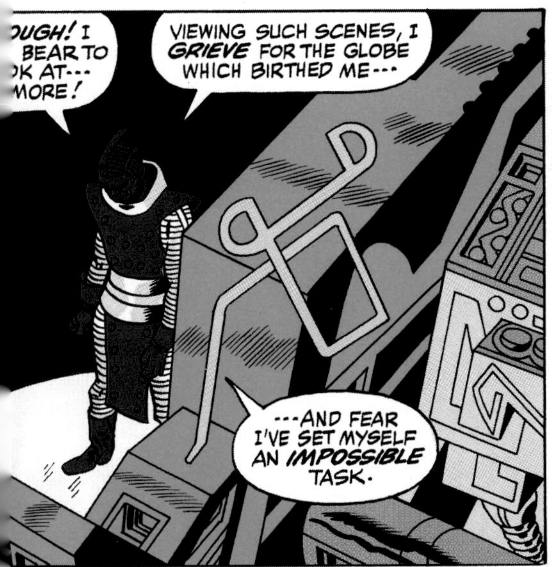

UGH! I
BEAR TO
K AT---
MORE!
VIEWING SUCH SCENES, I GRIEVE FOR THE GLOBE WHICH BIRTHED ME---
---AND FEAR I'VE SET MYSELF AN IMPOSSIBLE TASK.

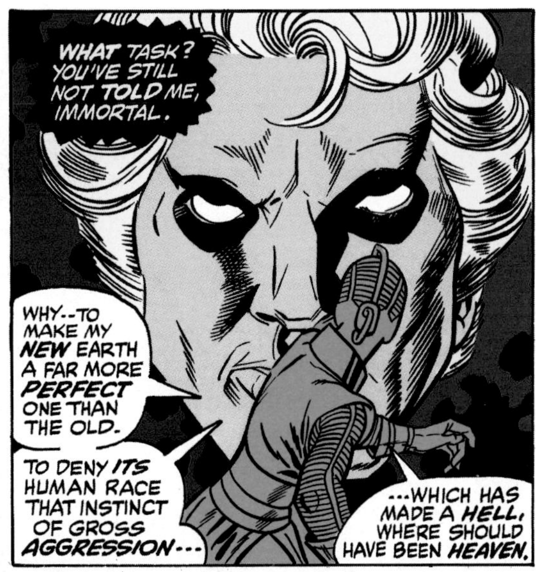

WHAT TASK? YOU'VE STILL NOT TOLD ME, IMMORTAL.
WHY--TO MAKE MY NEW EARTH A FAR MORE PERFECT ONE THAN THE OLD.
TO DENY ITS HUMAN RACE THAT INSTINCT OF GROSS AGGRESSION---
---WHICH HAS MADE A HELL, WHERE SHOULD HAVE BEEN HEAVEN.

HERE IN MY HAND
I HOLD A SINGLE
LECK OF EARTH'S
CARRED FLESH.
ST AS ONE
E HUMAN
L CONTAINS
GENETIC CODE
ICH WOULD
LOW ME END-
SSLY TO
PLICATE
OWNER---
SO THIS COLD, HARD ROCK IS ALL I
EED TO CREATE MY--- COUNTER-EARTH!

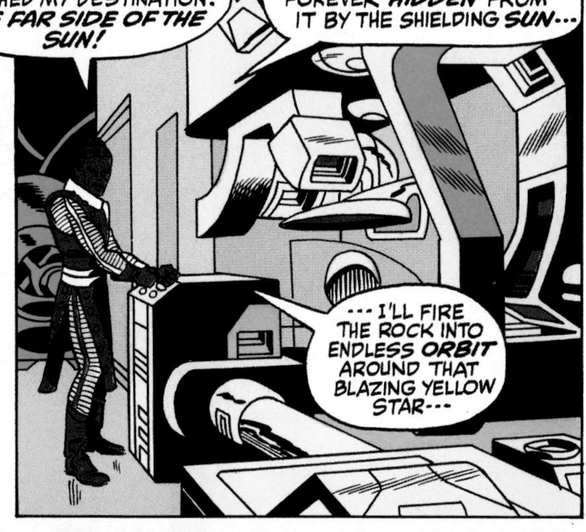

ALREADY RAAM SIGNALS ME THIS ASTEROID HAS REACHED MY DESTINATION: THE FAR SIDE OF THE SUN!
HERE, DIRECTLY OPPOSITE THE ORIGINAL EARTH, BUT FOREVER HIDDEN FROM IT BY THE SHIELDING SUN---
---I'LL FIRE THE ROCK INTO ENDLESS ORBIT AROUND THAT BLAZING YELLOW STAR---

"---AND MAKE OF IT A BRIGHTER, PURER PLACE THAN EVER SHONE BEFORE IN ANY SKY!

"BEHOLD, WAYFARER, AS I NOW BOMBARD THAT LIFELESS PEBBLE WITH RAYS WHICH WILDLY INCREASE ITS MASS---
"--AND THUS, ITS GRAVITY--
13

---UNTIL IT ATTRACTS SWARMS OF THE COUNTLESS METEORITES WHICH FLOAT ROOTLESS THRU THE ABYSS OF SPACE.
WHY, IMMORTAL? WHY WASTE EVEN A MOMENT'S THOUGHT UPON THIS GALACTIC FOLLY?
ALREADY, I CA SENSE THE STRA WHICH BEGINS T TELL UPON YOU

WASTE? NO, MY FRIEND---THE ACT OF CREATION IS ITS OWN END.
WITNESS NOW THE DARK DEBRIS WHICH PELTS MY TINY DEMI-WORLD, TILL IT GROWS AS LARGE AS ITS PROTOTYPE...

---TILL THIS EARTH, TOO, GIVES PAINFUL BIRTH TO A MOLTEN MASS WHICH ONE DAY SHALL BE CALLED--ITS MOON.

AND ALL THE WHILE, THE SEAS RUN RED LIKE SEETHING LAVA.

FINALLY, HOWEVER, MY WORLD BEGINS TO COOL--- DARK CLOUDS COVER THE FACE OF THE STONE-DISSOLVING DEEP---

---AND AT LAST THE RAINS COME.
RAINS WHICH SOOTHE A PLANET'S FEVERED BROW, AND MAKE OF IT A PLACE WHERE LIFE CAN BEGIN!

YES, GOLDEN ONE, I SPOKE OF LIFE.
FOR, LIFE IS THE PURPOSE OF THIS SECOND EARTH, EVEN AS IT WAS OF THE FIRST.
IN THE LIMITLESS SEAS IT BEGINS, SPAWNED BY THE MYRIAD BIO-RAYS WITH WHICH I BOMBARD THEM-- AND THE POWER OF MY OWN IMMORTAL BRAIN!
WATCH NOW AS UNNUMBERED AGES PASS BEFORE YOUR WONDERING EYES---A MILLION YEARS, A BILLION ---MORE---
---ALL AS I STAND HERE A MERE SEVEN-SCORE OF HOURS, WAITING FOR THAT INSTANT WHEN--
NOW! THE BEASTS OF THE LAND ARE EVOLVED--- A VAST KALEIDOSCOPE OF FORM, AND KIND, AND GEOLOGIC EON.
AND SO, THE TIME IS COME FOR ME TO SLOW THIS WORLD'S PROGRESS --- BEFORE THE STRAIN UPON ME-- BECOMES TOO GREAT TO BEAR.
THE TIME IS COME--- FOR MAN!!
15

BUT NOT MAN AS HE WAS.
RATHER, MAN AS HE COULD HAVE BEEN---
MAN AS HE OUGHT TO BE---

---MAN, IN SHORT--- AS HE SHALL BE!
YOU WERE EVER A VERY PROPHET.

MAN, INDEED, AS HE SHALL BE!
BUT NOT CAST ANEW IN YOUR INSIPID IMAGE, FATHER DEAR.
NO---MINE SHALL BE THE HAND THAT MOLDS THIS FINE NEW CLAY.

THE HAND O THE MA BEAST

YET, ALONE IN HIS GREAT CHAMBER, THE ONCE-MAN IN THE METAL MASK NEITHER HEARS NOR HEEDS THE QUASI-HUMAN SNARL OF THE MONITORING DEMON WHOM ONCE HE CREATED---

HIS MIND IS ELSEWHERE ---AND OTHER-WHEN---

COME DOWN, FRAIL APISH THING--- DOWN FROM THE SHELTERING TREES.

GROW TALL---GROW STRAIGHT--- AND SMILE!

YOU'VE COME FAR... SO VERY FAR... YET, STILL NOT FAR ENOUGH!

OTHER MOMENT--- EW THOUSAND TRY YEARS, AND---
IT IS DONE. NOW, MERELY ONE TASK REMAINS TO DO.
HE MUST BE PURGED, THIS NEW ADAM--- CLEANSED OF THE KILLER INSTINCT.
BUT---THAT WILL TAKE CONCENTRATION--- THE FULL FOCUSING OF MY MORE-THAN MORTAL MIND.
AND I HAVE DONE --SO MUCH...!
SO TIRED...
SO--- VERY--- TIRED---

EEP FOR M, KOHBRA FALLING SLEEP AT E INSTANT OF HIS REATEST RIUMPH---
--HIS PRICELESS CREATION LEFT TO THE TENDER MERCIES OF ANY PASSING PREDATOR.
HOW FORTUNATE IS OUR DEAREST MENTOR---

---THAT WE ARE NEAR, TO TAKE CARE OF THINGS FOR HIM.
17.

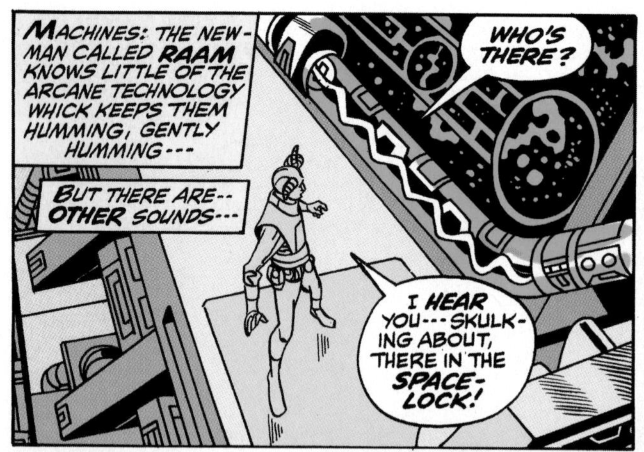
MACHINES: THE NEW-MAN CALLED RAAM KNOWS LITTLE OF THE ARCANE TECHNOLOGY WHICK KEEPS THEM HUMMING, GENTLY HUMMING---
BUT THERE ARE-- OTHER SOUNDS---
WHO'S THERE?
I HEAR YOU--- SKULKING ABOUT, THERE IN THE SPACE-LOCK!

STAND FORTH, BEFORE I'M FORCED TO---
NO! NO!
IT CANNOT BE. NOT YOU!

NOT YOU!!
YOU DISAPPOINT ME, SIR RAAM. NO OPEN ARMS, AFTER ALL THESE YEARS?
HAS NOT THE HIGH EVOLUTIONARY TAU YOU TO FORGIVE OLD ENEMIES--

---EVEN THOSE WHO HAVEN'T FORGIVEN YOU?
AAA ARR

SHALL WE TOSS THE VERMIN INTO THE OUTER DARKNESS, SIRE?
CERTAINLY NOT.
AND, STEP LIGHTLY NOW, MY CHILDREN---
--- HA YOU N RESPEC FOR T DEA

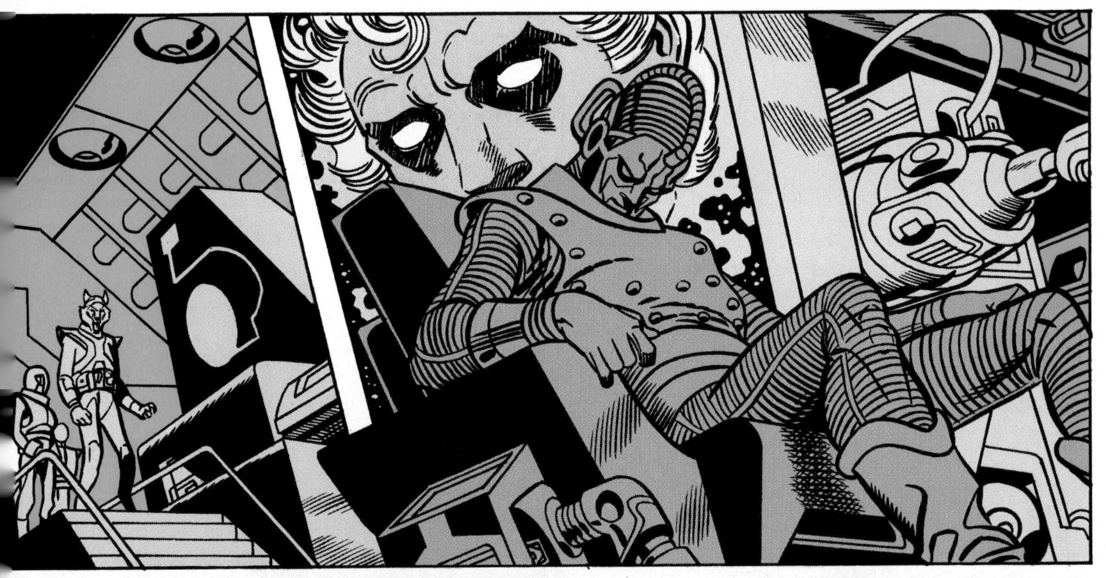

EP ON,
R PARENT.
AM SWEET
AMS ONLY.
IN THE FAR-OFF DROMISANA GALAXY, I'VE WAITED LONG FOR THIS MOMENT...

...AND, WHILE WAITING, GROWN STRONGER AND MORE SUBTLE.
SO NOW, AT LAST, I SHALL TAKE MY REVENGE.
BUT NOT ON YOU, FATHER MINE.
NEVER ON YOU.

S THRU THE MAN-WORMS
O CRAWL YOUR COUNTER-
ARTH THAT I SHALL CUT
U TO THE QUICK.
HAT'S
GHT,
U NAKED
PELING.
CK UP
AT WHICH
S AT
OUR
FEET...
...AND USE IT... SO!
THUS, IN ONE MAD, BLUDGEONING INSTANT...
MAN THE KILLER IS REBORN!
19.

THUS IT BEGINS! AND NOW, THRU TWICE-LIVED AGES, ONE CRIME FOLLOWS HARD UPON ANOTHER---
---EVEN UNTO--- THE ULTIMATE TRANSGRESSION!!

"AFTER THAT---THE REST IS ANTICLIMAX.
"AH, BUT WHAT ANTICLIMAX! HOW GLORIOUSLY MONOTONOUS!
"WAR---YES, AND RUMORS OF WAR. A WORLD WHERE HEROES SLAY, NOT SAVE---

"RAPINE--- MURDER--- INDISCRIMINATE SLAUGHTER---
"A DARK SPECTRUM OF CRIMSON BLOOD AND PIT-BLACK HEARTS---A WORLD CONCEIVED IN FIRE, AND BAPTIZED BENEATH THE SWORD---

"A WORLD ENFLAMED BY THE MAD DESIRES OF LITTLE MEN, WHO YEAR BY YEAR REFINE THEIR INSTRUMENTS OF TORTURE AND TERROR---
"---TILL ALL THE OLD FAITHS ARE BURNED AWAY, IN A WORLD WITHOUT HOPE---
"---A WORLD BEYOND REDEMPTION!

NOR SHOULD IT LOOK FOR ANY SHINING KNIGHT TO SAVE IT FROM TSELF-- TO PLUCK T BACK FROM THE ABYSS.
FOR, THAT TOO I HAVE DENIED TO IT!
AND NOW, I SHALL--

YOU HAVE DONE--- ENOUGH!
YOU!

WH... OOO..M!

, MAN-BEAST--- S YOUR RUEFUL REATOR WHO RUCK YOU THUS.
RSED BE THE THAT EVER YOU RE SPAWNED, U AND YOUR L NEW-MEN!
BUT-- THAT BLOW-- LIKE A TIGER'S SWIPE--
YOU WERE NEVER MY PHYSICAL EQUAL-- BEFORE.

YOU HAVE BEEN TOO LONG, MONSTER, AMONG FAR-FLUNG UNIVERSES.
NO LONGER AM I THE FRAIL MORTAL YOU ONCE COULD HAVE SLAIN WITH EASE.
IF YOU ARE A HYBRID OF SUPERIOR MAN-- AND SUPERIOR BEAST--

I AM THE HIGH EVOLUTIONARY...
---I AM THAT WHICH IS BEYOND BOTH MAN AND BEAST.
21.

TO ME, MY CHILDREN!
---AND I AM SUPREME!
WE HEAR AND OBEY, SIRE.
NAUGHT BUT BLOOD WILL EXPUNGE SUCH BASE ASSAULT!
BLOOD, FOOL? I'V
NONE TO SHED FO
THE LIKES OF YOU
I'VE ON
--THIS!
BUT ONE DANGER FACED IS ANOTHER FORGOTTEN--- AND SO, THERE IS TREACHERY THIS DAY---
---AS A BESTIAL MIND-BLAST WRACKS A WRITH-ING, METALLOID FORM!

ND, ALL THE WHILE,
S PROJECTED
SAGE A GOLDEN
ANCE OF MAD
ELECTRONS---
---THE ONE KNOWN ONLY AS HIM WATCHES---UN-NOTICED, UNFEARED---
---WEIGH-ING THE CHANCES OF THE SCARLET ONE AGAINST HIS DEMON-CREATION.

THAT LIVING ARMOR MIGHT WELL SURVIVE THE FERAL ON-SLAUGHT OF THE WOLF-THING ALONE---
---THE SLAVERING JAWS---THE CLAWS LIKE STEEL---

BUT, THERE ARE ALSO---THE OTHERS.
MURDEROUS MINIONS WHO WOULD DESTROY FIRST THEIR MAKER---THEN A PLANET.

GAIN, GOLD-FLAKED
YES SEEM TO SEE THE
AVAGES WROUGHT
Y THE MAN-BEAST ON
HE SPINNING GLOBE
BELOW---
AND IN THAT MOMENT,
A DECISION IS MADE---

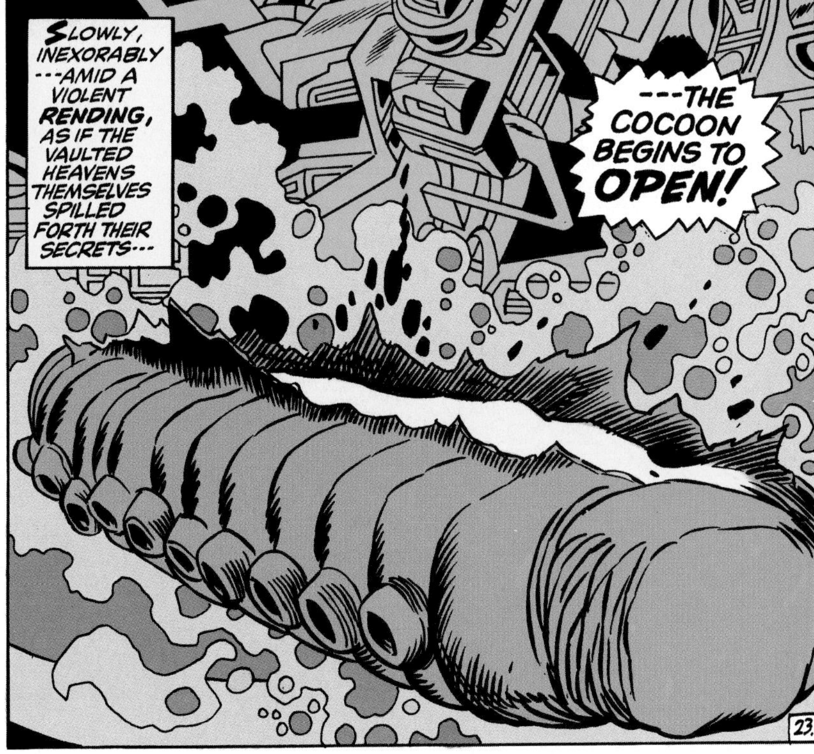
SLOWLY, INEXORABLY---AMID A VIOLENT RENDING, AS IF THE VAULTED HEAVENS THEMSELVES SPILLED FORTH THEIR SECRETS---
---THE COCOON BEGINS TO OPEN!
23.

AND, ONCE MORE, THE BEING WITHIN-- IS FREE!!
GLEAMING HIS BRONZED FLESH, BORN IN NIGHTED CAVERNS---
---RESPLENDENT HIS ARMOR AND ORNAMENTS, NEW-WOVEN ABOUT HIM AS NATURALLY AS HAD BEEN THE COCOON ITSELF.
NOW--HE SPEAKS:
YOU! WOLF THAT WALKS LIKE MOCKERY OF A MAN!
STAND AWAY FROM THE ONE WHO GAVE YOU LIFE!
BUT, EVEN THAT THUNDEROUS VOICE IS SCARCELY HEARD AMID THE HISSING AND SNARLING OF THOSE FLAILING ANIMAL FORMS---AS SAVAGE TALONS RIP AND SLASH AT THE HIGH EVOLUTIONARY---

T, WHERE ORDS MAY FAIL OF EARING---

Y NOT SOUND-LESS RAGE PREVAIL---?

THEY ARE GONE--- VANISHED!
HEN--- E HAVE WON!
I WISH THAT WERE TRUE, WAY-FARER.
BUT, IN THOSE FLEETING INSTANTS WHEN THE MAN-BEAST'S MIND MET MINE, HE TAUNTED ME WITH--- HIS PLAN OF CONQUEST.
HE'S FLED TO THE NEW-BORN WORLD BELOW ---AND HIS BRUTAL LACKEYS WITH HIM.

OF ICH ANS...
--THAT COUNTER-EARTH, MY SHINING JEWEL, IS FOREVER FLAWED.
ALREADY HE HAS CORRUPTED MY DEAREST DREAM ---THWARTED THE WORK OF LONG MONTHS.
AND, HE HINTED DARKLY OF OTHER DOOMS IN STORE FOR IT, AS WELL.

ONLY ONE COURSE IS OPEN TO ME.
WITH A FLICK OF A FINGER, I CAN DECIMATE MY COUNTER-EARTH---
---LEAVE IT NO MORE THAN COSMIC DUST, DRIFTING THRU THE HIGH-DOMED CORRIDORS OF SPACE.
YES. THAT IS WHAT I MUST--

NO. WAIT!
WHAT? YOU DARE?
25

I DARE! YOU MUST NOT DESTROY THIS PEOPLE YOU HAVE CREATED---AND WHICH DESERVES BETTER.

YET, IT WAS YOU WHO CALLED THEM "MEAN, BASE, AND MISERABLE"!

I WAS A FOOL---AND SPOKE AS A FOOL, HAVING WALKED BUT LITTLE AMONG MEN.

INDEED, IN THE PANORAMA WHICH THE MAN-BEAST PRESENTED, I BEHOLD THOSE QUALITIES ---YET OTHERS, AS WELL---

---SUCH AS PRIDE--- A SPARK, EVEN, OF GOODNESS.

THAT SPARK MUST BE NURTURED, AS THE FLICKERING EMBER IS SHIELDED FROM THE DRENCHING RAIN.

I PRAY YOU, LET ME SERVE THIS STRANGE RACE CALLED HUMAN---

THE PROSPECT IS TEMPTING. WHAT LABORER IS NOT LOATHE TO DESTROY HIS OWN HANDIWORK?

THEN SAY YES, GREAT ONE---AND SHOW THAT, WHETHER CORPOREAL OR NOT, A HEART BEATS WITHIN THAT ARMORED BREAST.

YOU ASK, PERHAPS, YOUR OWN DOOM, I FEAR.

FOR, THE WOLF-THING'S POWERS ARE FAR BEYOND EVEN YOURS.

YET, I CAN PROVIDE FOR THAT--- IF YOU TRULY WISH TO RISK YOURSELF FOR THE EARTH.

I-- WISH IT!

THEN, IT WOULD SEEM I FOUND A SON--- ONE WHO MIGHT HAVE SHARED MY GALACTIC WANDERINGS---

GO THEN, WHILE I END THIS WAKING TIME AS I BEGAN IT---
---APPRISING MY ELECTRONIC JOURNALS OF AN EXPERIMENT GONE WRONG--
---YET NOT, PERHAPS, BEYOND SALVAGING.

BUT FIRST, I SPOKE OF A BOON.
SOMETHING WHICH MAY PROTECT YOU FROM THE SNARES OF THE MAN-BEAST---
---OR WHICH MAY NOT.

---THIS EMERALD, BLAZING LIKE A GREAT, GREEN STAR UPON YOUR BROW---
---OF WHICH YOU SHALL LEARN MORE--- ANON.

AND NOW, PREPARE FOR PAIN, STRANGE-
ORN---FOR OTHER
IGHTS AND SENSES
OU HAVE NEVER
KNOWN BEFORE!

"FOR, UNCANNY YOUR SACRED MISSION--- UNEARTHLY YOUR WEIRDLING POWERS---
"AND, BEHOLDING THEM---

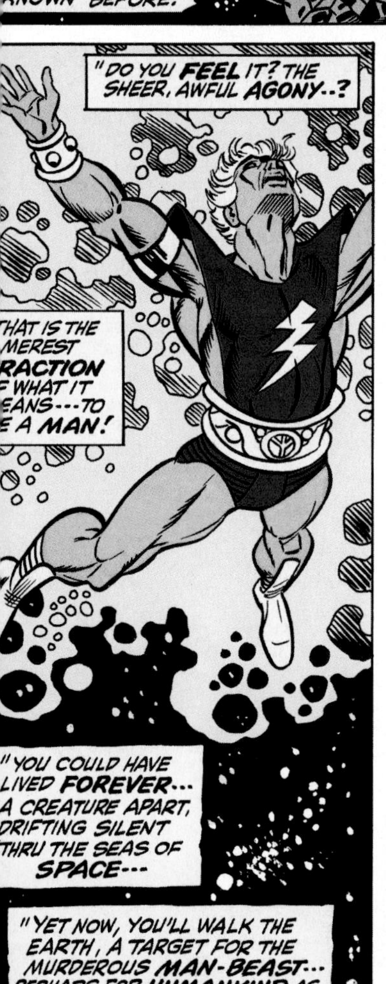
"DO YOU FEEL IT? THE SHEER, AWFUL AGONY--?
HAT IS THE
MEREST
RACTION
WHAT IT
EANS---TO
E A MAN!
"YOU COULD HAVE LIVED FOREVER... A CREATURE APART, DRIFTING SILENT THRU THE SEAS OF SPACE---
"YET NOW, YOU'LL WALK THE EARTH, A TARGET FOR THE MURDEROUS MAN-BEAST... PERHAPS FOR HUMANKIND AS WELL---

"...MEN SHALL CALL YOU WARLOCK!"
NEXT:
THE HOUNDS OF HELL!
27.

MARVEL PREMIERE
MARVEL COMICS GROUP
20¢
15
MAY
02142
MARVEL PREMIERE
FEATURING
IRON FIST
KUNG FU
ACTION--IN THE MIGHTY MARVEL MANNER!
YOU KARATE KILLERS WANTED A SHOWDOWN--
--NOW YOU'VE GOT IT!
ORIG

an Lee PRESENTS:
A SHINING NEW STAR IN THE FLAME-FLECKED MARVEL HEAVENS--
--PLANNED, PLOTTED, AND POLISHED BY-- ROY THOMAS AUTHOR/EDITOR & GIL KANE ARTIST
D. GIORDANO • INKER
G. WEIN • COLORIST
L.P. GREGORY • LETTERER
THE FURY OF IRON FIST!
YOU ARE IRON FIST. YOU STAND TENSELY--TOO TENSELY--AWARE OF THEIR EYES ON YOU: YÜ-TI, THE HOODED ONE, AND HIS FOUR DRAGON-KINGS...
AND, FACING YOU, FOUR OTHERS EDGE CLOSER, SEARCHING FOR AN OPENING--A MOMENT OF WEAKNESS--THE CARELESS FLICKERING OF AN EYELID.
FOR, THIS IS YOUR DAY OF DESTINY, IRON FIST. TODAY, YOU WILL EAT OF THE FRUIT OF THE TREE OF IMMORTALITY--OR ELSE DRINK DEEP OF THE ELIXIR OF DEATH--!

AND ALWAYS, ALWAYS UNDER THE BLAZING, SHROUDED EYES OF YÜ-TI--HE WHO IS CALLED THE AUGUST PERSONAGE IN JADE--
--YÜ-TI, AND THE LUNG-WANG--THE DRAGON-KINGS!
AGAIN YOUR FOUR STALKERS MOVE CLOSER, POISED TO STRIKE...
YOU ASSUME THE CAT STANCE.
YOU WAIT.
HAI!!
--AND THEY ATTAC
THEN--YOU MOVE!
A ROCK-SMASH BLOW FELLS ONE...
...THE SWORD HAND, ANOTHER...
FKAK!
...WHILE A THIRD IS DROPPED BY AN ELEPHANT KICK.
YOU WHIRL:
ONE MAN, STILL DOUBLED WITH PAIN, RECEIVES THE BLOW OF THE HAMMER...
THAP!
ANOTHER, ALREA REELING, YOU DISPO OF WITH THE MON BLOW.
KTHOK
THE FOURTH ATTACKER, MO CAUTIOUS THAN HIS FELLOW ONLY NOW MAKES HIS FORWA LEAP...
STILL, HE HAS MERELY DELAYED HIS PUNISHMENT, NOT EVADED IT...
PTHOW!
...AS A SINGLE LIGHTNING KICK GIVES HIM SORROW TO REMEMBER TILL THE END OF HIS DAY

, YOU HAVE GROWN CARELESS, IRON FIST, IN
OWING YOURSELF EVEN A MOMENT'S CON-
PLATION OF THE CARNAGE YOUR WEAPON-
BS HAVE WROUGHT...
FOR, NOW, ONLY A RUSH OF AIR WARNS YOU OF ATTACK FROM A NEW QUARTER...
...AND ONLY THUNDERBOLT REFLEXES, AND A SECOND SWORD HAND BLOW, SAVE YOU FROM THE VERY FATE YOU'VE OFT DEALT OUT TO OTHERS!
WAP!
R EYES DART UPWARD FOR AN
TANT, EXPECTING PERHAPS A
ETING GLANCE OF PRAISE...
...TO MEET ONLY WITH OTHER EYES THAT SAY...NOTHING.
THUS, YOU TURN ANEW TO YOUR ATTACKERS...
KEKK
...AND DIVERT THE FURY NOW BOILING WITHIN YOU...
...AGAINST THEM INSTEAD OF YÜ-TI.
LAST,
TWO
LONE
E LEFT
COME
YOU.
TWO ALONE--
--AND THESE, MADE RECKLESS BY RAGE--THEIR ASSAULT BORN MORE OF DESPERATION THAN OF THE KNOWLEDGE WHICH IS THE ONE TRUE PATH.
THEY ARE, PERHAPS, GOOD MEN... HONEST MEN.
ET THEM OUTSIDE
S AMPHITHEATRE,
D THEY MIGHT EVEN
VE BEEN YOUR
FRIENDS.
T, YOU CANNOT
FORD TO THINK
THAT NOW...
THROOM!
...AS YOUR COMBINED RAM'S HEAD BLOW AND DRAGON STAMP END FOREVER THEIR DREAMS OF MARTIAL-ARTS GLORY...
...AND THEY CRUMPLE, AS ONE MAN, TO THE ARENA FLOOR...

...NOR WILL ANY ONE OF THEM SOON RISE AGAIN.
IT HAS ALL TAKEN BUT A MINUTE, PERHAPS, AS MEN MEASURE TIME-- A SINGLE MINUTE, DURING WHICH YOU MUST HAVE SEEMED AN INHUMAN FIGHTING-MACHINE.
BUT NOW, T BEADS OF PERSPIRATIO WHICH DOT T DRAGON BRA ON YOUR CHE REMIND YOU T YOU ARE, AFT ALL, MERELY MAN.
PERHAPS THAT IS ENOUGH.
STANDING UPRIGHT, THOUGH BREATHING HARD, YOU ADDRESS AT LAST THE AUGUST PERSONAGE OF JADE...
O YÜ-TI--O FATHER-HEAVEN, AND LORD OF THE K'UN-LUN MOUNTAIN--I HAVE FACED THE CHALLENGE OF THE MANY, AND I HAVE PREVAILED.
I STAND READY NOW TO MEET THE CHAL-LENGE OF THE ONE!
THEN STAND, MY SON... STAND AND THINK.
IT IS NOT MEET THAT ONE SHOULD GO, PERHAPS, TO HIS DEATH... WITHOUT FIRST A MOMENT'S CONTEMPLATION.
THINK, HOODED ONE? OF WHAT? OF WHOM?
OF YOURSELF, MY SON... AND OF THOSE THINGS WHICH HAVE BROUGHT YOU TO THIS DAYS OF DAYS...!
THIN I SAY
AND SO, CLOSING YOURSELF TO OUTS EVENTS, YOU DO THIN
AND YOU SEE, WITH A MIND'S EYE MORE CLEAR THAN ANY SEAMAN'S GLASS:
YOU SEE... YOURSELF.
YOURSELF, AS YOU WERE.
IT WAS ALMOST EXACTLY TEN YEARS AGO...
...WHEN FOUR BLACK SPECKS MADE THEIR TRACKLESS WAY ACROSS THE SNOW-CRUSTED ASIAN WASTES.
YOU WERE A LAD OF NINE, THEN... AND YOU DIDN'T KNOW WHY YOU WERE THERE, THOUGH YOU WERE SOON TO LEARN.
...WENDELL, IF OUR FACTORY-WORKERS COULD SEE US NOW, THEY'D THINK WE WERE ALL CRAZY!
YOU, FOR SCOURING HALF THE HIMALAYAS, IN SEARCH OF YOUR OWN MAD VERSION OF SHANGRI-LA...
...YOUR WIFE AND CHIL FOR ALLOWING THEMSE TO BE DRAGGED ALO
...AND I, MOST OF AL FOR NOT STAYING IN NE YORK, WHERE THE WO THING THAT COULD HAP TO ME MIGHT BE A STALLED LIMOUSINE IN WINTER!
OTHERS SEEMED TO KNOW LITTLE MORE THAN YOU.
PERHAPS YOU'RE RIGHT, HAROLD...

CT, I'LL NEVER ERSTAND WHY, R YOU FAILED ALK ME OUT RINGING THER AND ANNY...
...WHY I ENDED UP TRAILING ALONG, AFTER ALL?
WHERE'S THE MYSTERY? WE'RE BUSINESS PARTNERS, AREN'T WE-- RAND & MEACHUM--
-- AND FRIENDS, TO BOOT!
WHAT ARE FRIENDS FOR, IF NOT TO INDULGE EACH OTHER'S DELUSIONS?
I KNOW I INSISTED ON COMING, WENDELL--BUT IF ONLY IT WEREN'T SO COLD! AND THE WIND--!
IT BLOWS US THE SILENT MUSIC OF THE K'UN-LUN MOUNTAIN, DARLING... IF ONLY YOU OTHERS COULD HEAR IT, AS I CAN.
SOMETIMES... I THINK I HEAR IT, DAD.
DO YOU, SON?
DEAREST HEATHER... PLEASE.. JUST BEAR WITH ME A LITTLE WHILE LONGER...
WE'LL REACH OUR GOAL... AND EVERYTHING WILL BE CLEAR TO YOU, AT LAST!
WHEREVER YOU GO, MY DARLING..!
AND WE'D BETTER GO--NOW!

EN AS A CHILD, YOU KNEW YOUR FATHER HAD ALWAYS BEEN AN ENIGMA TO EVERYONE:
APPEARING OUT OF NOWHERE, NEARLY A DECADE BEFORE-- BECOMING AN INSTANT ENTREPRENEUR, WITH MYSTERIOUS FUNDS--
EN WINNING YOUR MOTHER'S HAND--YOUR MOTHER, NCE THE BELLE OF NEW YORK SOCIETY.
BUT THIS WAS DIFFERENT--THIS SEARCH FOR THE K'UN-LUN MOUNTAIN, THE MYTHICAL DWELLING-PLACE OF THE IMMORTALS, IN CHINESE LEGEND.
N OLD TALES, THE MOUNTAIN LIES AT EARTH'S CENTER. BUT YOUR FATHER SEEMED CONVINCED IT WAS SITUATED IN ASIA ITSELF...
...THAT IT UNDERLAY SUCH COLORFUL VISIONS AS SHANGRI-LA, WHICH THE WORLD THOUGHT A CREATION OF FICTION.
PERHAPS YOU WERE THINKING OF THESE THINGS EVEN AS YOU TOOK A MISSTEP CROSSING A DEEP GORGE--AND PULLED YOUR MOTHER BEHIND YOU!
HEATHER! DANNY!
EEEEEE!
THEN, OUR COMBINED WEIGHT PULLED OVER YOUR FATHER, AS WELL..

THE NEXT MOMENT, THE ROPE THAT HELD THE THREE OF YOU TOGETHER SNAPPED-- LEAVING YOUR FATHER DANGLING PRECARIOUSLY FROM THE NATURAL BRIDGE--
--AND YOU AND YOUR MOTHER ROLLING OVER AND OVER AGAIN, DOWN THE SNOW-PACKED MOUNTAINSIDE.

SOMEHOW, THE TWO OF YOU CAME TO REST ON A LEDGE NOT FAR BELOW, YOUR MOTHER STUNNED BY THE IMPACT FROM WHICH SHE HAD MANAGED TO SHIELD YOU.
HAROL PULL ME FAST
THEN, AS YOU GAZED AT HER, FORLORN AND SHOCKED, YOU HEARD SOUNDS FROM FAR ABOVE...

WE'VE GOT TO GET--ANOTHER ROPE! THROW IT TO HEATHER-- AND DANNY!
WH-WHY ARE YOU STARING AT ME THAT WAY, MAN? FOR GOD'S SAKE-- DO SOMETHING!!

OH, I'LL DO SOMETHING ALL RIGHT, OLD FRIEND...

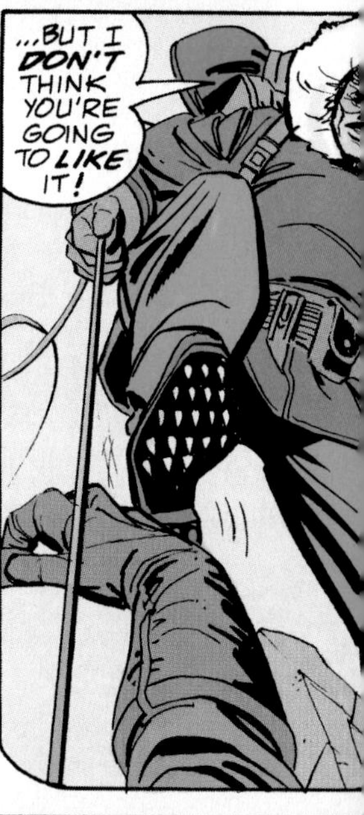
...BUT I DON'T THINK YOU'RE GOING TO LIKE IT!

YOUR FATHER WAS A STRONG MAN... STRONG IN BODY, STRONG OF WILL.
IT TOOK LONG SECONDS FOR THE CRUSHING PRESSURE OF HAROLD MEACHUM'S BOOT TO LOOSEN HIS GRIP ON THE ICE-COLD ROCK.

BUT, AT LAST, YOUR FATHER FELL.
WENDELL! OH MY GOD-- WENDELL

YOU REMEMBER IT CLEARLY, DON'T YOU, IRON FIST?
YOUR FATHER FELL FOR A LONG TIME...
...AND THE LAST YOU COULD SEE OF HIM WAS A VIEW OF SOMETHING VERY LIKE A BROKEN DOLL, CAROMING LUDICROUSLY FROM AN OUTCROPPING OF JAGGED ROCK.

PERHAPS YOU KNEW, EVEN THEN, THAT YOU'D SEE THAT HORRIBLE SIGHT AGAIN AND AGAIN, EVERY NIGHT OF YOUR LIFE...
AND ALWAYS, THE DREAM WOULD END THE SAME WAY:
WITH A MUFFLED, THROAT-CAUGHT SOB FROM THE HUSBAND-LESS WOMAN BEHIND YOU.

THEN, A VOICE INTRUDED ONCE MORE UPON YOUR OWN PRIVATE HELL...
AND YOU WONDERED WHY I ACCOMPANIED YOU, WENDELL RAND?
WELL, NOW THERE IS NO MORE MEACHUM & RAND-- ONLY RAND, INC.--
-- AND NO ONE WILL EVER BE ABLE TO PROVE I KILLED YOU!

EXHILARATION WAS SWEEPING OVER HAROLD MEACHUM ...EXHILARATION, AND A SENSE OF POWER...
--WHEN THE FIRST ROCK STRUCK AND BLOODIED HIS CHEEK.
THUK!
PERHAPS THAT IS WHY HE LOOKED MORE SHOCKED THAN TRULY HURT--

T STILL, ERE WAS RY HATRED THE HAND AT FLUNG IT.
HEATHER! STOP!! YOU'VE GOT ME ALL WRONG!
I DON'T WANT TO HARM YOU--EITHER OF YOU! IT WAS FOR YOU THAT I DID IT-- I'VE ALWAYS LOVED YOU!
DON'T YOU HEAR ME, WOMAN? I LOVE YOU!
BUT YOUR MOTHER KEPT RIGHT ON HATING--AND THROWING ROCKS.
MANY OF THEM FOUND THEIR RGET, OF COURSE.
S IS YOUR LAST ANCE, WOMAN. E WITH ME--IF T FOR YOUR OWN KE--THEN FOR THE BOY'S!
DO YOU WANT HIM TO DIE OUT HERE, IN THE MIDDLE OF NOWHERE?
DO YOU??
AT LAST, YOUR MOTHER ANSWERED.
YES!
THAT'S WHAT I DO WANT--IF LIVING MEANS SHARING THE SAME WORLD WITH YOU!
LET MY SON GROW UP TO KILL YOU WITH HIS OWN TWO HANDS--OR LET HIM DIE, LIKE HIS FATHER!
ANY WAY YOU WANT IT, HEATHER...
STILL, I RATHER SUSPECT YOU'LL FEEL DIFFERENTLY, WHEN YOU SEE THE FIRST SIGNS OF NUMBNESS SET IN.
GOOD-BYE, HEATHER.
'M GLAD U THREW CKS AT M, MOTHER. M GLAD!
DON'T TALK, DARLING. SAVE YOUR STRENGTH... FOR CLIMBING BACK UP... IF WE CAN.
ARE YOU READY, DANNY? ARE YOU READY TO TRY??
YES, MOTHER. YES, I'M...
...READY!

THAT IS GOOD. FOR, TO BECOME ONE OF US--TO EAT OF THE TREE OF IMMORTALITY, AND THUS TO GAIN ETERNAL LIFE HERE IN K'UN-LUN YOU FIRST MUST MEET--
--THE CHALLENGE OF THE ONE!
I HAVE FELLED MANY MEN WITH EASE, O YÜ-TI.
SHALL I FLINCH AT ONE?

BE CERTAIN, MY SON, THAT SUCH FALSE BRAVADO IS NOT THE VOICE OF A DEMON AT YOUR EAR...

FOR, ONE MAY PER HAPS BE MANY.. AYE, AND MORE THAN MANY...

...WHEN THAT ONE IS SHU-HU!
HE WHOSE LIPS ARE PLEDGED TO SILENCE, AND WHOSE NAME MEANS THE LIGHTNING...
...AND WHOSE FISTS ARE LIKE TWIN THUNDER-BOLTS!

WELL, MY SON? WILL YOU FACE SHU-HU...
OR SHALL MY DRAGON-KINGS AND I DELAY THIS CHALLENGE UNTIL ANOTHER DAY, WHEN YOU ARE RESTED?
NO, AUGUS ONE. MY T BY COMBA MUST B TODAY. I W NOT DEL IT.
THEN PROCEED. LET IT BE AS IT IS WRITTEN.

CALMLY, RESOLUTELY, YOU STRIDE TO THE CENTER OF THE EERIE INDOOR AMPHI-THEATRE.
YOU AND THE LIGHT-NING-LORD BOW TO EACH OTHER, FOR THAT IS THE WAY OF THE EAST...
...AND NOWHERE MORE SO THAN IN K'UN-LUN.

THEN--THE BATTLE!
SHU-HU IS SWIFT--NEARLY AS SW AS THE THUNDERCLAPS FOR WHICH HE IS NAMED.
YET, YOU WHO ONC WERE DANNY RAND EVADE HIS MAM-MOTH FIST, AND STRIKE HOME A SOLID BODY BLOW
--TO NO EFFECT!

MOST UN-
ELIEVING
N, YOU SEEK
O TAKE
VANTAGE OF
HE SLOW
NDEROUSNESS
THE HOODED
N'S VAST
BULK.

THOP

HAI-YA!

YOUR NIMBLE FEET FIND THEIR TARGET, SURELY ENOUGH--

T, ONCE MORE,
HU-HU SEEMS
ARCELY SHAKEN
THE IMPACT--

WOM

IS OWN CLENCHED
STS ARE FAR FROM
SLOW--

ND ONLY A NEAR-DECADE
F INTENSIVE TRAINING ENABLES
OU TO REGAIN YOUR
FOOTING--

THUD!

SO, AUGUST ONE... THIS GAUDILY-FESTOONED WEAKLING IS HE WHOM YOU WOULD WELCOME INTO THE COMPANY OF THE IMMORTALS!?

PHUK THIK THIK THIK!

--INSTEAD OF BEING SMASHED AGAINST THE WALL, LIKE A WORRISOME BUG.

RATHER, IT SEEMS TO **THIS** ONE THAT HE SHOULD BE TURNED OUT AGAIN INTO THE **END-LESS SNOWS** THAT DRIFT BE-YOND THE **GATE OF DREAMS.**

THE AUGUS PERSONAGE OF JADE SAY **NOTHING.**

AND, IF THE B BEHIND HIS SO HOOD IS **FURRO** NOT EVEN THE **DRAGON-KINGS** CLOSE ENOUGH T

MEANWHILE, WITH SURPRISING **QUICKNESS,** THE GIANT HURLS HIM-SELF **BODILY** TOWARD YOU.

WITH AN AGILE LEAP, YOU **DODGE** FEET WHOSE SHEER MASS COULD CRUSH A **TIGER'S SKULL...**

...ONLY TO BE FELL IN TURN BY A FAST DARTING **FIST.**

IT SEEMS TO BE SLIPPING AWAY NOW--YOUR GRIP ON CONSCIOUSNESS.
WOULD IT NOT BE SIMPLER FAR TO LET IT GO-- TO COLLAPSE INTO SWEET OBLIVION?
BUT WHY, THEN, DOES YOUR MIND RACE BACK ONCE MORE TO THAT WINDBLOWN LEDGE?
WHY DO YOU HEAR AGAIN YOUR MOTHER'S VOICE, FROM OUT OF THE DEAD PAST?
COME ON, DANNY! WE'RE GOING TO CLIMB NOW...!
YOUR HEART BEATS FASTER WITHIN YOUR BREAST...

T, IS IT HERE THAT IT BEATS... RE, WITHIN THE ARENA YOUR THROBBING PAIN...
...OR IS IT THERE, WHERE TWO PEOPLE MADE THAT MOST INHUMAN EFFORT, TEN YEARS GONE?

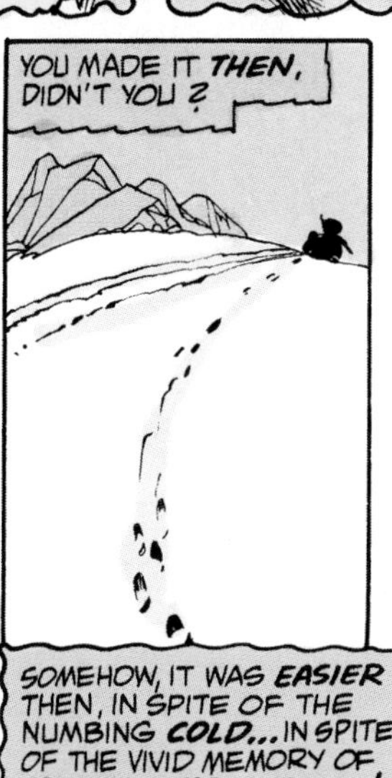
YOU MADE IT THEN, DIDN'T YOU?
SOMEHOW, IT WAS EASIER THEN, IN SPITE OF THE NUMBING COLD... IN SPITE OF THE VIVID MEMORY OF MURDER MOST FOUL!

FOR, THOUGH YOU KNEW YOU BOTH WERE LOST...
...THAT YOU WERE HEADING FORWARD, INTO THE UNKNOWN, INSTEAD OF BACK TOWARD MEACHUM AND THE DEATH THAT WAITED SURELY AT HIS HANDS...

STILL, YOU HAD ACH OTHER.
DANNY, I... I WANT YOU TO PROMISE ME SOME-THING.
PROMISE ME YOU DON'T HATE YOUR FATHER FOR BRINGING YOU HERE!
FOR, HE HAD A VISION OF A BETTER WORLD, WAITING SOME-WHERE FOR THE THREE OF US...
...SOMEWHERE ALWAYS JUST BEYOND THE NEXT RIDGE.
PROMISE ME, DANNY!
I...PROMISE, MOTHER.
AND SO YOU WANDERED ALONE, FOR DAYS. THEN, EVEN AS YOUR STRENGTH GREW EVER WEAKER...

...YOUR STEPS EVER MORE FALTERING...
...SUDDENLY, YOU BOTH WEREN'T ALONE ANY LONGER.

THE WOLVES MUST HAVE TRAILED YOU BOTH FOR HOURS, IN PATIENT, SINISTER SILENCE.
BUT NOW, THEY BEGAN TO RU AS IF SENSIN SOMEHOW THA THEY HAD LITT TIME LEFT.

MOTHER... WHAT KIND OF PLACE WAS FATHER LOOKING FOR? I... I NEVER KNEW...
IT WAS A DREAM PLACE, DANNY. IT NEVER REALLY EXISTED, EXCEPT IN HIS OWN MIND...
...ALTHOUGH ONCE... JUST FOR A LITTLE WHILE... I THOUGHT THAT PERHAPS IT DID.

IT WAS THE VERY NEXT SECOND THAT SHE SAW IT...
NO! I IT CAN BE--!

A BRIDGE! OUT HERE IN THE MIDDLE OF NOWHERE!
COULD IT BE THE ONE THAT LEADS TO--NO! THAT'S IMPOSSIBLE!
THAT PLACE DOESN'T EXIST! IT COULDN'T!
IT'S... JUST A BRIDGE... NOTHING MORE.
IT WAS THEN, YOU REMEMBER, THAT THE HOWLING BEGAN...

...THE HOWLING THAT WAS SCARCELY MORE HORRIFYING THAN THE SUDDEN, TERRIBLE KNOWLEDGE THAT THEY HAD BEEN THERE, ALL ALONG.
ARROOO
WOLVES!

RUN, DANNY! RUN FOR THE BRIDGE!
HURRY, DARLING! HURRY!

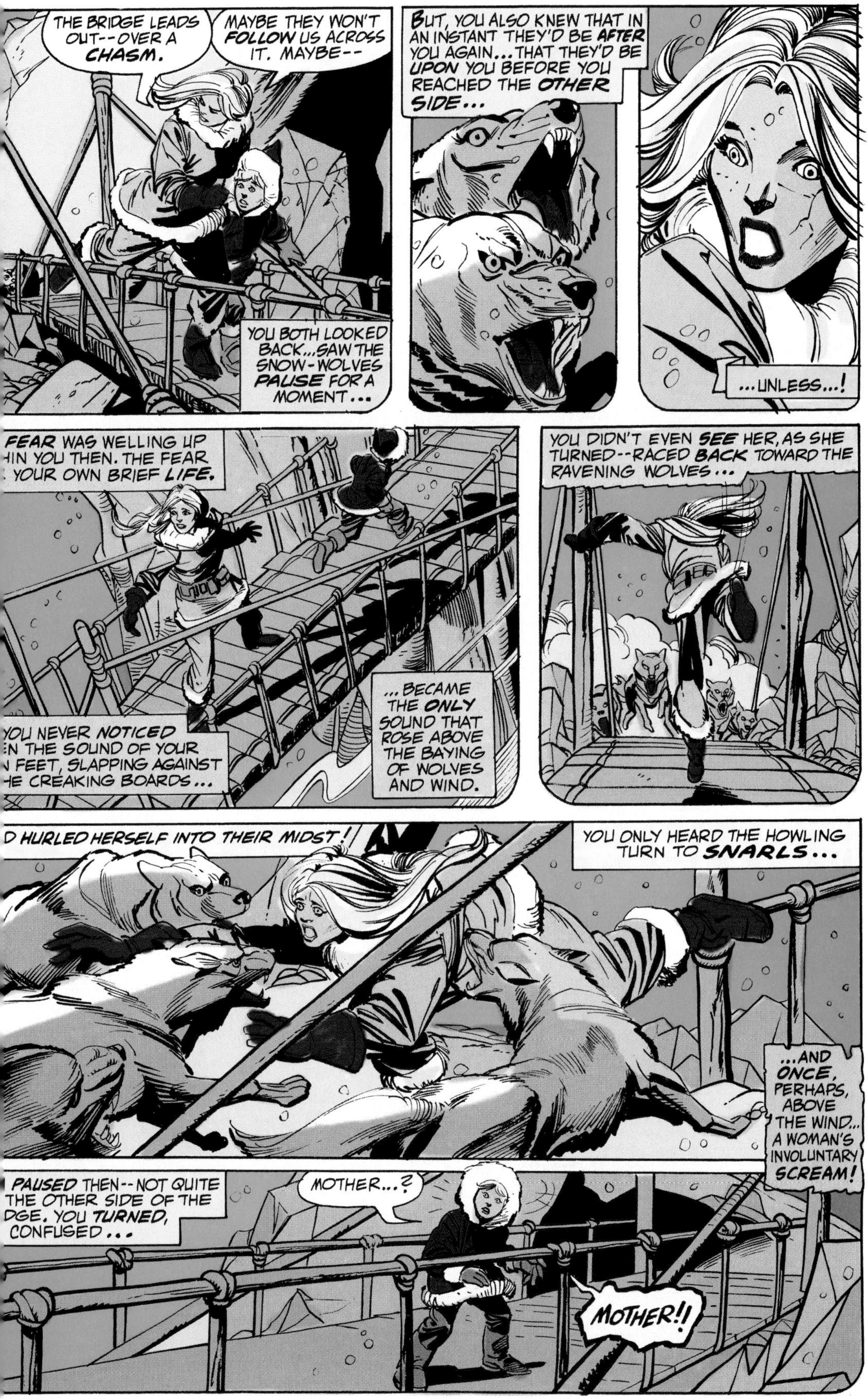

THE BRIDGE LEADS OUT--OVER A CHASM.
MAYBE THEY WON'T FOLLOW US ACROSS IT. MAYBE--
YOU BOTH LOOKED BACK...SAW THE SNOW-WOLVES PAUSE FOR A MOMENT...

BUT, YOU ALSO KNEW THAT IN AN INSTANT THEY'D BE AFTER YOU AGAIN...THAT THEY'D BE UPON YOU BEFORE YOU REACHED THE OTHER SIDE...

...UNLESS...!

FEAR WAS WELLING UP
HIN YOU THEN. THE FEAR
YOUR OWN BRIEF LIFE.
YOU NEVER NOTICED
EN THE SOUND OF YOUR
N FEET, SLAPPING AGAINST
HE CREAKING BOARDS...
...BECAME THE ONLY SOUND THAT ROSE ABOVE THE BAYING OF WOLVES AND WIND.

YOU DIDN'T EVEN SEE HER, AS SHE TURNED--RACED BACK TOWARD THE RAVENING WOLVES...

D HURLED HERSELF INTO THEIR MIDST!

YOU ONLY HEARD THE HOWLING TURN TO SNARLS...

...AND ONCE, PERHAPS, ABOVE THE WIND... A WOMAN'S INVOLUNTARY SCREAM!

PAUSED THEN--NOT QUITE THE OTHER SIDE OF THE DGE. YOU TURNED, CONFUSED...

MOTHER...?

MOTHER!!

MOTHER--!

YOU SAW THEN-- WHAT YOU SAW. AND YOU'LL NEVER FORGET IT. YET, AS YOU STARTED BACK TO HER, HEEDLESS OF THE COST, MINDLESS OF THE FANGED PERIL--
--SUDDENLY, STRONG HAN WERE THERE--GRIPPIN HOLDING--

AND, THE NEXT INSTANT--
THWISSSH!

YOU DIDN'T WONDER THEN AT THE MEN WHO HAD APPEARED AS IF FROM NOWHERE--AT THE WEAPON OF ANOTHER AGE WHICH HAD FIRED--TOO LATE!
SHE... DEAL
MOTHER--!? I--I'VE GOT TO--
BUT YO ARE AMC THE LIVI ONCE MO
WELCO LAD

...WELCOME TO K'UN-LUN!
YOU DIDN'T EVEN HEAR HIM THEN, DID YOU? YOUR TEARS WERE TOO LOUD, YOUR SORROW TOO STRIDENT... YOUR YOUNG BODY TOO WRACKED...
...WITH TOO MANY KINDS OF PAIN...PAIN OF A DIFFERENT KIND FROM THAT YOU FEEL TODAY, THOUGH NO LESS REAL FOR ALL THAT.
BUT NOW, THE REALITIES COME POURING OVER YOU AGAIN, LIKE A TIDAL WAVE OF AGONY...
...LIKE A THUNDERCLOUD OF DARK DESPAIR...

...LIKE THE SHADOW OF DEATH ITSELF!
I AM IRON FIST! I WA TRAINED TO BE A LIVING WEAPON-- TO DEFEND MYSELF FROM ANYTHIN HUMAN!
YET YOU TOSS ME ABOUT-- LIKE A CHILD'S BROKEN PLAYTHING!
WHO ARE YOU??

R ONLY
SWER :
A BLUR OF DEADLY MOTION, STREAKING FROM OUT OF YOUR TORMENTOR'S VERY HAND--
ZZUP!

--TO TAKE SOLID FORM IN YOUR OWN PAIN-WRACKED SHOULDER!
THEN, EVEN AS YOU REALIZE AT LAST THAT YOUR OPPONENT IS NOT HUMAN--
THUK!
--SOMEONE ELSE IS MYSTERIOUSLY THERE!

RHAPS IT IS THE SIGHT OF HER--MORE REAL
N THAN THE DUST AND CARNAGE OF THE
ENA--WHICH BRINGS YOU INSTANTLY TO
R SENSES--
TUNK!
O THAT THE
ECOND
FT-HURLED
ADE DOES
T FIND
MARK!
IT IS FOR HER YOU HAVE BEEN FIGHTING, ALL ALONG!

SHE DIED TO BRING YOU TO THIS PLACE CALLED K'UN-LUN--A PLACE IN WHICH SHE DID NOT EVEN BELIEVE, AND WHICH SHE THUS COULD NEVER HOPE TO ENTER.
YOU HEAR HER VOICE ONCE AGAIN, FROM OUT OF THE PAST--AND IT DULLS THE PAIN YOU FEEL--

LLS IT INTO INSENSITIVITY, THEN
LIVION.
NO LONGER DO YOU FEEL THE PAIN--
D THE BLOOD WHICH DROPS
LD AS EASILY BELONG TO A
LD WHO PERISHED TEN
YEARS AGO.

NOW, YOU ARE MERELY--
IRON FIST!
AND, YOU ARE AS WELL--
A MAN GONE BERSERK!
HAI--
--YAH!
DRAK
YOU KNOW YOU FAILED BEFORE--WITH BLOWS YOU THOUGHT YOUR STRONGEST.
BUT THAT DOESN'T MATTER NOW, AS YOU LEAP ANEW INTO THE JAWS OF STEEL-FLESHED DOOM--

--AS YOU STRIKE AGAIN--
WHUMP

--AND AGAIN--

--AND YET AGAIN--
NOW, YOU CAN FEEL THE HARD, MAN-FORGED METAL BENEATH THE HOOD--FEEL IT START TO GIVE AND BEND AND TWIST.
AND, IF HE--IF IT COULD FEEL PAIN--
THE PONDEROUS GIANT'S MOVES BECOME SLUGGISH--SLOW--MECHANICAL--
--ITS PAIN WOULD DWAR ANY THAT YO HAVE EVER KNOWN!

AT LAST IT TOTTERS--REELS--YET, IT IS STILL TOO STRONG TO FALL.
AND NOW, AN ICY CALM SETTLES OVER YOU--
--A CALM WHICH IS, FINALLY, YOUR GREATEST STRENGTH.

YOU CALL SILENTLY, INWARDLY, UPON THE INVINCIBLE WIL WHICH FORMS THE VERY CORE OF YOUR BEING.
UNFATHOMED RESERVES CONCENTRATION AND RE SOLVE FLOW FROM YOUR BRAIN, YOUR SHOULDERS YOUR LEGS, FROM EVERY OF A BODY HONED FOR LONG YE

--FLOW, MELD, AND MERGE INTO ONE PLACE--
--INTO YOUR HAND--
--UNTIL IT BEGINS TO SMOULDER AND GLOW--

--UNTIL IT BECOMES LIKE UNTO--
--A THIN OF IRON

THIS SERIES IS AFFECTIONATELY DEDICATED TO THE MEMORY OF BILL EVERETT... A MOST AMAZING MAN!

WHAT IF™
MARVEL® COMICS GROUP
50¢
CC
3
JUNE
02686
WHAT IF™
THE AVENGERS
HAD NEVER BEEN?
ALL NEW!
NEVER SEEN BEFORE!!
THOR! GIANT-MAN! WASP! YOU CAN'T QUIT NOW--!
--NOT WHILE THE HULK AND SUB-MARINER HAVE UNITED TO DESTROY MANKIND!
K S
A TALE OF TRIUMPH AND TRAGEDY IN THE TITANIC MARVEL TRADITION!

AN LEE
ESENTS: A STUNNING SAGA OF AN ALTERNATE REALITY!
WHAT IF... The AVENGERS HAD NEVER BEEN?
I AM THE WATCHER!
FOR EONS I HAVE DWELT ON EARTH'S DESOLATE MOON, OBSERVING AND RECORDING THE HISTORY OF THIS SECTOR OF THE UNIVERSE, FOR SUCH IS MY SWORN DUTY!
THUS, I WITNESSED WITH PROFOUND INTEREST THE TENTATIVE, HESITANT ORIGIN OF THE SUPER-HERO GROUP CALLED THE AVENGERS! BEHOLD AGAIN, HOW, IN YOUR REALITY, THEY MET A CRITICAL POINT IN THEIR EARLY DAYS...
I DON'T NEED ANY OF YOU! I'M STILL THE HULK!
I'M STILL THE STRONGEST THING WALKIN' THE EARTH! AND WHATEVER I DO FROM NOW ON, I DO ALONE!
CO-PLOTTED BY
JIM SHOOTER WRITER * GIL KANE PENCILER
K. JANSON INKER * DENISE W. LETTERER
G. ROUSSOS COLORIST * A. GOODWIN EDITOR
TAKE A LONG LOOK AT IRON MAN'S OLD-STYLE GOLDEN ARMOR, FAITHFUL ONE, 'CAUSE THIS SCENE FROM AVENGERS #2 IS THE LAST TIME YOU'LL SEE IT -- ASSEMBLIN' ARCH.

"THE LOSS OF A MEMBER AS MIGHTY AS THE HULK COULD HAVE BEEN A CRIPPLING BLOW TO THE FLEDGLING TEAM IN THOSE TROUBLED DAYS! INSTEAD, IT UNITED THEM IN PURPOSE!"
HE'S O JOKER YO CAN'T FI IN THE CLASSIFI ADS!
I TELL YOU WE'VE GOT TO FIND THE HULK! SO LONG AS HE IS RUNNING WILD, THERE'S NO TELLING WHAT HE'LL DO!
IRON MAN IS RIGHT! SO SAYS THOR!
BUT HOW DO WE FIND HIM?

"WITH THE AID OF YOUNG RICK JONES THE RAMPAGING HULK WAS FOUND IN NEW MEXICO.
"ATTEMPTS TO REASO WITH THE GREEN-SKINNED BEHEMOT FAILED--AND SO, A ALMOST LEGENDAR BATTLE WAS FOUGH IN AN EFFORT TO CAPTURE HIM!
"THE HULK ESCAPED, AND FLED, SEEKING A PLACE APART, TO BROOD AND PLAN. BUT WHEN THE MIGHTY CREATURE REACHED A BARREN ISLE IN THE ATLANTIC..."
THE SUB-MARINER!
I HAVE BEEN WAITING FOR YOU HULK! AN YOU SHOULD B FLATTERED! FO NORMALLY, THE SUB-MARINE WAITS FOR NOBODY!

"AT FIRST, THE HULK LASHED OUT IN RAGE AT THE INTRUDING SEA-PRINCE...
"...BUT THEIR BRIEF CONFRONTATION ENDED IN A DRAW -- AND SOON AFTERWARD, THEY FORMED AN UNEASY ALLIANCE, BONDED BY THEIR MUTUAL HATRED FOR HUMANS!

"THEY BEGAN THEIR CAMPAIGN AGAINST MANKIND BY CHALLENGING THE AVENGERS TO BATTLE IN THE SHADOWS OF GIBRALTAR!
"NEVER HAS ANY GROUP OF HEROES FACED A STERNER TEST!

IN THE END, THE
HULK AND SUB-
MARINER WERE
DRIVEN OFF,
EACH GOING HIS
SEPARATE WAY--
AN INDECISIVE
VICTORY, PERHAPS--
"--BUT A VICTORY, NONETHELESS. THUS THOR, IRON MAN, GIANT-MAN, AND THE WASP WENT ON TOGETHER, BECOMING THE NUCLEUS AND FOUNDATION FOR ONE OF THE MOST VARIED AND SUCCESSFUL TEAMS EVER!"

SO IT WAS... IN YOUR WORLD!
BUT THERE ARE COUNTLESS BILLIONS OF WORLDS PARALLEL TO YOUR OWN, THAT DIVERGE FROM YOUR CONTINUUM AT CRITICAL POINTS--!
--AND IN THESE OTHER REALITIES, WHAT MIGHT HAVE HAPPENED ON YOUR WORLD IS, INDEED, WHAT DID HAPPEN!
I HAVE WINDOWS INTO THESE ALTERNATE PLANES...

...AND I HAVE OBSERVED A WORLD--AN ALTERNATE EARTH, IF YOU WILL--WHERE THE FATEFUL MOMENT OF THE HULK'S ABRUPT DEPARTURE FROM THE AVENGERS CAUSED A RIFT...
...WHICH, IN TURN, SEVERAL DAYS LATER--

--LED TO THE END OF THE AVENGERS!"
HOLD IT, GUYS! WAIT A MINUTE!
ARE YOU CRAZY, GIANT-MAN? WE'VE GOT TO GO AFTER THE HULK!
UNHAND ME, MORTAL!

CALM DOWN AND THINK A LITTLE, TROOPS!
THIS IS STRICTLY A VOLUNTEER ORGANIZATION! WE CAN'T FORCE THE HULK TO STAY!
BUT...WITHOUT THE AVENGERS TO KEEP HIM IN CHECK, WHAT WILL HE DO NEXT?
I TELL YOU WE'VE GOT TO FIND THE HULK!
A MOMENT AGO, I AGREE BUT GIANT-MAN'S WOR RING TRUE! SO SAYS THO
NONE OF US ARE BOUND BY OATH!
I NEVER FIGURED IT WAS NECESSARY! I GUESS WHAT YOU'RE DRIVING AT IS THAT YOU PLAN TO LEAVE, TOO!
SO GO AHEAD AND QUIT, LONGHAIR! I'VE JUST ABOUT HAD IT WITH YOUR BLASTED SUPERIORITY COMPLEX, ANYWAY!
STAY YOUR BITTERNESS, IRON MAN!
YOU CANNOT KNOW WHAT IT MEANS TO BE GOD!
MAYHAP THE SON OF ODIN WAS NOT MEANT TO BATTLE ALONGSIDE MORTAL ALLIES!
THE GOD OF THUNDER HAS DUTIES TO PERFOR IN REALMS MERE HUMANS DARE NOT ENTER! 'TIS FAREWELL, THEN! MAY TH PATH BE NOT DARK!
WELL, THAT JUST ABOUT WRAPS IT UP, SHELLHEAD! WITHOUT THOR AND THE HULK, THE "MIGHTY AVENGERS" IS PRETTY MUCH A JOKE!
YEAH...I SUPPOSE! STILL, YOU AND I MIGHT ACCOMPLISH A LOT TOGETHER, GIANT-MAN!
HEY! THE WASP IS STILL HERE! DON'T FORGET ME!

IET, JAN! THIS IS SERIOUS!
OOK, IRON MAN... I KNOW AT TEAMING UP WAS MY IDEA THE FIRST PLACE, BUT NOW, I-- ONDER IF THE WASP AND I SHOULDN'T LEAVE TOO!
RIGHT! WHY STICK AROUND IF THAT DREAMY THOR IS GONE!! ≈SIGH≈
JAN, PLEASE!
E FACT OF THE MATTER IS, THAT HANGING AROUND TH FOLKS AS POWERFUL AS YOU, THE HULK AND OR HAS SORT OF GIVEN ME A NEW PERSPECTIVE!
BEING TWELVE FEET TALL ISN'T ALL THAT GREAT A POWER! I'M NOT A BIG-LEAGUER! I WOULDN'T BE MUCH MORE THAN COMPANY FOR YOU, IRON MAN!
BUT--BUT, GIANT-MAN!
IT'S BEEN GREAT, PAL... BUT MAYBE IT'S TIME I STOPPED KIDDING MYSELF AND WENT BACK TO BEING A PLAIN, OLD BIO-PHYSICIST!
GET THE FEELING HAT WE'RE THROWING WAY SOMETHING RREPLACEABLE
BUT WHAT CAN I DO?
"THUS IN THIS ALTERNATE REALITY, HENRY PYM RETURNED TO HIS LABORA-TORY--
--TO RECONSIDER HIS CAREER AS A SUPER-HERO, WHILE THOR BECAME EMBROILED IN ASGARDIAN CONFLICTS!"
BACK, BASE ONE!
ARRGH!
YOU SHALL MENACE THE GOLDEN REALM WITH YOUR EVIL NO LONGER! SO SWEARS THOR!

"AND SO, IRON MAN WAS LEFT ALONE IN THE PLUSH TOWNHOUSE HE OWNED AS ANTHONY STARK WHI IN YOUR REALITY, EVENTUALLY BECAME KNOWN AS AVENGERS' MANSION--AND ALONE, HE SET O TO FIND THE HULK!"
HMM... I WAS GOING TO USE M NEW IMAGE PROJECTOR TO SEARCH FOR THE HULK, BUT I HAVE A BETTER IDEA!
YOUNG RICK JONES SEEMS TO BE THE HULK'S FRIEND... IF THAT'S POSSIBLE! I'LL CONTACT HIM!
HE'S A SHORT-WAVE HAM RADIO OPERATOR! HE'S PROBABLY AT HIS SET RIGHT NOW!
"HALFWAY ACROSS THE COUNTRY, IN THE GREAT SOUTHWEST, THE GRIM-FACED TEEN-AGER RECEIVED IRON MAN'S MESSAGE!"
I UNDERSTAND! THE HULK IS TOO DANGEROUS TO ROAM OUT OF CONTROL! I'LL START SEARCHING AT ONCE!
"IT WAS NOT LONG UNTIL RICK LOCATED THE HULK--
"--BUT AT FIRST HE ATTEMPTED TO HANDLE THE BRUTE HIMSELF, JUST AS HE DID ON YOUR WORLD!
"IN BOTH CONTINUUMS, HE FAILED!"
HULK! WAIT! STOP!
NO USE! HE DOESN'T EVEN HEAR ME! HE'S COMPLETELY OUT OF CONTROL!

...NLY THEN DID RICK ...LL FOR IRON MAN!"
RICK SAID THE HULK'S ON A RAMPAGE! AND STRONGER THAN EVER!
THIS IS IT! THE HULK MUST BE STOPPED!
HOW I'M GOING TO DO THAT ALONE, I JUST DON'T KNOW YET!
...SOME TIME LATER, ...ON MAN ARRIVED AT ...E APPOINTED PLACE..."
THERE'S RICK! BUT, WHY IS HE TRYING TO WAVE ME AWAY?
WHAM
"THE IRON-GARBED HERO GOT HIS STAGGERING ANSWER A SECOND LATER!"
"THE BATTLE PROGRESSED MUCH AS IT DID IN YOUR WORLD..."
THIS WON'T STOP HIM, BUT IT'S SURE TO SLOW HIM DOWN!
BAH! IS THAT THE BEST YOU CAN DO?
"IRON MAN COULD NOT CONVINCE THE HULK TO END HIS VENDETTA AGAINST HUMANITY--
"--NOR COULD HE COPE WITH THE MONSTER'S MATCHLESS STRENGTH, OR THE SAVAGERY OF HIS ATTACK!"

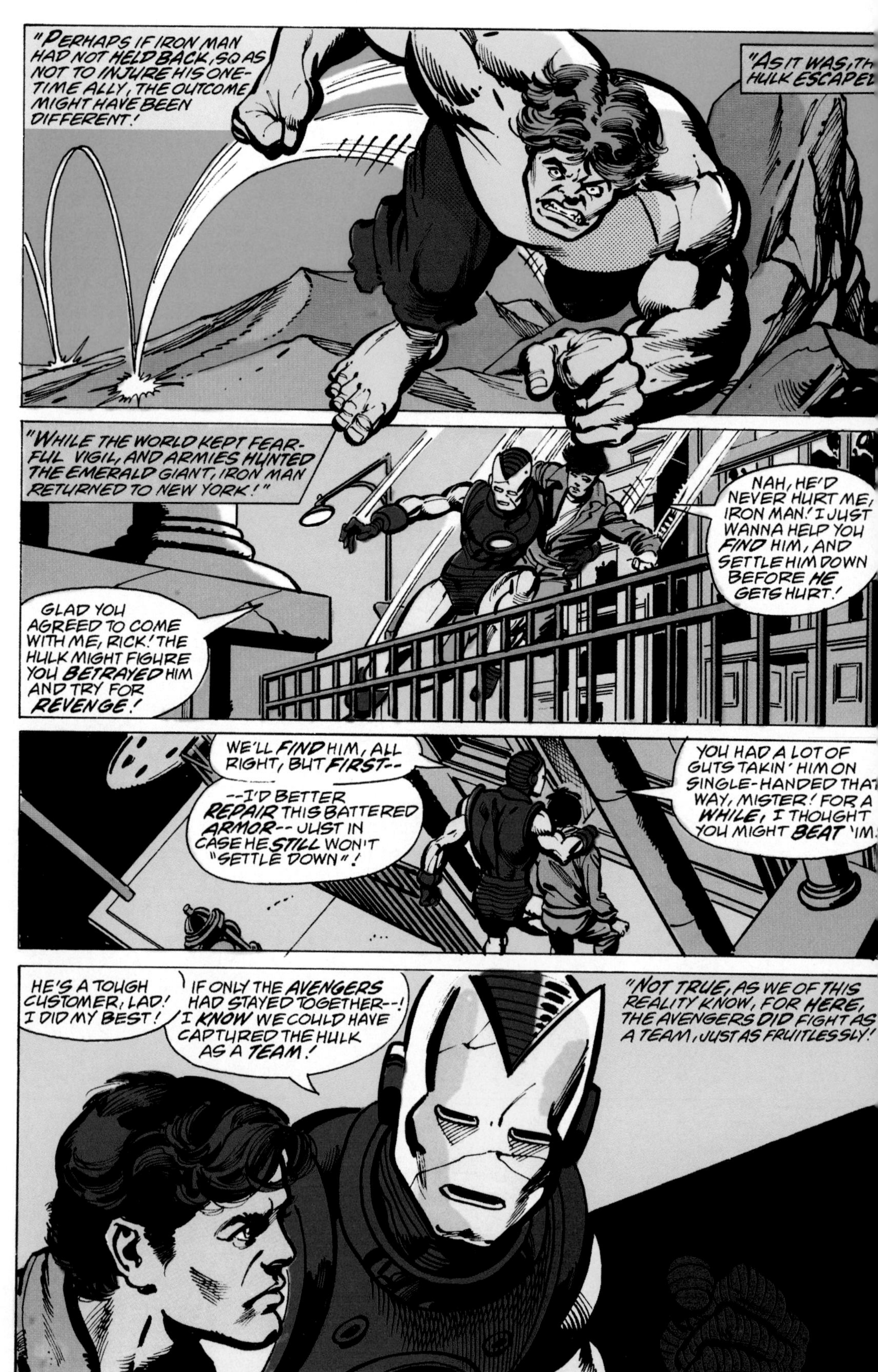
"PERHAPS IF IRON MAN HAD NOT HELD BACK, SO AS NOT TO INJURE HIS ONE-TIME ALLY, THE OUTCOME MIGHT HAVE BEEN DIFFERENT!
"AS IT WAS, TH HULK ESCAPED
"WHILE THE WORLD KEPT FEARFUL VIGIL, AND ARMIES HUNTED THE EMERALD GIANT, IRON MAN RETURNED TO NEW YORK!"
GLAD YOU AGREED TO COME WITH ME, RICK! THE HULK MIGHT FIGURE YOU BETRAYED HIM AND TRY FOR REVENGE!
NAH, HE'D NEVER HURT ME, IRON MAN! I JUST WANNA HELP YOU FIND HIM, AND SETTLE HIM DOWN BEFORE HE GETS HURT!
WE'LL FIND HIM, ALL RIGHT, BUT FIRST--
--I'D BETTER REPAIR THIS BATTERED ARMOR-- JUST IN CASE HE STILL WON'T "SETTLE DOWN"!
YOU HAD A LOT OF GUTS TAKIN' HIM ON SINGLE-HANDED THAT WAY, MISTER! FOR A WHILE, I THOUGHT YOU MIGHT BEAT 'IM!
HE'S A TOUGH CUSTOMER, LAD! I DID MY BEST!
IF ONLY THE AVENGERS HAD STAYED TOGETHER--! I KNOW WE COULD HAVE CAPTURED THE HULK AS A TEAM!
"NOT TRUE, AS WE OF THIS REALITY KNOW, FOR HERE, THE AVENGERS DID FIGHT AS A TEAM, JUST AS FRUITLESSLY!

NDEED, EVENTS ON THIS ALT-
RNATE PLANE ARE IN
RIKING ACCORD WITH THOSE

"AND THE PARALLELS DO NOT YET END!
"THERE, THE HULK ENCOUNTERED NAMOR, THE SUB-MARINER, JUST AS IN OUR HISTORY--

"--AND BATTLED HIM, JUST AS INCONCLUSIVELY--

--AND JOINED HIM IN THE SAME, TREACHEROUS ALLIANCE!"

I'LL STRING ALONG FOR A WHILE AND THEN SMASH HIM WHEN HE'S OFF GUARD!

HE'S TOO STRONG! TOO UNDEPENDABLE! WHEN HE'S SERVED HIS PURPOSE, I'LL DESTROY HIM!

"BOTH NAMOR AND THE HULK WERE UNAWARE THAT THE AVENGERS HAD DISBANDED--

--AWAIT YOU THOR GIANT-MAN AND THE WASP AT GIBRALTAR! WE WILL FIGHT TO THE DEATH!

-AND SO THEIR HISTORIC CHALLENGE WAS ISSUED TO A GROUP THAT WAS NO MORE! IRON MAN RECEIVED THE COMMUNIQUE IN HIS LAB AT WHAT HAD BEEN AVENGERS H.Q."

YOUR ANSWER? SPEAK QUICKLY, ARMORED ONE!
WE'LL BE THERE, FISH-FACE... IN 48 HOURS!

COULDN'T TELL HIM THE AVENGERS DOESN'T EXIST ANYMORE! HE WOULD HAVE INTERPRETED IT AS COWARDICE!
ON THE OTHER HAND--

--I'D BE A FOOL NOT TO BE AFRAID OF GOING IT ALONE AGAINST THE HULK AND NAMOR!
BUT... WHAT CAN I DO?

"IT WAS IN THAT BLEAK MOMENT OF NEAR-DESPAIR THAT FINALLY THE COURSE OF FATE DEVIATED--IN THE FORM OF A DESPERATE IDEA!"
OF COURSE IF I CAN'T CALL OUT THE OLD AVENGER
--MAYBE I CAN CREATE NEW AVENGE

"THE ALTERNATE-EARTH IRON MAN SPENT THE NEXT FORTY HOURS WORKING NON-STOP ON HIS SCHEME
HEY, IRON MAN! DIG IT! THE GANG'S ALL HERE!
RICK! GIANT-MAN... WASP! GLAD YOU ALL COULD MAKE IT!
WE'RE JUST PLAIN HENRY PYM, BIOCHEMIST AND JANET VAN DYNE, AIRHEAD HEIRESS NOW, IRON MAN! BUT WHAT'S UP?

"IRON MAN QUICKLY EXPLAINED..."
--AND I CAN'T EMPHASIZE ENOUGH THE IMPORTANCE OF STOPPING THEM NOW!
AGREED. BUT HOW?
TOGETHER, THEIR POWER IS NEARLY UNIMAGINABLE!

RIGHT! AND YOU'RE WONDERING HOW WE COULD EVER MATCH IT!
WELL, RIGHT BEFORE YOUR EYES IS A WAY WE CAN EASILY SURPASS THEIR MIGHT--BY A COUNTRY MILE!
TRANSISTORIZED ARMOR--LIKE MINE--DESIGNED AND PROVIDED BY MY BOSS, TONY STARK, THE BEST ELECTRONIC WEAPONRY WHIZ IN THE WORLD! THERE'S OUR POWER, GROUP! ALL YOU HAVE TO ADD IS THE GUTS!

WELL? WHAT'S WRONG? SAY SOMETHING!
OKAY. YOU'RE CRAZY!
I DON'T KNOW, JAN! THE IDEA IS SOUND!
HENRY PYM! CAN'T YOU SEE THAT THIS COLOR CLASHES WITH MY EYE SHADOW!

SOON..."
LMOST EADY, SHELL UH, IRON AN! BUT... SURE FEELS TRANGE!
WHEEE! THIS IS FUN!
JUST GET USED TO MOVING AROUND WITH THE EXTRA WEIGHT, FIRST!
REMEMBER THOUGH, THE ARMOR AMPLIFIES THE FORCE OF YOUR MOVEMENTS.

OOK, MA, O WINGS!
I WISH TONY HAD CONSULTED WITH MY FASHION DESIGNER, THOUGH.
THIS DOES NOTHING FOR MY FIGURE, AND--
WHOOPS! GLAD HE PUT A MASK ON IT! THIS IS GETTING... EMBARRASSING!
OH... GOODNESS! I-I'M REALLY OUT OF CONTROL! HANK! SOMEBODY! HELP!

OWW!
CLANG!
RICK! LOOK OUT FOR THE WASP! WATCH WHERE YOU'RE--

NO, NO! YOU DON'T HAVE TO FLAP YOUR ARMS! LET THE ARMOR DO THE WORK!
THINK! USE YOUR HEAD!

FLYIN'S COOL, BUT I THINK I'M STARTIN' TO GET... AIRSICK!
HOLD ON, WASP! I'LL CATCH YOU!
WHOA! I-I'M AIRBOR
I MUST HAVE ACCIDENTA
ACTIVATED THE BOOSTE
JETS!
LOVER, HELP ME! I CAN'T TURN IT OFF!

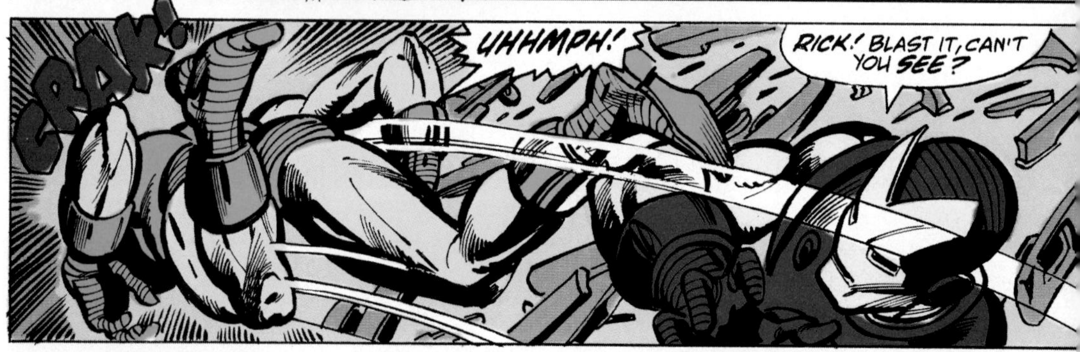

CRAK!
UHHMPH!
RICK! BLAST IT, CAN'T YOU SEE?

I THOUGHT I EXPLAINED EVERYTHING TO EACH OF YOU! DIDN'T ANYBODY LISTEN? YOU'VE GOT TO CONCENTRATE!
IT'S HARD TO WOR
THESE SUITS! WE'R
TRYING!
DON'
BE S
MEAN

DAMN IT! I WORKED DAY AND NIGHT ON THAT ARMOR--!
--UH, WITH STARK! ALL I ASK IS THAT YOU GIVE IT SOME RESPECT! NOW LET'S TAKE IT FROM THE TOP!
GEE, IRON MAN, WE--
SHUT UP!

HAT DOES IT! I'M LEAVING! IF YOU ANTED PERFECTION, YOU SHOULD VE BUILT ROBOTS, YOU... YOU TIN-PLATED TYRANT!
JAN! WAIT!
YOU GO WITH HIM IF YOU WANT, HENRY PYM--BUT I'M NOT!
GIANT-MAN, LOOK... I-I-M SORRY!
DON'T SWEAT T, RUST-POT! IN WAY, I'M GLAD IT APPENED! I WAS EGINNING TO HAVE Y DOUBTS ABOUT IS WILD SCHEME ANYWAY!
JAN AND I HAD DECIDED TO GIVE UP THE HERO BIZ... I GUESS WE'LL STICK TO OUR DECISION!
GEE, IRON, MAN...
ALWAYS WANTED BE A SUPER-HERO, IT... WELL, THIS RMOR JUST ISN'T Y GIG, Y'SEE! AYBE... IF YOU COULD OMEHOW GIVE ME IPER-POWERS--?
NO, LAD... I'M AFRAID I DON'T HAVE ANY MAGIC POTIONS! I THINK YOU'D BETTER GO WITH THE OTHERS, NOW!
YEAH, I GUESS... BUT WHAT ABOUT THE HULK AN' SUBBY?
I'LL, UH, THINK OF SOMETHING! MAYBE I CAN GET SOME HELP FROM THE FANTASTIC FOUR!
HEY, THAT WOULD BE THE COOLEST! GOOD LUCK!
MOMENTS LATER...
THEY'VE ALL SHED THEIR ARMOR AND DESERTED ME! AND I REALLY CAN'T BLAME THEM!
SO TIRED... HAVEN'T SLEPT FOR TWO DAYS! NO WONDER MY HEAD ACHES! STILL, I SHOULDN'T HAVE YELLED AT THEM!
SO I'M ALONE AGAIN! AS IT BEGAN... SO IT IS ONCE MORE!

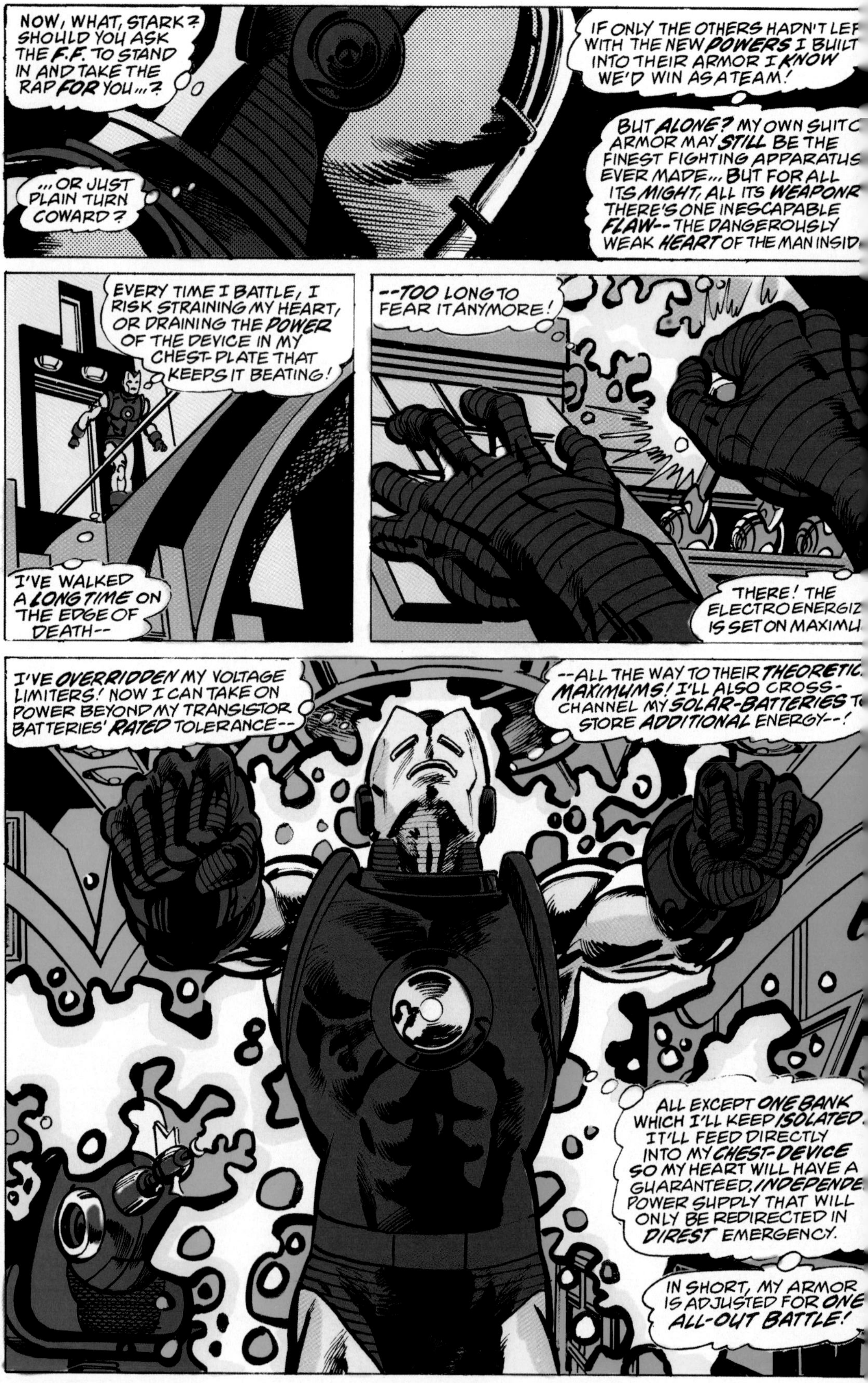

NOW, WHAT, STARK? SHOULD YOU ASK THE F.F. TO STAND IN AND TAKE THE RAP FOR YOU...?
...OR JUST PLAIN TURN COWARD?
IF ONLY THE OTHERS HADN'T LEF WITH THE NEW POWERS I BUILT INTO THEIR ARMOR I KNOW WE'D WIN AS A TEAM!
BUT ALONE? MY OWN SUIT C ARMOR MAY STILL BE THE FINEST FIGHTING APPARATUS EVER MADE... BUT FOR ALL ITS MIGHT, ALL ITS WEAPONR THERE'S ONE INESCAPABLE FLAW-- THE DANGEROUSLY WEAK HEART OF THE MAN INSID

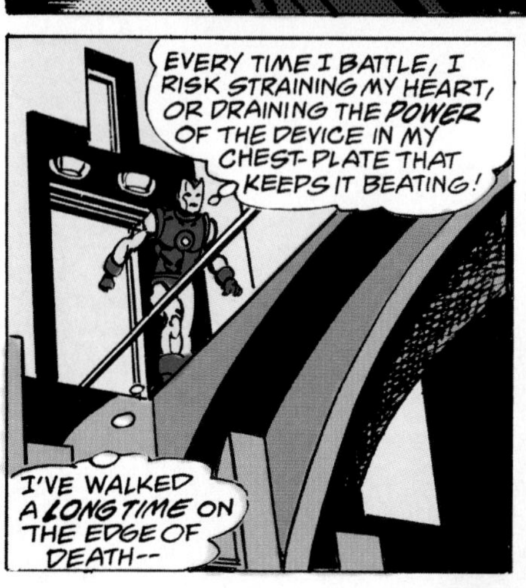
EVERY TIME I BATTLE, I RISK STRAINING MY HEART, OR DRAINING THE POWER OF THE DEVICE IN MY CHEST-PLATE THAT KEEPS IT BEATING!
I'VE WALKED A LONG TIME ON THE EDGE OF DEATH--

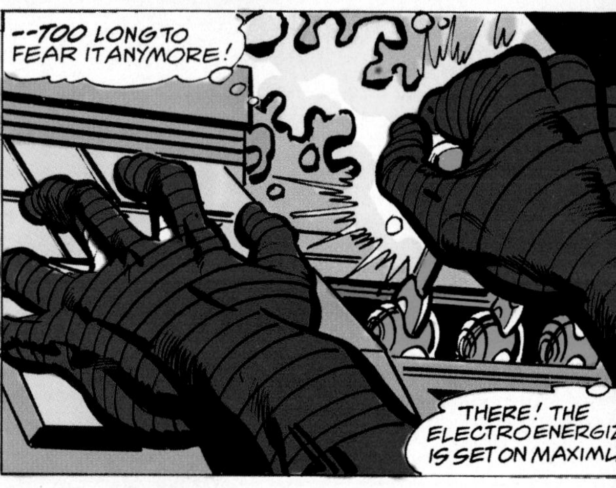
--TOO LONG TO FEAR IT ANYMORE!
THERE! THE ELECTRO ENERGIZ IS SET ON MAXIMU

I'VE OVERRIDDEN MY VOLTAGE LIMITERS! NOW I CAN TAKE ON POWER BEYOND MY TRANSISTOR BATTERIES' RATED TOLERANCE--
--ALL THE WAY TO THEIR THEORETIC MAXIMUMS! I'LL ALSO CROSS-CHANNEL MY SOLAR-BATTERIES T STORE ADDITIONAL ENERGY--!
ALL EXCEPT ONE BANK WHICH I'LL KEEP ISOLATED. IT'LL FEED DIRECTLY INTO MY CHEST-DEVICE SO MY HEART WILL HAVE A GUARANTEED, INDEPENDE POWER SUPPLY THAT WILL ONLY BE REDIRECTED IN DIREST EMERGENCY.
IN SHORT, MY ARMOR IS ADJUSTED FOR ONE ALL-OUT BATTLE!

I'VE NEVER BEEN THIS POWERFUL BEFORE!
I'M READY--!

--AND TODAY IS THE DAY THE WORLD FINDS OUT--
--WHETHER THE "INVINCIBLE IRON MAN" IS TRULY INVINCIBLE!

MEANWHILE..."
HEY! PUFF WAIT UP! PUFF
IT'S THE FASTEST WAY ACROSS TOWN AT RUSH HOUR, RICK! THAT'S WHY WE DIDN'T CHANGE BACK TO OUR CIVVIES!
S'HARD TO PUFF CATCH A GUY TAKIN' GIANT STRIDES LIKE YOURS!
HAT'S THE ROBLEM!
WELL, I BEEN THINKIN' ABOUT WHAT IRON MAN SAID--
--ABOUT GETTIN' HELP SOMEWHERE ELSE--? THE F.F. MAYBE, AN' WELL--
CAN'T IT WAIT? BLUE EYES, HERE, AND I HAVE A DATE!

YOU'VE KNOWN 'IM ONGER'N I HAVE, UT IT DON'T SEEM O ME THAT PASSIN' HE BUCK IS HIS STYLE, MAN!
NO, IRON MAN'S TOO LEVEL-HEADED TO DO ANYTHING... RASH...
...BUT...

"NOT LONG AFTERWARDS, IN THE SHADOWS OF GIBRALTAR...
IT'S IRON MAN! SOONER THAN I'D EXPECTED!
WE MUST LURE HIM TO THE CAVES WHERE THE WEAPONS I HAVE PREPARED AWAIT!
FORGET IT! I'VE HANDLED HIM BEFORE! BUT... WHERE ARE THE OTHERS? ARE THEY PULLIN' SOMETHIN'?

WATCH WHILE I TWIST THAT ARMOR PLATE INTO--
UHHH!!
HULK, YOU PONDEROUS SLOW MOVING CLOD! YOU MUST NO BE INJURED WHILE I HAVE A NEED OF YOUR BRUTISH STREN
HE THINKS I'M JUST SOME KIND OF STOOGE! BUT HE'LL LIVE TO REGRET THOSE WORDS BEFORE I'M DONE!
JUST LIKE IRON MAN'S GONNA REGRET BLASTIN' ME WITH THOSE REPULSER RAYS OF HIS!
UHH!
THEY NEVER SEEMED SO STRONG BEFORE THOUGH!
I WILL PROVE A MORE DIFFICULT FOE THAN MY SLOW WITTED ALLY, AVENGER!
FASTER! CAN'T LET HI CONNECT WITH THOSE BATTERING RAM FISTS.
WHA--?
AT LEAST NOT BEFORE I GET IN A FEW LICKS!
I HAVE ALWAYS SUSPECTED THAT YOU WERE THE MOST COLDLY DANGEROUS AVENGER, IRON MAN!
HERE, ON LAND I'M CERTAIN I COULD SL IT OUT WITH NAMOR AND WIN... BUT I CAN'T AFFORD TO WASTE THAT MUCH JUICE, JUST YET!
COME AND GET IT, FIN-BRAIN
YOUR SUPPLY OF WEAPONS SEEMS LIMITLESS... AND YOUR CUNNING IS LEGENDARY!
AND YET... YOU HAVE FOOLISHLY TRAPPED YOURSELF!

WHAT? NO ARMORED MAN CAN MOVE THAT--
UNNGH!
FAST? SURE I CAN!

E'S DOWN! OUT COLD! OW FOR THE HULK!

HE'S NOWHERE IN SIGHT!
BLAST! HE'S AWARE OF MY INCREASED POWER AND HE'S TRYING TO AMBUSH ME AGAIN!
HAVE TO GAIN ALTITUDE ...USE MY BUILT-IN RADAR TO SPOT HIM!

"BUT BEFORE IRON MAN COULD IMPLEMENT HIS PLAN..."
I BEEN ITCHIN' TO PROVE TO THAT FISH-MAN WHAT THE HULK CAN DO--
--AN' I'M GONNA START BY TAKIN' YOU APART!
KANG
UHHH!

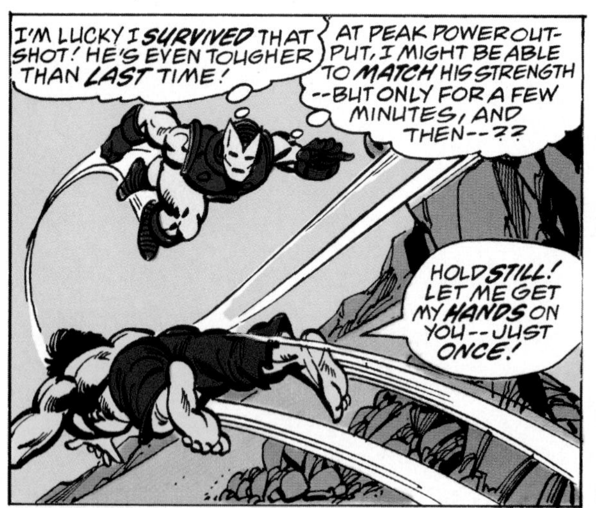

I'M LUCKY I SURVIVED THAT SHOT! HE'S EVEN TOUGHER THAN LAST TIME!
AT PEAK POWER OUT-PUT, I MIGHT BE ABLE TO MATCH HIS STRENGTH --BUT ONLY FOR A FEW MINUTES, AND THEN--??
HOLD STILL! LET ME GET MY HANDS ON YOU--JUST ONCE!
THAT POND! I HAVE AN IDEA!
THERE'S NO PLA YOU CAN GO I CAN'T FOLLO TIN MAN!
AND WHEN I CATCH YOU I'LL RIP YOU TO SHREDS!
ENOUGH THREATS, BIG MAN, LET'S HAVE IT OUT RIGHT HERE AND NOW!
HOL THAT POS
HUH?
YOU LILY-LIVERED, PUNY, WEAKLING! GO AHEAD AND RUN WHILE YOU CAN!
WHO'S RUNNING?
SLIME ON THE BOTTOM O THIS POOL! CAN PLANT MY FEE TO LEAP OUT!
I'VE GOT YOU RIGHT WHERE I WANT YOU... AND NOW--

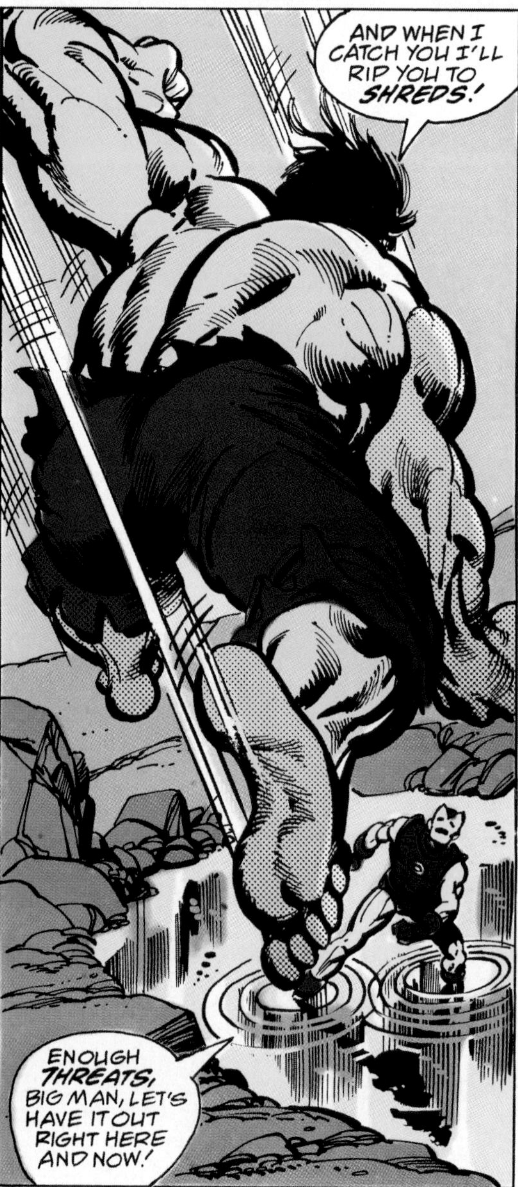

ARRRGH!
ZZZZZZZT
"HOPELESSLY GROUNDED IN THE STAGNANT, BRINE-FILLED POOL, THE HULK WRITHED IN UTTER AGONY AS IRON MAN SENT A HIGH-VOLTAGE ELECTRIC CHARGE CRACKLING FROM HIS TRANSISTORIZED GAUNTLETS!"

I'VE HIT HIM WITH ENOUGH JUICE TO LIGHT A SMALL CITY-- AND STILL HE STANDS!
AHHH!
GOT TO KEEP POURING IT ON--!
AHH-H--
--EVEN IF IT DRAINS MY MAIN POWER PACK! I HAVE TO GIVE IT ALL I CAN!
I MAY NOT GET ANOTHER CHANCE!
I DID IT! HE'S OUT! I WON!
CAN'T WASTE TIME PATTING MYSELF ON THE BACK! I MUST SECURE THE SUB-MARINER, THEN RE-VIVE THE HULK AND TRY TO REASON WITH HIM AGAIN!
"BUT IRON MAN'S VICTORY WAS SHORT-LIVED!"
OH, NO!
FEW COULD HAVE ACCOMPLISHED WHA YOU HAVE, HUMAN! IT IS A PITY YOUR VALOR HAS ONLY EARNED YOU DEATH!

OR THE AVENGING
ON WILL NOT TOLERATE
EING HUMBLED BY
ANY MAN!

UHH-H!

COULDN'T DODGE
HIM! THAT... HURT!

SPENT TOO
MUCH POWER
AGAINST THE
HULK!

I STILL HAVE
ENOUGH ENERGY
LEFT TO
SPLATTER THAT
ARROGANT
FISH-MAN...

BUT IT'LL TAKE A
FEW MINUTES FOR
MY TRANSISTORS TO
BUILD UP TO PEAK
OUTPUT AGAIN!
UNTIL THEN--

--GOT TO STAY OUT OF HIS--AHHGH!

YOUR SPEED
AND STRENGTH
HAVE DIMINISHED
IRON MAN...

WHILE
AM AS
IGHTY AS
EVER! AND
SO YOUR DOOM
S SEALED!

IF... ONLY MY ARMOR...
WILL WITHSTAND THIS
POUNDING... A FEW
MORE SECONDS!

BAH! IT WOULD TAKE TOO LONG
O PEEL AWAY YOUR PRO-
TECTIVE STEEL SHEATH
HERE, IN THE AIR!

IN THE
WATER, MY
STRENGTH
IS ITS
GREATEST!

OH, NO!

HERE, MANY FATH-
OMS IN THE DEEP
YOU ARE AT MY
MERCY! HERE, I
AM SUPREME!

CAN'T OUT-MANEUVER
HIM! HE'S LITERALLY
SWIMMING RINGS
AROUND ME!

THUS I FINISH THIS CHARADE!

SPLASH!

LET ME AT HIM! WHERE IS HE?!

THERE HE IS, MY BRUTISH ALLY, AMONG THE ROCKS!
HEY! HE'S LYING SO STILL! IS HE--?
DEAD? OF COURSE!
AND NOW THAT MY IMPERIAL RAGE SUBSIDES I AM... SADDENED HE WAS VALIANT! AT ONE POINT HE HAD BEATEN US BOTH!

ERE IS LITTLE HONOR IN THIS
CTORY", HULK... FOR IF THE OTHER
ENGERS HAD ARRIVED, SURELY WE--
AIT!
HAT'S
HAT?
A NOISE LIKE
IRON MAN'S JETS,
BUT--

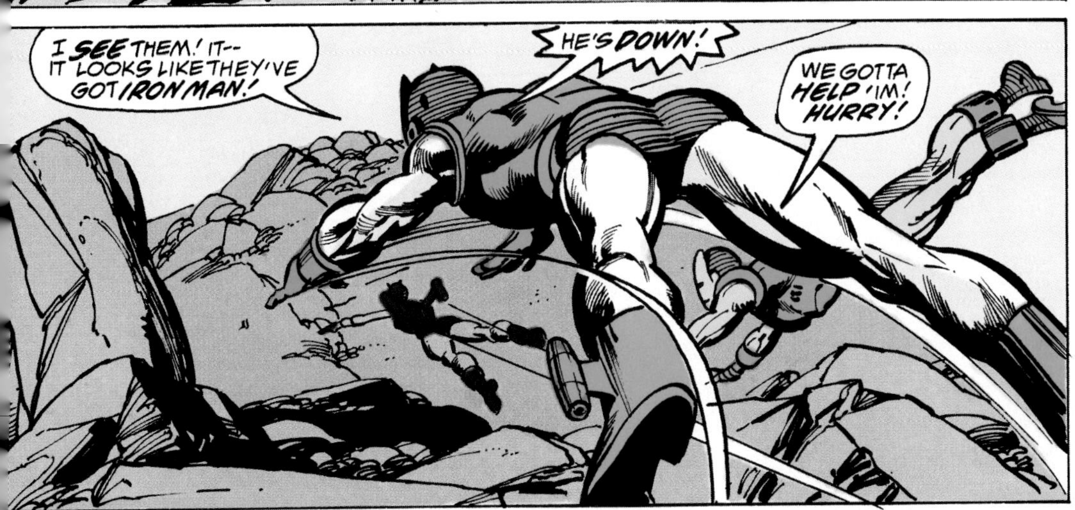
I SEE THEM! IT--
IT LOOKS LIKE THEY'VE
GOT IRON MAN!
HE'S DOWN!
WE GOTTA
HELP 'IM!
HURRY!

MORE ARMORED
FOES! THE
AVENGERS--?
CAN THIS BE?
WHO CARES,
FISH-MAN?
GET READY
FOR 'EM!
-NO! DON'T L-LET
HEM... C-COME NOW!
I-I CAN'T...
H-HELP THEM
...N-NOW! CAN'T...

IRON MAN'S ALIVE! I
SAW HIM MOVE! BUT
THESE TWO ARE GOING
TO PAY FOR HURTING
HIM!
WHA--?
A TINY--
AHH!

EVERYTHING'S
SPINNING!
GETTING...
DIZZY!
MY SKIN HAS
BEEN PIERCED BY
DOZENS OF DRUGGED
STINGERS! THIS MUST
BE THE WASP'S DOING!

SHE NEVER COULD DO SUCH A THING BEFORE! HOW--?
CAN'T STAND UP... SICK... OHHH-H!
YOU BETTER QUIT WHILE YOU'RE AHEAD GILL-PUSS!
IT WOULDN'T TAKE MUCH TO MAKE ME WANNA FILET YOU!

A PRINCE OF THE BLOOD NEVER YIELDS! ONCE I HAVE YOU IN MY GRASP
WHAT? HOW-HOW COULD MISS?
YOU DIDN'T SHARK FACE!

YOU WENT THROUGH ME! STARK DESIGNED SOME SPECIAL TRICKS INTO MY ARMOR!
GUHHH!
THERE'S A GADGET BUILT INTO THIS SUIT MAKES ME IMMATERIAL WHEN I WANT! A "MOLECULAR OSCILLATOR" ...OR SOM'PIN.
OH, YEAH, IT'S ALSO GOT YOUR STANDARD REPULSERS!

"ELSEWHERE..."
WHA--? NEEDLES HITTING MY FACE! IT'S GIANT-MAN'S PARTNER!
MY STINGS WON PENETRATE HIS SKIN! BETTER GET OUT OF RANGE BEFORE HE GRAB ME.
HANK, IF I EVER NEEDED YOU--
STUPID BUG-WOMAN! YOU CAN'T HURT THE HULK--!

BACK OFF, WASP! THE HULK'S MY DEPARTMENT!
YES, SIR!
OH, HANK! BE CAREFUL! HE'S SO POWERFUL SUDDENLY I'M WORRIED FOR THE FIRST TIME
YOU DON'T SCARE ME, BIG MAN, ARMOR OR NOT!

OBODY IS
S STRONG
AS THE
HULK!
OBODY!
UFF!
KEEP THINKING THAT, UGLY!
I'M GAINING STRENGTH! BROKEN INSIDE... BUT NOT AS BAD AS... I THOUGHT!
HAVE TO PULL MYSELF TOGETHER! THEY--THEY MAY NEED ME... TO HELP WITH--ARMOR!
SO... HARD TO... MOVE!
OU ALWAYS
VERE A CLOWN,
GIANT-MAN!
MAYBE YOU'RE
TRONG NOW--
--BUT I DON'T NEED NO TIN SUIT!
I'M THE HULK! THE HULK!
BLAST IT! AGILITY ISN'T
MY FORTE AS JUST PLAIN
GIANT-MAN! IN THIS
ARMOR, WITHOUT THE
EARS OF PRACTICE
RON MAN HAS HAD, I'M
OWNRIGHT AWKWARD!
BUT IF I CAN KEEP THE HULK ENRAGED--LUNGING WILDLY AT ME--
WHAM!
--I CAN NEGATE HIS SPEED, AND GET THE MOST OUT OF MY STRENGTH!
UNHHNGH!

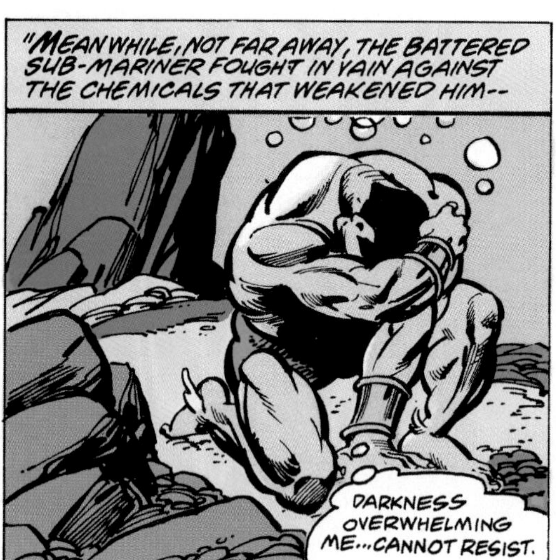
"MEANWHILE, NOT FAR AWAY, THE BATTERED SUB-MARINER FOUGHT IN VAIN AGAINST THE CHEMICALS THAT WEAKENED HIM--
DARKNESS OVERWHELMING ME...CANNOT RESIST.

THE SEA--! IF I CAN JUST MAKE IT...TO THE SEA!

LOSING CONSCIOUSNESS! MUST LEAP...TRY TO REACH... MY NATURAL ELEMENT... FEEL ITS ALL-CLEANSING, ALL-HEALING EMBRACE!

IT'S... WORKING! I FEEL NEW STRENGTH SURGING THROUGH MY SINEWS...
...MY MIND CLEARING! I AM WHOLE ONCE MORE!

THEY WILL PAY FOR THIS INDIGNITY!
FIRST THEY WILL DIE, AND THEN THEIR ENTIRE SURFACE DWELLING RACE SHALL SUFFER FOR THE ATROCITIES COMMITTED AGAINST MY ATLANTEAN SUBJECTS!
FOR I AM NAMOR, THE SUB-MARINER, PRINCE OF ATLANTIS, AND SO I HAVE SWORN!

LAST IT! I LOST
E ADVANTAGE!
HULK KNOWS MY STRENGTH, NOW, AND HE'S EVADING ME, RUNNING ME RAGGED!
HE'S MAKING ME WASTE POWER! GOT TO FIND A WAY TO BOX HIM IN BEFORE IT'S TOO LATE!
WHAT'S A MATTER GIANT-MAN? YOU WINDIN' DOWN?
THE HULK NEVER GETS TIRED! I ONLY GET STRONGER!
YOU'VE HAD IT, BIG MAN!
UHH!

IRON MAN WOULD KNOW WHAT TO DO! I CAN'T THINK-- REACT FAST ENOUGH!
IT DOESN'T MATTER HOW BIG YOU ARE, OR HOW POWERFUL!
SOONER OR LATER, I'LL WEAR YOU DOWN... AND THEN I'LL SMASH YOU--
WHUFFF!
--LIKE THIS!
SO MUCH FOR THAT CLOWN!
HANK! OH MY GOD! HANK!
VICTORY... WAS IN OUR GRASP! NOW ONLY RICK... LEFT!
W-WHAT CAN I DO? INJURED... CAN'T FIGHT... CAN'T MOVE!

BUT HE-- HE ISN'T BREATHING!
THE HULK KNOCKED THE WIND OUT OF HIM... AND WITH HIS POWER EX-HAUSTED, HIS ARMOR'S DEAD WEIGHT!
IT'S KEEPING HIM FROM GETTING HIS BREATH!
UNLESS I REENERGIZE HIS ARMOR... HE'LL DIE!

IT HURTS WHEN I TRY! GOT TO REACH HIM... DESPITE THE PAIN.
ONLY... HE CAN SAVE ALL OF THEM!

B-BLACKING OUT! MUST F-FIGHT IT! REACH... INDUCTION GRID!

DID IT!
COME ON, HANK! IT'S ALL ON THE LINE, NOW--! ALL UP TO YOU!

WOOZY... BUT IRON MAN, YOU--?
OH, HANK! YOU'RE ALL RIGHT!
F-FORGET ABOUT ME! GE THE H-HULK... BEFORE HE HURT WASP OR... RICK S-STOP HIM!
ALL... UP... TO... YOU...
YES... IT IS UP TO ME! I CAN'T FAIL AGAIN... CAN'T WASTE THIS SECOND CHANCE!
MY OWN GIANT STRENGTH IS MULTI-PLIED A HUNDRED FOLD BY THIS ARMOR! I'M THE MOST POWERFUL BEING ON EARTH! I CAN DO IT--I KNOW I CAN!
YOU WON'T ESCAPE ME AGAIN, GARGOYLE!
WHAT? YOU AGAIN?!
THIS TIME I HAVE MY ATTACK PLANNED! I'M USING MY HEAD!
SURPRISE, HULK! UP AGAINST THIS CLIFF, YOU CAN'T ROLL AWAY FROM MY PUNCHES AND EVADE ME!
UHHG
YOU'RE GOING TO HAVE TO STAND AND SLUG IT OUT!
AND YOU'RE GOING TO LOSE!
GUHH!

S THE HULK REELED
DER GIANT-MAN'S
NEWED ATTACK,
CK JONES WAS
RD PRESSED BY
E REVITALIZED
B-MARINER!"
HE'S RIGHT! I BETTER TRY SOMETHIN' ELSE BEFORE MY POWER-PACK RUNS DOWN!
YOU CANNOT EVADE ME, THUS, FOR LONG! SURELY THAT TRICK USES UP YOUR ENERGY VERY QUICKLY!
WHY DON'TCHA GO STICK AN OCTUPUS IN YOUR POINTY EAR FISH-FACE?
ROM YOUR VOICE, IT
OULD SEEM THAT YOU ARE
OUTH! THAT IS A PITY--
FOR NAMOR
EXPECTS NO
ERCY, AND HE
IVES NONE!
CRIPES! HE'S GOT ME!
I BETTER FIGURE OUT ANOTHER ONE OF THESE BUILT-IN GIMMICK, FAST!
KTANG!
EEEEEEE!
YOU ARE FINISHED, HUMAN! YOU WILL BE CRUSHED WHEN YOU HIT THOSE ROCKS! NO ONE CAN SAVE YOU!

"BUT AS HE HURTLED TO HIS DOOM, RICK JONES' SCREAM OF PAIN AND TERROR PIERCED THE DIN OF BATTLE..."
RICK--?!
EEEEEEEEEE
THAT'S RICK!
"THERE WAS ONE WHO MIGHT SAVE THE LAD!"
CAN'T... PULL UP! I'M GONNA GET PULPED!
NO! NOT THE BOY!

GOT YOU!
UHH!

NAMOR!
NAMOR--! YOU DIRTY, FLAT-HEADED SCUM! I'LL KILL YOU FOR THIS!
OHHH-H!

TRIED TO
HIM! HE'S
A KID!
HE IS AN ENEMY!
HE MUST DIE, SO THAT I CAN AID YOU AGAINST THE GIANT ONE! VICTORY CAN STILL BE OURS, YOU LUMBERING OAF!

NEVER CALL
NAMES LIKE THAT
GAIN, NAMOR!
I DON'T CARE ABOUT THE AVENGERS ANYMORE! I'M GOING SMASH YOU!
SO! YOU BETRAY ME! NOW I REALIZE NO HUMAN CAN BE TRUSTED! I DESPISE YOU ALL!

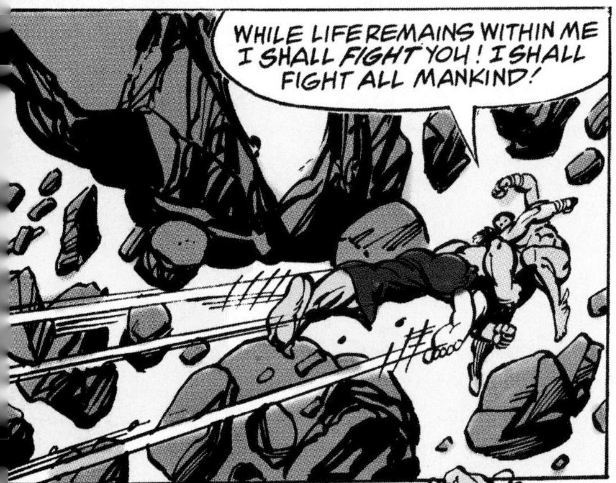

WHILE LIFE REMAINS WITHIN ME I SHALL FIGHT YOU! I SHALL FIGHT ALL MANKIND!

FWOOSH!

IDIOT! YOUR BLIND, UNTHINKING ATTACK HAS CARRIED US BENEATH THE WAVES, WHERE NONE CAN DEFEAT THE MONARCH OF THE SEA!
"NAMOR STRUCK BACK, HIS POWER AGAIN AT ITS VERY PINNACLE. BUT THE HULK'S MATCHLESS STRENGTH WAS FUELED BY A SEETHING RAGE!"

"THE SEA ITSELF REFLECTED THE MAGNITUDE OF THEIR FURY...

"...UNTIL, FINALLY..."
BAH! THERE IS NO PURPOSE IN THIS! ALL IS NOW RUINED!
I MUST DEPART AND PLAN ANEW!
HE'S RUNNIN' BUT...NEED AIR

"THUS IT ENDED. AS IN OUR OWN CONTINUUM, THE HULK AND NAMOR SUNDERED THEIR ALLIANCE AND QUIT THE FIELD OF BATTLE...
"...LEAVING THE 'VICTORS' BEHIND.

"IN OUR REALITY, THIS CONFLICT PROVED TO BE THE MIGHTY AVENGERS' BAPTISM OF FIRE... BUT IN THIS ALTERNATE REALITY, ITS SIGNIFICANCE LOOMED EVEN GREATER...
"...FOR THA DAY, HENR PYM, JAN VAN DYNE AND RICK JONES DEDICAT THEM- SELVES

"--TO THE MEMORY OF ANTHONY STARK, THE FIRST IRON MAN...
"...WHOSE DAMAGED HEART FINALLY STOPPED AS HE SACRIFICED THE POWER OF HIS CHEST DEVICE TO SAVE THE LIVES OF HIS ARMORED AVENGERS."

DEVIL
MARVEL® COMICS GROUP
APPROVED BY THE COMICS CODE AUTHORITY
146
JUNE
02459
DAREDEVIL®
THE MAN WITHOUT FEAR!
ATCH
REFULLY,
E-VIEWERS!
F FROM
YORK, IT'S
REDEVIL'S
EATH--!
--BROUGHT TO YOU IN GLORIOUS LIVING COLOR BY BULLSEYE!
GK + DEC

He dwells in eternal night— but the blackness is filled with sounds and scents other men cannot perceiv
Though attorney MATT MURDOCK is blind, his other senses function with superhuman sharpness—h
radar sense guides him over every obstacle! He stalks the streets, a red-garbed foe of evil!
Stan Lee PRESENTS: DAREDEVIL, THE MAN WITHOUT FEAR!
DUEL!
CAN'T BE SURE FROM THIS HIGH UP--TOO MANY PEOPLE, TOO MUCH NOISE, OVERLOADING MY SUPER-HEARING CAN'T CLEARLY FOCU ON JUST ONE VOICE OR HEARTBEAT!
BUT I COULD HAVE SWORN I HEARD BULLSEYE MUTTERING TO HIMSELF DOWN I THAT CROWD!
JIM SHOOTER WRITER
GIL KANE ARTIST
JIM MOONEY INKER
DENISE WOHL LETTERER
DON WARFIELD COLORIST
ARCHIE GOODWIN EDITOR

I WAS RIGHT! THERE HE IS!
HEAR
E RUSTLE
F LOOSE-
TTING
OTHES AS
WALKS--
--HE'S IN CIVVIES, WHICH EXPLAINS WHY NOBODY SEEMS TO BE NOTICING HIM!

NOBODY SEEMS TO HAVE NOTICED ME, YET EITHER!
GOOD! HOPEFULLY I CAN GET OUT OF SIGHT BEFORE SOME KID SPOTS ME--

--AND YELLS "THERE'S THE DAREDEVIL" AT THE TOP OF HIS LUNGS--
--WHICH MIGHT MAKE BULLSEYE NERVOUS ENOUGH TO SPLIT IN A HURRY, THEN I'D HAVE TO ATTACK HIM NOW--

--INSTEAD OF CAPITALIZING ON THIS CHANCE TO FOLLOW HIM INCONSPICUOUSLY!
MATT MURDOCK IS A BIT HARDER TO SPOT IN A CROWD THAN D.D.

ECONDS LATER, A BLIND AWYER SETS OUT TO TALK THE WORLD'S MOST DANGEROUS KILLER-FOR-HIRE...
BULLSEYE DROPPED OUT OF SIGHT AFTER HIS ATTEMPTED MURDERS OF FOGGY AND ME--*
--WHILE WE WERE DIGGING FOR CLUES TO THE IDENTITY OF THE KIDNAPPER OF FOGGY'S FIANCE DEBORAH HARRIS!
D.D. #141--ARCH.

GUNS
IF HE WAS WORKING FOR THE KIDNAPPER THEN, MAYBE HE STILL IS, AND HE'LL LEAD ME TO--
HE'S GOING INTO THAT STORE! IT MAY BE A CONTACT POINT! I'LL HAVE TO FOLLOW HIM IN!

--EVEN THOUGH THERE IS A CHANCE HE'LL RECOGNIZE ME AS A FORMER MARK!
--THE SALZBURG MODEL?
CERTAINLY SIR! UH... ONE MOMENT PLEASE!
HMM! SMELLS OF CORDITE AND BLUING! A GUN SHOP!
PARDON ME, MISTER ARE YOU SURE YOU'R IN THE RIGHT PLACE
THIS IS A GUN SHOP!

UH... YES! I'M HERE FOR... A GIFT!
I SEE-- ER, I MEAN I UNDERSTAND! I'LL BE WITH YOU IN ONE MOMENT!
BULLSEYE'S UP TO SOMETHING! I HEAR HIS PULSE QUICKENING.

HE'S IGNORING ME! AND WHY NOT? A BLIND MAN IS NO THREAT!
REACHING IN HIS POCKET--?
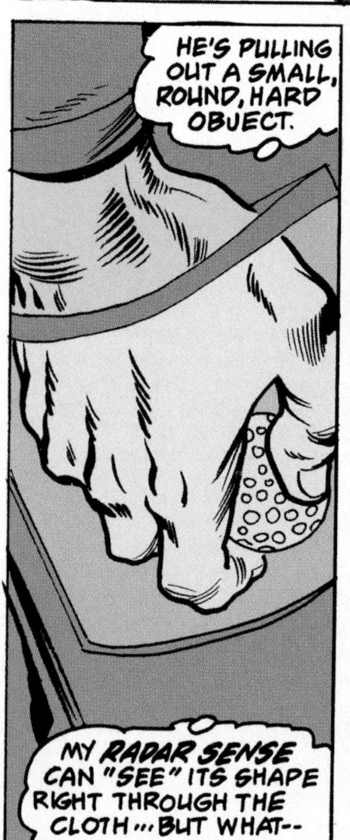
HE'S PULLING OUT A SMALL, ROUND, HARD OBJECT.
MY RADAR SENSE CAN "SEE" ITS SHAPE RIGHT THROUGH THE CLOTH... BUT WHAT--

A GOLF BALL!
HE'S GOING TO BEAN THE PROPRIETOR AND ROB THE PLACE!
NO!!
WHA--?
I-I DON'T BELIEVE IT! A BLIND MAN IS MUGGING ONE OF MY CUSTOMERS.

ECONDS LATER...
WELL, I'LL BE--
I OUGHT TO BREAK THAT CANE OVER YOUR HEAD!

WRIGHT, AWRIGHT, BREAK IT UP!
E ATTACKED ME, OFFICER.
THIS MAN WAS ABOUT TO ROB THE STORE!
FORGIVE ME, PAL, BUT IF YOU'RE BLIND, HOW DID YOU KNOW BEFORE THE PROPRIETOR DID?
HE'S CRAZY!
UH...HIS...UH, VOICE...SOUNDED ...THREATENING!

LAST IT! BULLSEYE IS ONE OF HE MOST WANTED MEN IN THE COUNTRY! WHY DOESN'T THE OFFICER RECOG-NIZE HIM!
HMM! YOUR I.D. SEEMS TO BE IN ORDER, MR. PONDEXTER! YOU CAN GO IF YOU WISH!
THANKS.
B-BUT--

OU BE QUIET! HERE AIN'T NO AW AGAINST ARRYING A CONCEALED OLF BALL!
I OUGHTTA RUN YOU IN FOR DISTURBING THE PEACE-- BUT SINCE YOU'RE BLIND--!
HE BELIEVED THAT PHONEY I.D. --AND THERE'S NO WAY I CAN TELL HIM WHO'S SLIPPING THROUGH HIS FINGERS WITH-OUT SPILLING MY SECRET!

ONE BRIEF LECTURE LATER...
GONE! NO SIGN OF HIM!

I THINK HE WENT THIS WAY-- BUT IT'D BE A MINOR MIRACLE TO PICK OUT HIS HEARTBEAT AMID ALL THIS STREET-LEVEL RACKET!
I'D HAVE A BETTER SHOT SWINGING ABOVE THE CROWD AS DAREDEVIL!
--BUT B THE TIME I CHANGE HE COULD B IN QUEENS
GREAT! JUST GREAT! MY BIG CHANCE AND I FLUB IT-- WITH SOME HELP FROM A COP WHO DOESN'T LOOK AT WANTED POSTERS!
BULLSEYE'S PROBABLY ON A CROSSTOWN BUS RIGHT NOW, LAUGHING HIS HEAD OFF!
MIGHT AS WELL GO TO WORK AND--
WHAP!
GNNH!
OHH--H!

N HOUR LATER, IN A COMFORTABLE ST SIDE APARTMENT LEASED TO E BENJAMIN PONDEXTER...
BAH! A SCHEME OF THE FEARSOME MAN CALLED BULLSEYE FOILED BY A BLIND MAN!

A BLIND MAN! I STILL CAN'T FIGURE HOW HE KNEW!
I REMEMBER HIS FACE NOW--AND IT IS A BITTER IRONY THAT A MAN I ONCE FAILED TO ASSASSINATE SHOULD OBSTRUCT ME NOW!

IT WASN'T AN IMPORTANT CRIME! I JUST INTENDED TO STEAL A PARTICULAR RARE PISTOL FOR MY COLLECTION.
I'M LIVING PRETTY WELL OFF OF LOOT I STASHED A LONG TIME AGO.

--BUT I'M TIRED OF LAYING LOW WAITING FOR A BIG MONEY CONTRACT THAT'LL NEVER COME.
SINCE I BLEW MY LAST JOB, AND THEN LET DAREDEVIL ESCAPE ME WHEN I HAD THE CHANCE TO KILL HIM,* MY REP IS GONE.
BUT I'M GOING TO GET IT BACK-- IN A WAY THAT'LL MAKE EVERYBODY IN THIS TOWN TREMBLE AT THE NAME BULLSEYE!
*D.D. #142. --A.G.

ATER THAT DAY AT THE STOREFRONT LAW FFICE OF NELSON AND MURDOCK...
FOGGY? HEATHER?
MATT! WHA-- WHAT HAPPENED TO YOU?

HOW SHOULD I KNOW? I COULDN'T SEE WHAT HIT M-- OWW!
WHY DIDN'T YOU TELL ME THIS DARN CHAIR WAS IN MY WAY?
BUT IT'S ALWAYS BEEN THERE--AND YOU HAVE THE OFFICE MEMORIZED.
NO, I DON'T-- BECAUSE I'VE NEVER HAD TO COUNT STEPS AND MEMORIZE LIKE A NORMAL BLIND MAN!

I'VE ALWAYS HAD MY RADAR SENSE TO GUIDE ME--
--TILL NOW.
I-I'M A LITTLE CONFUSED GUYS! I TOOK A PRETTY BAD RAP ON THE SKULL!
IS THERE ANYTHING WE CAN DO? UH--WHY DON'T YOU SIT DOWN--AND I'LL GET YOU A GLASS OF WATE

OR MAYBE I SHOULD CALL A DOCTOR?!
NO! LOOK, UH, IT'S NO BIG DEAL. I'LL BE ALL RIGHT!
OH, MATT! IF YOU'RE HURT, IT IS A BIG DEAL... TO ME!

PLEASE DON'T DRAW AWAY FROM ME WHEN YOU NEED HELP! I LOVE YOU! I WANT TO BE THE ONE YOU TURN TO.
SHE MEANS IT...

...BUT MY RADAR SENSE COULD BE GONE FOR GOO AND MY OTHER SUPER-SENSES DON'T BEGIN TO MAKE UP FOR MY BLINDNESS BY THEMSELVES.
I CAN'T... I WON'T LET HEATHER WASTE HER LIF PITYING ME!
I... THINK I'LL JUST GO HOME!
OH, NO DON'T GO OUT ALON PLEASE.

WHY? WHAT'S TO BE--
HAVEN'T YOU HEARD? THAT LUNATIC WHO TRIED TO KILL US--BULLSEYE--HAS TAKEN OVER A T.V. STUDIO! HE'S DEMANDING DAREDEVIL COME AND FIGHT HIM, OR HE'LL WIPE OUT HIS HOSTAGES!
AS LONG AS HE'S LOOSE, YOU MAY BE IN DANGER, MATT!
OH.
HEY, MATT! IT'S NOT THAT BAD! YOU LOOK LIKE A CONDEMNED MAN ON HIS WAY TO THE GALLOWS.
I'M SURE DAREDEVIL WILL TAKE CARE OF BULLSEYE! I DIDN'T MEAN TO WORRY... YOU...
...MATT?

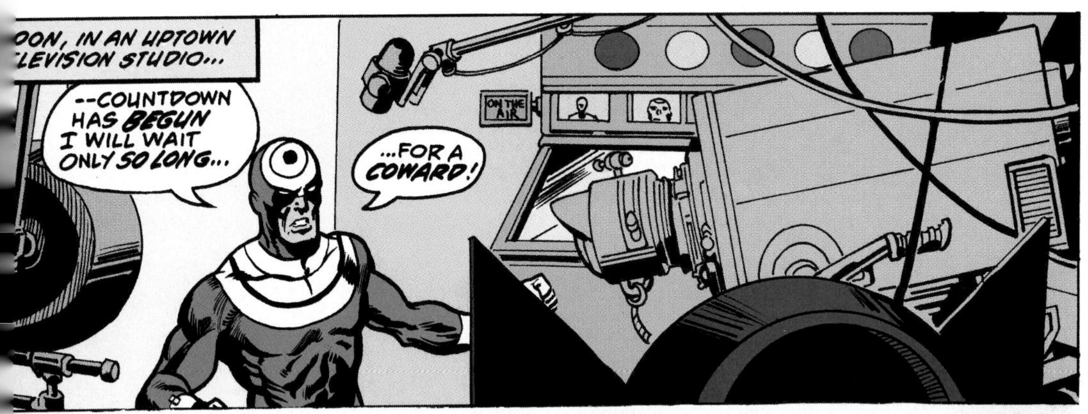
OON, IN AN UPTOWN
LEVISION STUDIO...
--COUNTDOWN HAS BEGUN I WILL WAIT ONLY SO LONG...
...FOR A COWARD!
ON THE AIR

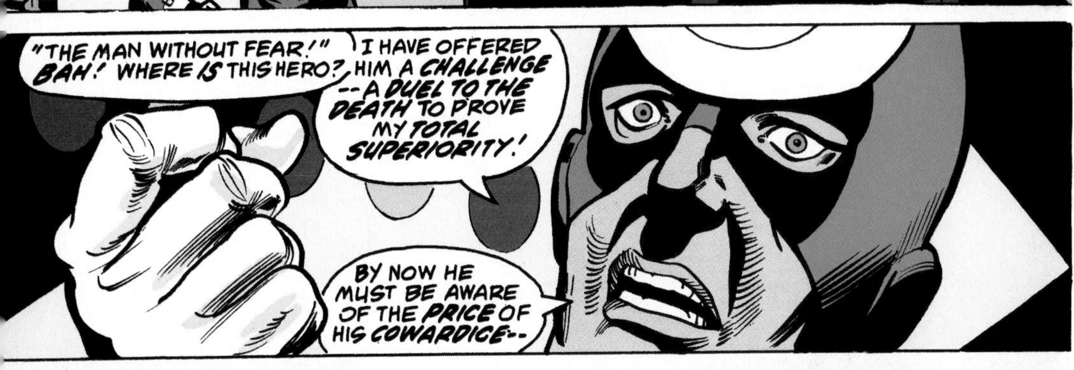
"THE MAN WITHOUT FEAR!" BAH! WHERE IS THIS HERO?
I HAVE OFFERED HIM A CHALLENGE --A DUEL TO THE DEATH TO PROVE MY TOTAL SUPERIORITY!
BY NOW HE MUST BE AWARE OF THE PRICE OF HIS COWARDICE--

THESE
REE PEOPLE
LL DIE WHEN
RELEASE
ESE WEIGHTED
KNIVES--

"--IN SEVEN MINUTES!"
WE'RE READY TO RUSH HIM SIR, IF--
YEAH. I CAN'T FIGURE IT, THOUGH. WHY IS D.D. CHICKENING OUT?
BULLSEYE CLAIMS HE DOESN'T EVEN HAVE A GUN!

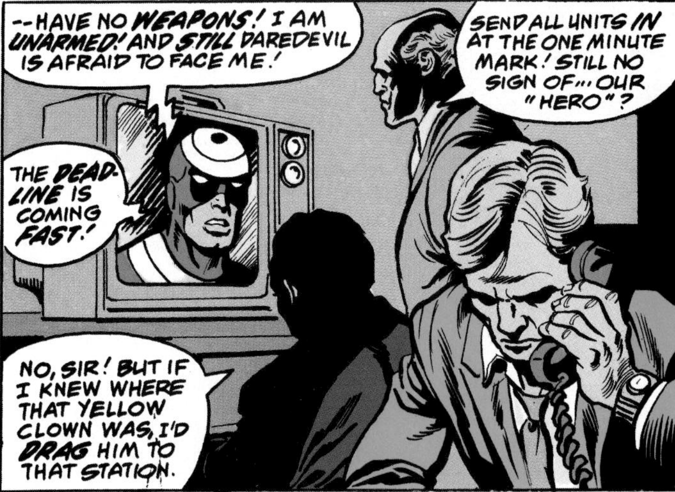
--HAVE NO WEAPONS! I AM UNARMED! AND STILL DAREDEVIL IS AFRAID TO FACE ME!
SEND ALL UNITS IN AT THE ONE MINUTE MARK! STILL NO SIGN OF... OUR "HERO"?
THE DEAD-LINE IS COMING FAST!
NO, SIR! BUT IF I KNEW WHERE THAT YELLOW CLOWN WAS, I'D DRAG HIM TO THAT STATION.

IT'S NO *WONDER* THAT DAREDEVIL IS *HIDING* IN TERROR SOMEWHERE! HE BARELY ESCAPED OUR *LAST* ENCOUNTER WITH HIS--
WELL, WELL...
WHA--?

YOU SHOULD *KNOW* THAT YOUR *SACRIFICE* IS NOT IN *VAIN*, FOOL.
I WOULD HAVE KILLED THESE PEOPLE--

--BUT I WILL *ENJOY* KILLING *YOU* MUCH MORE!
SO *QUIET*, DAREDEVIL! THAT'S NOT *LIKE* YOU!

BUT IT *IS* LIKE A MAN WHO KNOWS HE'S GOING TO *DIE*!!
UFF!
GNNGH!
WHAT'S *WRONG* WITH YOU
FIGHT BACK, BLAST IT!

HEN...
I-I DID IT! I FOUND THE RANGE--
--FROM THE SOUND OF HIS VOICE ALONE!
IT IT TOOK TOTAL ONCENTRATION! HOW NG CAN I KEEP IT UP?

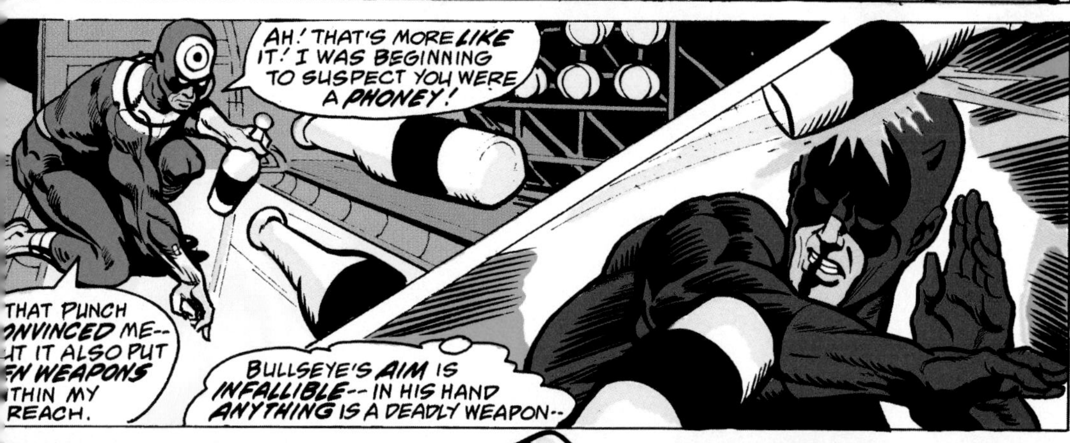
AH! THAT'S MORE LIKE IT! I WAS BEGINNING TO SUSPECT YOU WERE A PHONEY!
THAT PUNCH ONVINCED ME-- IT IT ALSO PUT EN WEAPONS THIN MY REACH.
BULLSEYE'S AIM IS INFALLIBLE-- IN HIS HAND ANYTHING IS A DEADLY WEAPON--

OT TO FIND COVER! AN'T ANTICIPATE HIS ROWS WITHOUT RADAR ENSE--AND BY THE ME I HEAR THE HOOSH--AS THEY--
WHA-- TRIPPED!
SOMETHING MUFFLING BULLSEYE'S HEARTBEAT! THERE'S SOME FURNITURE BETWEEN US! GOOD!

UT...
WHAM
DIOT! EVEN HE TALK SHOW ET PROVIDES ME ITH WEAPONS!
UH!

HE'S... ALREADY GOT ME ON THE ROPES! NEVER... LETS GO... NEVER RUNS OUT OF WEAPONS.
THERE... MUST BE DOZENS OF WAYS HE COULD KILL ME... RIGHT NOW...
...BUT HE'S TOYING WITH ME... HOPING I'LL CRAWL...
AND THAT'S HIS MISTAKE!
GOT TO HOME IN ON HIS BREATHING -- HIT HIM!
WHA-- UHH!!
GOT TO CHARGE RIGHT THROU WHATEVER H THROWS AT M --ATTACK RECK LESSLY AGAIN AND AGAIN.
HE'S COUNTING ON FEAR TO HOLD ME BACK, KEEP ME CRINGING AND HIDING!
NO! I AM THE MAN WITHOUT FEAR--AND BY GOD I'LL PROVE IT!
WHAM!
UHHH!

THAT TINGLING--! MY--MY RADAR SENSE--! IT'S COMING BACK! I CAN FEEL IT!

I'M BEGINNING TO PICK UP RADAR IMAGES-- SILHOUETTES OF OBJECTS AROUND ME--

--BUT THEY'RE BLURRED, HAZY! MAYBE IF I CONCENTRATE!

BUT AS DAREDEVIL WAGES HIS INNER STRUGGLE--

THE GREATER CONFLICT VERTAKES HIM...

THAT WAS THE LAST TIME YOU'LL EVER HIT ME, FOOL!

UHH!

THERE IS NO TIME TO CONCENTRATE... NO TIME AT ALL BETWEEN WHITE FLASHES OF PAIN AS BULLSEYE PRESSES HIS ATTACK.

THE MASTER OF ALL WEAPONS MISSES NOT ONCE-- AND DAREDEVIL REELS UNDER A AIL OF MUNDANE MISSILES!

E FEELS HIMSELF BEING BATTERED AND PIERCED BY OOKS AND PENCILS FROM THE JR. HIGH QUIZ SHOW SET--

AND THEN THE BLOWS BECOME LESS ISTINCT, MERGING INTO A STEADY TREAM OF AGONY...
FINALLY THROUGH HIS REY, SEMI-CONSCIOUS AZE, HE REALIZES THE UMMELING HAS NDED... A MOMENT FTER IT ENDS!

A SOUND FILTERS THROUGH THE BUZZING IN HIS HEAD--
--FOOTSTEPS FAINT... AS IF FAR AWAY.
STILL YOU STAND?!

BULLSEYE'S WORDS SOMEHOW REACH DAREDEVIL...YES, HE STILL STANDS, BUT NOW TRULY BLIND. PAIN AND DIZZINESS HAVE OVERWHELMED ALL HIS SENSES.
WHAT HE DOES PERCEIVE HE CANNOT TRUST. HE KNOWS BULLSEYE IS CLOSER THAN THE DISTANT DISBELIEVING VOICE SEEMED.

HE STRIKES AT THE NOTHINGNESS HOPING FOR--
WHA--UFF!
WHAM!
--CONTACT!

NO! YOU CAN'T-- UHHNNH!
I CAN! NOW THAT I KNOW WHERE TO SWING!
MY WHOLE BODY HURTS-BUT I BOUGHT THE SECOND I NEED TO RECOVER MY SENSES
ALREADY...I CA SENSE...ROPES AND I CAN SMEL ROSINED CANVA I KNOCKED HIM INTO THE STUDIO WRESTLING RING.

THERE'S NOTHING HERE FOR YOU TO USE AS A WEAPON, BULLS! IT'S JUST YOU AND ME!

IT DOESN'T MATTER! YOU MUST BE HALF DEA FROM THE POUNDING I GAVE YOU! I'LL FINISH YOU WITH MY BARE HAND

GH-HH!
KRAK
MAYBE I AM HALF DEAD--

URRGH!
--MAYBE I SHOULD HAVE LAID DOWN AND DIED A LONG TIME AGO--
UFF!

--BUT I DIDN'T! AND I WON'T--!
RAK
--EVER!
NNNGH!

GUHHN!
WOK!
REMEMBER THIS, BULLSEYE! REMEMBER THAT DAREDEVIL HAD THE GUTS TO GO ON AND BEAT YOU AFTER HE SHOULD HAVE GIVEN UP AND DIED!
--BECAUSE THAT'S WHY DAREDEVIL WILL ALWAYS BEAT YOU!

N-NO! TH-THIS WASN'T SUPPOSED TO COME OUT LIKE THIS!
YOU'RE YOU'R CRAZY
GOT TO KILL...NOW!

HE'S PULLING SOMETHING METALLIC FROM HIS BOOT!
A GUN!

HE NEVER MISSES--NEVER FAILS! I'M DEAD UNLESS--
--MY RADAR SENSE CAN DETECT THE SLIGHT INITIAL MOVEMENT OF HIS TRIGGER FINGER--
--AND I CA TIME MY LEA TO AVOID--WHA

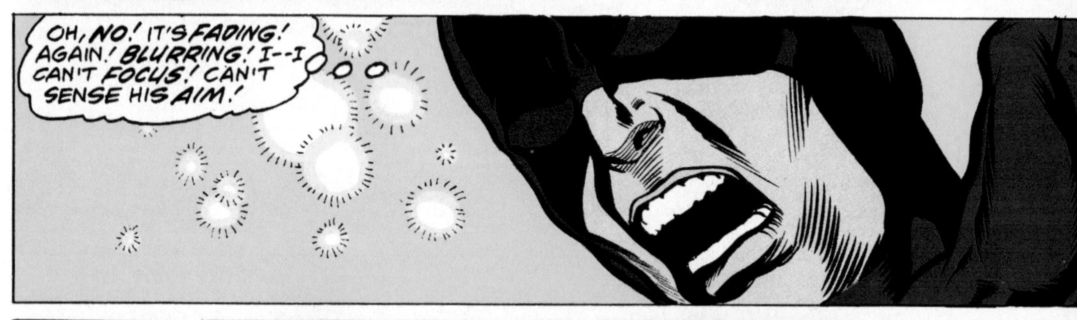
OH, NO! IT'S FADING! AGAIN! BLURRING! I--I CAN'T FOCUS! CAN'T SENSE HIS AIM!

GOT TO LEAP SUDDENLY--BLINDLY AND HOPE TH--
ARRHH!
BLAM

WHAK!
EEYARRHH!
RADAR SENSE FOCUSING AGAIN. THE FADE-OUT WAS JUST FOR A MOMENT!
THE WRONG MOMENT!

-CAN'T STOP -HIM... CAN'T ILL HIM. ONLY -ONE THING... EFT... TO DO!
HE'S GOING FOR THE GUN AGAIN--!
--BUT HE'S NOT GOING TO FIRE AT ME!

--THE HOSTAGES! HIS SHOT SEVERED A THREAD--!
GOT IT!
CAN'T LET HIM FIRE AGAIN! NO TIME TO DRAW MY BILLY CLUB!
NO!
OHH-HN!
SH-SHOULD HAVE FIRED AT HER! WHY--WHY DID I... SHOOT THE THREAD?
HE MEANT TO KILL ONE HOSTAGE AND THREATEN THE OTHERS SO I'D STOP SHORT AND LET HIM ESCAPE--
--BUT HIS OW
SHOWMANSHI
FOULED HIM U
AND NOW--WHO HIRE
YOU TO KILL NELSON AND
MURDOCK, CREEP? TALK
SOON...
WHAT'S HE BABBLIN' ABOUT, SARGE?
WHO KNOWS? SOUNDS LIKE A NAME-- SOMEBODY "GLENN"!
WHO CARES?
EVERYTHIN'S JUST FINE, NOW--
--RIGHT-- DAREDEVIL?

A STUNNING SAGA OF AN ALTERNATE REALITY!
NY ISABELLA WRITER | GIL KANE & FRANK GIACOIA ARTISTS | GAFFORD colorist | ORZECHOWSKI letterer | O'NEIL EDITOR | SHOOTER Ed.-IN-CHIEF
HIS NAME IS PETER PARKER... AND HE HAS DEDICATED HIS LIFE TO BATTLING INJUSTICE AS THE AMAZING SPIDER-MAN. WHILE HE HAS HAD MANY SUCCESSES, THERE HAVE ALSO BEEN FAILURES... BUT NONE MORE POIGNANT THAN THE ONE WHICH DRAWS HIM HERE.
HERE, ON THIS NIGHT ONE YEAR AGO, HE LOST THE WOMAN HE LOVED. *
AND IF HIS SORROW OVER THAT TRAGIC PASSAGE WERE NOT STILL SO FRESH IN HIS MIND, PERHAPS HE TOO COULD PONDER WHAT MIGHT HAVE BEEN...
PERHAPS HE TOO COULD ASK:
WHAT IF GWEN STACY HAD LIVED?
SPIDER-MAN #121-122. -- D/M.
ART ASSIST BY GAFFORD, POPLASKI, ZALME & ALBELO.

THE CHILL NIGHT AIR FRAMES HIS HALTING WORDS AS HE ADDRESSES THE FACE THAT LOOMS BEFORE HIS MIND'S EYE...
HI, GWEN -- IT'S ME. I HAVEN'T FORGOTTEN...
I'VE TRIED TO FORGET YOU, GWEN -- I KNOW YOU'D WANT IT THAT WAY -- I'VE REALLY TRIED.
SOMETIMES I EVEN MANAGED TO GO FOR WEEKS AT A TIME WITHOUT THINKING OF YOU.
THEN I SEE SOMETHING THAT REMINDS ME OF YOU -- SOME LITTLE RESTAURANT WE WENT TO -- SOME "CUTE" PRESENT YOU GAVE ME -- AND THAT'S WHEN IT ALL COMES BACK.
THAT'S WHEN IT STARTS TO HURT.
BUT I CAN LIVE WITH THE HURT, GWENDY.
BECAUSE I DON'T WANT TO FORGET YOU.
I WANT TO REMEMBER IT ALL. THE UNCERTAINTY OF OUR FIRST MEETING. THE FIRST CLUMSY STEPS IN OUR RELATIONSHIP. THE HAPPINESS AND THE PAIN THAT CAME WITH LOVING YOU.
THE JOY WHEN WE WERE ABLE TO FORGET OUR TROUBLES AND JUST BE WITH EACH OTHER.
MOST OF ALL, I WANT TO REMEMBER THE JOY--

BECAUSE IF I
SE THAT, THEN
I'LL HAVE
FT IS THE
ORROR.
IT'S QUITE SIMPLE, WEB-SPINNER...
YOUR PRESENCE IN THIS WORLD HAS BEEN A SOURCE OF CONSTANT AGONY TO ME.
I WISH YOU TO LEAVE IT-- PERMANENTLY.
OR ELSE... GWEN STACY ***DIES!***
"THE GOBLIN ALMOST GOT HIS WISH. A BAD CASE OF THE ***FLU*** HAD ME SO DIZZY I COULD HARDLY KEEP MY BALANCE.
"I KNEW THAT ONCE THE GOBLIN DOPED OUT HOW SICK I REALLY WAS, IT WOULD BE ALL OVER FOR US.
"I'D ONLY HAVE ONE CHANCE. I HAD TO PUT EVERYTHING I HAD LEFT INTO A SINGLE PUNCH.
"IT WASN'T ENOUGH.
GWEN!
NO!

"I WATCHED IN HORROR AS YOU PLUMMETED. THE GOBLIN VANISHED FROM MY THOUGHTS--
"THE ONLY REALITIES WERE YOU *FALLING* AND THAT MURKY RIVER BELOW.
I'VE GOT TO *CATCH* HER--
-- STOP HER FALL BEFORE SHE HITS THE *WATER!*
I'VE GOT TO!
I'VE GOT TO!
"MY WEBBING CAUGH YOUR LEG. I THOUG I HAD DONE IT. I THOUGHT I HAD *WO*
"I HADN'T CONSIDERED WHAT THE *SHOCK* OF THAT SUDDEN FALL COULD *DO* TO SOME-ONE WITHOUT MY OWN SPIDER-STRENGTH.
SPIDER-POWERS, I LOVE YOU!
NOT ONLY AM I THE MOST DASHING HERO ON TWO LEGS--
-- I'M EASILY THE MOST VERSATILE.
WHO ELSE COULD SAVE A FALLING GIRL FROM CERTAIN *DEA--*
GWEN?
HEY, KID--WHAT'S WRONG? DON'T YO UNDERSTAND?
I SAVED YOU--
--YOU CAN'T BE--

I SAVED YOU, HONEY... DON'T YOU SEE?
I saved you...
BUT I DIDN'T SAVE YOU, DID I, GWEN?
LIKE YOUR FATHER-- LIKE MY OWN UNCLE BEN-- THE SPECTRE OF SPIDER-MAN CROSSED YOUR PATH--
--AND BROUGHT YOU DEATH.
I GUESS I CAME HERE TO TELL YOU I'M SORRY-- TO TELL YOU THAT A PART OF ME DIED HERE WITH YOU.
TO TELL YOU THAT NO MATTER WHAT I HAVE WITH ANYONE ELSE, IT'LL NEVER BE AS GOOD AS WHAT I HAD WITH YOU.
I DON'T KNOW WHAT THE FUTURE WILL BRING.
MAYBE SOMEDAY I WILL FIND HAPPINESS.
SOMEHOW.
BUT NO MATTER WHAT HAPPENS TO ME, HONEY, I WANT YOU TO KNOW SOMETHING:
I'LL NEVER FORGET YOU...
... AND I'LL ALWAYS LOVE YOU.
HE IS NOT A HOLLOW MAN, THIS PETER PARKER. HE WILL, INDEED, CARRY THIS GRIEF ALL THE DAYS OF HIS LIFE.
HE WILL NEVER BE ABLE TO ESCAPE THE GNAWING FEELING THAT THERE WAS SOMETHING HE MIGHT HAVE DONE...
THWIP!
...THAT HE IS, AT LEAST IN PART, RESPONSIBLE FOR THIS TRAGEDY...

I AM THE WATCHER-- AND I TOO KNOW SOMETHING OF RESPONSIBILITY. FOR YEARS BEYOND RECKONING, IT HAS BEEN MY RESPONSIBILITY TO OBSERVE AND RECORD THE ETERNAL TABLEAU OF HISTORY ON THE PLANET EARTH.
BUT RECENTLY I LEARNED THAT THERE ARE OTHER EARTHS THAN THAT WHICH EXISTS IN YOUR UNIVERSE... EARTHS WHICH DIVERGE FROM ONE ANOTHER AT CRITICAL POINTS TO CHART ALTERNATE HISTORIES.
EXAMINING THE REALITY OF THESE DIVERGENT EARTHS HAS OFTEN PROVIDED ME INSIGHTS INTO THE MEN OF YOUR WORLD -- FOR THESE WERE THE SAME BEINGS UNTIL THEIR LIVES TOOK OTHER PATHS.
ON YOUR WORLD, THE COSTUMED YOUTH NAMED SPIDER-MAN FEELS REMORSE AT HIS FAILURE TO SAVE THE WOMAN HE LOVED.
BUT IF HE COULD SEE, AS I CAN, THAT A REALITY AWAY GWENDOLYN STACY HAD A DIFFERENT DESTINY-- ONE THAT IRREVOCABLY ALTERED HIS OWN--
--WOULD THAT KNOWLEDGE COMFORT HIM OR EMBITTER HIM?
THAT IS NOT FOR ME TO DECIDE. I FEAR THAT FEW HUMAN MINDS COULD EVEN COPE WITH THE KNOWLEDGE OF THE MULTI-PLICITY OF EXISTENCE.
LET US RETURN TO THE FATEFUL MOMENTS THAT LED, IN ONE REALITY, TO GWEN STACY'S DEATH -- AND WITNESS A WORLD OF DIFFERENCE...

...E GEORGE ...ASHINGTON ...RIDGE!
IT FIGURES OSBORN WOULD PICK SOMETHING NAMED AFTER HIS FAVORITE PRESIDENT.
HE'S GOT THE SAME SORT OF HANGUP FOR DOLLAR BILLS.
SPIDER-MAN! OR SHOULD I SAY-- MISTER PARKER?
I HAVE YOUR WOMAN UP HERE, MY FRIEND--
I TRUST YOU UNDERSTAND WHAT THAT MEANS?
THAT CUTS IT, PUMPKIN BOY.
UP TO NOW, I'VE BEEN REAL FRIENDLY -- CONSIDERING YOUR PROBLEM, AND ALL THAT.
BUT, BUSTER-- WHEN YOU START THREATENING MY GIRL--
-- THE KID GLOVES ARE OFF!
A MOST CHIVALROUS ATTITUDE.
PITY YOU WON'T LIVE TO ENACT IT!
YOU KNOW SOMETHING, GOBLIN?
SPLUNCH
I THINK YOU MEAN IT!

ONCE THE GOBLIN CATCHES ON TO HOW SICK I AM-- I'VE HAD IT!
SO I'VE GOT TO MOVE NOW!
I MAY NOT GET ANOTHER CHANCE!

AND FOR GWENDY'S SAKE--

-- I'VE GOT TO MAKE THIS ONE COUNT!
WHAP

GWEN!
LOOKS LIKE SHE'S IN A STATE OF SHOCK!
I'D BETTER GET HER TO A HOSPITAL!
YOU CURSED INTERLOPER!
YOU'LL NEVER TAKE THAT GIRL ANYWHERE!
SHE'S DOOMED, DO YOU HEAR ME?
WHAK
GWEN!

DOOMED--
AND SO
ARE YOU!
NO!

"FOR ONE FLEETING INSTANT TIME SEEMS CRYSTALLIZED AS A THOUSAND POSSIBLE COURSES OF ACTION FLIT THROUGH SPIDER-MAN'S MIND. HIS FIRST IMPULSE IS TO STOP HER DESCENT WITH HIS CHEMICAL WEB--
"--BUT, EVEN AS HIS MIDDLE FINGERS TOUCH HIS WEB-SHOOTER, THAT NOTION IS DISPELLED BY A TINY MOTE OF CAUTION. THE NEXT MOMENT, THE REALITY WITH WHICH WE ARE FAMILIAR IS NO MORE...

LEG MUSCLES, DON'T FAIL ME NOW! GWENDY'S ONLY CHANCE IS FOR ME TO REACH HER BEFORE SHE HITS--
-- WHICH ISN'T GOING TO BE EASY, WHAT WITH HER HEAD-START!
"HIS POWERFUL LEG MUSCLES PROPELLING HIM DOWNWARD...

"SPIDER-MAN POURS EVERY ERG OF HIS BEING INTO OVERTAKING THE FALLING FIGURE...
I- I'M DOING IT!!

GOT HER!
NOW IF I CAN SNAG THE NEAREST BRIDGE PYLON WITH MY TRUSTY WEB, WE'LL BE HOME FREE!

MY FOE'S ATHLETIC PROWESS IS INCREDIBLE, BUT EVEN HE IS ONLY HUMAN. HE FORGOT TO ALLOW FOR THE WIND CURRENTS--

--AND HIS WEBBING MISSED THE BRIDGE ENTIRELY!

OH, GOD-- WHEN IT MATTERED MOST--

--I BLEW IT!

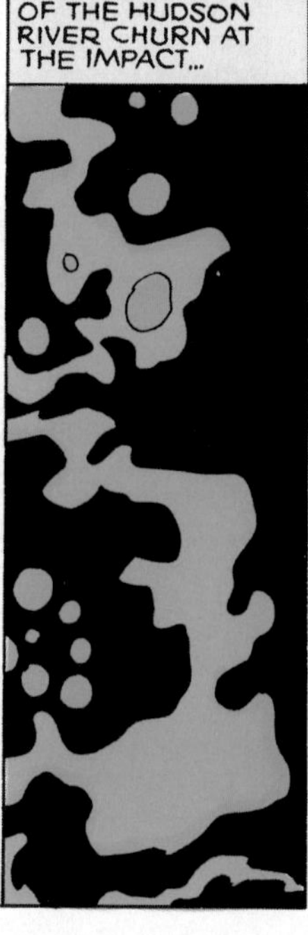

AT LAST--I'VE WON!
A FALL FROM THAT HEIGHT WOULD KILL ANYONE!
THERE'S NO WAY ON EARTH THAT CURSED WALL-CRAWLER COULD HAVE SURVIVED!

AFTER ALL THESE YEARS, PARKER IS OUT OF MY HAIR FOREVER!
AND WITH SPIDER-MAN DEAD--

--THERE'S NOTHING TO PREVENT ME FROM ASSUMING MY RIGHTFUL, IF LONG-DENIED, POSITION--
--AS CRIME-BOSS OF ALL NEW YORK!

"AS A GLEEFUL GOBLIN CLIMBS EASILY INTO THE NIGHT...
...A DARK SHAPE WRITHES BENEATH THE WATER, STRUGGLING FOR THE SURFACE.

FRESH AIR kaff kaff I LOVE YOU!
WE MADE IT, GWENDY! WE MADE IT!
GWENDY?
GWEN!

SH-SHE'S NOT BREATHING!
I'VE GOT TO GET HER TO SHORE!

THERE'S NO TIME TO CALL AN AMBULANCE!
GWEN'S LIFE DEPENDS ON *ME!*
SHE LOOKS SO STILL-- SO *LIFELESS!*
NO! I CAN'T START THINKING LIKE THAT!

SHE'S *GOT* TO MAKE IT!
SHE'S GOT TO!

"HE BENDS TO HIS TASK, HIS HEART POUNDING IN HIS EARS... AN UNSPOKEN PRAYER ON HIS LIPS...
"THIS WOMAN MEANS THE WORLD TO HIM. AND SO HE FORCES HIS LIFE'S BREATH INTO HER LUNGS, HE REALIZES JUST HOW FRAGILE HIS WORLD IS.

"SECONDS STRETCH LABORIOUSLY INTO MINUTES.
"MINUTES LENGTHEN INTO AN ETERNITY.
"HE WILL NOT ACCEPT DEFEAT.
"HE *CANNOT* ACCEPT DEFEAT.
cough cough
PETER?
"HIS WORLD IS WHOLE ONCE MORE... AS HIS GENTLE SOBS ATTEST.
THANK YOU.

JUST RELAX, HONEY. EVERYTHING'S GOING TO BE OKAY NOW. I WON'T LET ANYBODY HURT YOU AGAIN.
PETER? WHAT...

OH MY GOD-- THAT COSTUME!
YOU-- YOU'RE SPIDER-MAN!
THE MAN WHO KILLED MY FATHER!

DIDN'T -- I FORGOT THAT SHE TILL BLAMES SPIDER-MAN FOR E DEATH OF HER FATHER! *
STAY AWAY FROM ME, YOU MURDERER!
*SPIDER-MAN #90. -- D/M.

NO!
YOU'VE GOT TO LISTEN TO ME, GWEN! TURN ME IN TO THE POLICE IF YOU LIKE--
-- BUT LISTEN TO ME!
PLEASE?

ND LISTEN SHE DOES, S A DESPERATE ETER PARKER ARES HIS SOUL O ANOTHER UMAN BEING OR THE FIRST ME SINCE HE SSUMED HIS OUBLE LIFE.
SHE IS NO STRANGER TO PAIN--
--YET THE SORROWS HE DESCRIBES BRING A DULL ACHE TO HER HEART.
SHE TOUCHES HIS HAND SOFTLY...

LATER...
YOUR DAD WAS THE BRAVEST MAN I'VE EVER KNOWN.
HE SAVED THAT BOY, BUT THE RUBBLE DOC OCK KNOCKED OFF THE EDGE OF THE BUILDING HIT **HIM** INSTEAD.
I COULDN'T GET HIM TO A DOCTOR IN TIME.
DID-- DID HE SAY ANYTHING BEFORE HE...

HE CALLED ME PETER.
BUT TH
MEAN

HE KNEW WHO I WAS. HE MUST HAVE KNOWN ALL ALONG, BUT HE NEVER GAVE ME AWAY.
HE ASKED ME TO BE GOOD TO YOU. I PROMISED THAT I WOULD LOVE YOU-- AND CHERISH YOU-- AS LONG AS I LIVED.
I HAVEN'T DONE TOO GOOD A JOB OF THAT UP TO NOW, BUT THAT'S ALL GOING TO CHANGE.

WHAT DO YOU MEAN, PETER?

I DO LOVE YOU, GWEN-- AND MAYBE A CONDEMNED, OUT-OF-THE-WAY PIER ISN'T THE BEST PLACE TO ASK WHAT I SHOULD'VE ASKED A LONG TIME AGO, BUT--
THIS ISN'T GOING TOO WELL, IS IT?

I GUESS WHAT I'M TRYI
TO ASK YOU IN MY TYPIC
STUMBLE-MOUTHED
FASHION IS:
Ms. STACY
WILL YOU
MARRY M

KNOW THERE'S A THOUSAND ASONS YOU SHOULD TURN ME WN, HONEY, SO YOU DON'T E TO ANSWER RIGHT AWAY.
TAKE ALL THE TIME YOU...
YE --
Uh-uh, MR. PARKER. YOU DON'T BACK OUT OF THIS ONE THAT EASILY.
MY ANSWER IS: YES!
YES!

Mmmmm...

WHAT'S THE MATTER, GWEN? YOU'RE SHAKING!
I JUST REMEMBERED. Mr. OSBORN-- THE GREEN GOBLIN -- IS STILL ON THE LOOSE--
--AND HE KNOWS WHO YOU ARE, TOO!

DON'T WORRY ABOUT GOBBY, PRETTY LADY. A CERTAIN WEB-SLINGING PAL OF OURS WILL SETTLE UP WITH HIM.
CAN'T THE POLICE HANDLE HIM?

WISH THEY COULD, UT THE GOBLIN IS AY OUT OF THEIR AGUE. LIKE IT OR OT, THIS IS MY JOB.
AND, BELIEVE ME, GWEN, I'VE NEVER LIKED IT LESS THAN RIGHT NOW--

-- WHEN I'M THIS CLOSE TO MARRYING THE BEST LADY IN THE WHOLE WORLD.
DO WHAT YOU HAVE TO DO, PETER.
I'LL BE WAITING.

BY WAY OF CONTRAST, "WAITING" IS THE LAST THING ON THE TRIUMPHANT GREEN GOBLIN'S MIND.
FOR THAT VERY EVENING, IN SURROUNDINGS SOME-WHAT LESS THAN AUSPICIOUS, HE HAS CALLED...
...A BUSINESS MEETING.
GOBLIN, YOU'RE CRAZY-AND-A-HALF!

WHY SHOULD WE TURN OVER CONTROL OF OUR RACKETS TO YOU--
--A COSTUMED KOOK WHO COMES OUT OF HIDING ONCE A YEAR TO GET HIS BUTT KICKED BY SPIDER-MAN?
YOU'LL LIVE TO REGRET THOSE WORDS, MERRICK.

AS FOR SPIDER-MAN, THAT WALL-CRAWLING DOLT WON'T BE PLAGUING US ANY LONGER. HE'S FINISHED--
--AND IT WAS I WHO KILLED HIM!

THAT'S YOUR STORY, BIG SHOT, AND MAYBE IT WAS GOOD ENOUGH TO GET US DOWN HERE FOR A MEET--
--BUT IT'S GONNA HAVE TO GET A LOT BETTER BEFORE WE'D GO ALONG WITH THE KIND OF DEAL YOU'RE TALKING!
YEAH!

WILL THIS DO, BOYS?
CRIPES! I KNEW SOMETHING LIKE THIS WAS GONNA HAPPEN TONIGHT!
I KNEW IT!

S IMPOSSIBLE! U CAN'T BE ALIVE!
NO ONE COULD HAVE SURVIVED THAT FALL!
NO ONE!
Aw... YOU'RE JUST TRYIN' TO FLATTER ME!
ulp
WHUMPH!
UUNNGGHH!

YOU'LL PAY FOR THAT, SPIDER-MAN!
YOU KNOW WHAT YOU BIGGEST PROBLEM IS, CHUM? YOU'RE SO BLASTED PREDICTABLE
EVERY TIME I KNOCK YOU DOW YOU TRY TO BROI ME WITH THOS SPARKLERS OF YOURS..
YOU THINK MAYBE I HAVEN'T FIGURED OUT HOW TO DUCK AFTER ALL THE FUN TIMES WE'VE HAD TOGETHER --
-- OR THAT I NEVER NOTICED IT TAKES A FEW SECONDS FOR THEM TO RECHARGE AFTER EACH BLAST?
FACE IT, GOBBY! IF YOU CAN'T COME UP WITH A NEW ACT EVERY NOW AND THEN --
-- IT'S TIME TO GET OFF THE STAGE!
OOOFF!
AND WITH THESE LITTLE TOYS SMASHED --
SKASH
-- I THINK WE CAN CALL IT A WRAP!
NOT SO FAST, SPIDER-MAN. MAYBE YOU'RE NOT CONCERNED ABOUT YOUR OWN SAFETY --
-- BUT WHAT HAPPENS TO THOSE YOU LOVE --
-- WHEN THESE ASSOCIATES OF MINE LEARN YOUR TRUE IDENTITY!

YOU ARE POSITIVELY NOT FOR REAL!
AFTER ALL THE GRIEF YOU'VE AL-READY GIVEN ME, YOU HAVE THE GALL TO MAKE A THREAT LIKE THAT?!
HANKS FOR EMINDING ME HAT YOU'RE EVERY T AS SCUMMY AS WANT YOU TO E, GOBLIN...
IT MAKES IT THAT MUCH EASIER FOR ME TO TAKE CARE OF YOU PERMANENTLY!
NOT SO FAST, BOYCHIK! I DON'T GIVE TWO SHAKES ABOUT THE GOBLIN ONE WAY OR THE OTHER--
--BUT, IF HE KNOWS WHO YOU ARE, THEN IT'S WORTH OUR WHILE TO KEEP HIM HEALTHY!
ETTER E-DO YOUR RITHMETIC, CREEP!
BECAUSE EVEN AFTER I'VE PUT YOU AND YOUR BUDDIES IN THE EMERGENCY WARD--
--I'LL STILL HAVE ENOUGH MAD LEFT TO MAKE DARN SURE THE GOBLIN NEVER HARMS ANYONE AGAIN!
DO YOU HEAR ME, OBLIN?!
IT'S UNCANNY! THOSE ARE THE DEADLIEST KILLERS IN THE CITY AND THEY'RE NOT EVEN SLOWING PARKER DOWN!
CAN NOTHING STOP HIM?

NO! THAT KIND OF SPECULATION IS PUREST INSANITY! SPIDER-MAN IS JUST ANOTHER MORTAL FOOL!
ONLY THE GOBLIN IS INVINCIBLE!

AND NOW--WHILE THAT UNWITTING INSECT IS OCCUPIED WITH MY WOULD-BE ALLIES--
--I'LL PROVE IT!

BUT THE GOBLIN'S ASPIRATIONS ASIDE...
THWAK!
HHUUNNFF?!?

BWHOOM!
BLAST! I KEPT ONE EYE ON OSBORN 'CAUSE I EXPECTED HIM TO GO FOR THE BACK SHOT--
--BUT I FORGOT HIS PUMPKIN-BOMBS DON'T HAVE TO HIT THEIR TARGET TO BE EFFECTIVE!
NO SMOKE-SCREEN IS GONNA SAVE HIM FROM ME THIS TIME, THOUGH...

NOT EVEN IF I HAVE TO PUT DOWN A THOUSAND OF THESE CHEAP PUNKS--
--BEFORE I WRAP MY HANDS AROUND NORMAN OSBORN'S SLIMY GREEN THROAT!
HE -- HE CAN'T BE STOPPED!
I'VE GOT TO GET AWAY!

T WHY PROLONG
S AGONY ANY
RTHER? I CAN'T
CAPE SPIDER-
N... AND I WAS
VER MEANT TO!
HILL'S BAK
SEE IT
L SO VERY
ARLY NOW!

THE GODS RAISED ME TO GREATNESS-- REMOVED ME FROM THE SHACKLES OF MY WEAKER SELF-- ONLY TO DASH MY DREAMS OF CONQUEST TO THE DUST!
THE MIGHTY GREEN GOBLIN! AN UNWITTING FOIL IN A GHASTLY COSMIC JEST!
DEAD END
ONE WAY
GORDON SPEAKS

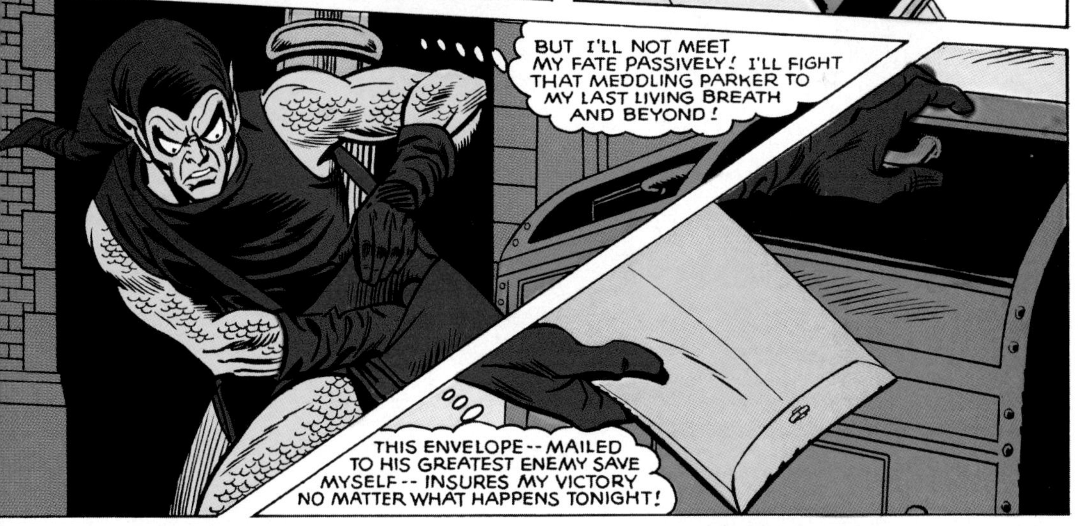
BUT I'LL NOT MEET MY FATE PASSIVELY! I'LL FIGHT THAT MEDDLING PARKER TO MY LAST LIVING BREATH AND BEYOND!
THIS ENVELOPE-- MAILED TO HIS GREATEST ENEMY SAVE MYSELF-- INSURES MY VICTORY NO MATTER WHAT HAPPENS TONIGHT!

LL ME IF YOU CAN,
PIDER-MAN!
ENGEANCE
ILL STILL
BE MINE!

MEANWHILE...
SO MUCH FOR MINDLESS RAGE. THE GOBLIN MADE HIS ESCAPE WHILE I WASTED TIME WITH THESE CREEPS.
BUT MAYBE THAT'S FOR THE BEST. IF I HAD KILLED OSBORN, I WOULDN'T BE ANY BETTER THAN HE IS.
AND I'VE GOT TO BE BETTER THAN THAT--
--FOR GWEN.

ON THE OTHER HAND, I'VE STILL GOT TO FIND OSBORN BEFORE HE CARRIES OUT HIS THREAT TO EXPOSE MY IDENTITY.
WHICH BRINGS ME FULL CIRCLE TO A PROBLEM I DON'T EVEN WANT TO THINK ABOUT...
NAMELY, HOW DO I PROTECT THE PEO I CARE ABOUT FROM A MANIAC LIKE THE GREEN GOBLIN WHEN HE'S THE FATHER OF MY BEST FRIEND?

IT IS NOT MUCH LATER WHEN THE FIRST RAYS OF THE DAWN PENETRATE THE LUXURIOUS TOWNHOUSE OF NORMAN OSBORN.
INSIDE, HIS SON HAS JUST LEARNED THE TERRIFYING SECRET OF THE GREEN GOBLIN.
AND NOW, HIS SOUL SHAKEN TO THE CORE, HARRY OSBORN TRIES SO HARD TO UNDERSTAND...

WE DON'T HAVE MUCH TIME, HARRY. SPIDER-MAN WILL BE HERE BEFORE LONG AND WE HAVE TO BE READY FOR HIM.
PARKER ***MUST*** DIE -- OR WE'LL ***NEVER*** BE SAFE!
IT DOESN'T ***HAVE*** TO BE THAT WAY, DAD!

EVEN IF HE ***IS*** WH YOU SAY HE IS, PETER PARKER IS STILL OUR FRIEND I KNOW HE WON TRY TO HURT US--
-- IF ONLY YOU'L GIVE UP BEING THE GOBLIN!

YOU SPINELESS JELLYFISH! I GIVE YOU THE CHANCE TO STAND BESIDE ME AGAINST MY MOST HATED FOE--
--TO SHARE IN THE ALMOST LIMITLESS POWER OF THE GREEN GOBLIN--
-- AND YOU WANT ME TO ***GIVE IT UP?!***
PLEASE, DAD! I ONLY WANT TO--

SHUT UP, YOU SNIVELLING WEAKLING!
WOK!
AGGHH!

ELL ME,
SBORN,
IS IT
YERYBODY
DU HATE--
--OR ONLY THE PEOPLE WHO CARE ABOUT YOU?
PIDER-MAN!

CONGRATULATIONS, NORMIE! YOU JUST PASSED RECOGNITION 101!
YOU WERE A FOOL TO COME HERE, PARKER!

IO ONE CAN
EFEAT ME
N MY HOME
ROUNDS!
THIS ISN'T GOING TO SOLVE ANYTHING, DAD!
YOU'VE GOT TO LET US HELP YOU!
GET AWAY FROM ME, YOU GUTLESS COWARD--

-OR YOU'LL DIE WITH YOUR
AEDDLING FRIEND!
ZASP!
STAY BACK, HARRY! WHEN YOUR FATHER IS THE GOBLIN, HE'S MORE DANGEROUS THAN YOU CAN IMAGINE!

YOU SURPRISE ME, WALL-CRAWLER!
I'M OVERWHELMED BY YOUR SHOW
OF RESPECT FOR A SUPERIOR FOE!
PERHAPS I'LL EVEN GRANT YOU THE MERCY OF A RELATIVELY PAINLESS DEATH!

OSBORN, YOU ARE ELEVEN KINDS OF CRAZY--
THWIP
THWIP
NOOOOO!
--AND ALL OF 'EM ARE WEARIN' PRETTY THIN!

SPAM

ON YOUR FEET, GOBLIN.
I WON'T LET YOU KILL HIM!

I DON'T CARE WHAT HE'S DONE!
NO!

SWAK
I-- I STRUCK OUT INSTINCTIVELY!
DIDN'T REALIZE IT WAS HARRY!
UNGHHH!

ARRY--?
THAT MASKED CRETIN! IN HIS CONCERN FOR MY WORTHLESS OFFSPRING, HE'S FORGOTTEN ABOUT ME!
HE'S GIVEN ME AN OPPORTUNITY TO PLAY MY LAST--AND DEADLIEST--GAMBIT!

THIS DEVICE WILL REDUCE MY TOWNHOUSE TO A SMOLDERING RUIN! AND THOUGH I'LL NOT SURVIVE THAT MOMENT--
--NEITHER WILL PARKER!

GET YOUR ANDS OFF ME, PIDER-MAN!
MY SON--STANDING UP TO PARKER?!
HE DOESN'T STAND A CHANCE!

DON'T YOU SEE? HE'S MY FATHER--THE ONLY WAY YOU'RE GONNA GET TO HIM AGAIN IS OVER MY DEAD BODY!
HARRY, PLEASE...!
HE'S RISKING HIS LIFE FOR ME!

OR ME!
WHAT HAVE I DONE?!
HARRY?

WHAT'S GOING ON HERE? OSBORN'S BACK TO NORMAL, BUT HE REMEMBERS BEING THE GREEN GOBLIN!
DAD! IT'S *YOU!* IT'S REALLY *YOU!*
AFTER EVERYTHIN I'VE SAID-- EVERY THING I'VE DONE THE GOBLIN-- YOU STUCK BY ME WH IT MATTERED MOST!
YOU-- YOU'RE THE BRAVEST S A MAN COULD EVER ASK FO HARRY!

IT'S LIKE SOME KIND OF MIRACLE!
WHEN ALL MY POWER WAS USELESS, IT WAS A SON'S LOVE FOR HIS FATHER THAT CURED NORMAN OSBORN.
AND, THIS TIME, I'VE GOT A FEELING HE'S GOING TO STAY CURED.
BUT IS THAT MY DECISION TO MA
I... *uh*... HATE TO BE A SP SPORT, HARRY, BUT I'M AFRAID YOUR DAD ISN'T OUT OF THIS YET.
I KNOW TH SPIDER-M

WE KNOW THAT, PETE, BUT WE NEED A LITTLE TIME TO KIND OF SORT THINGS OUT.
YOU'LL NEVER REGRET GIVING US THAT TIME.
YOU'VE GOT MY *WORD* ON IT.
SO

YOU'LL ALWAYS BE WELCOME IN OUR HOUSE, PETE, BUT RIGHT NOW, IF YOU DON'T MIND--
--I'D LIKE TO BE ALONE WITH MY DAD.
YOU GOT IT, PAL.

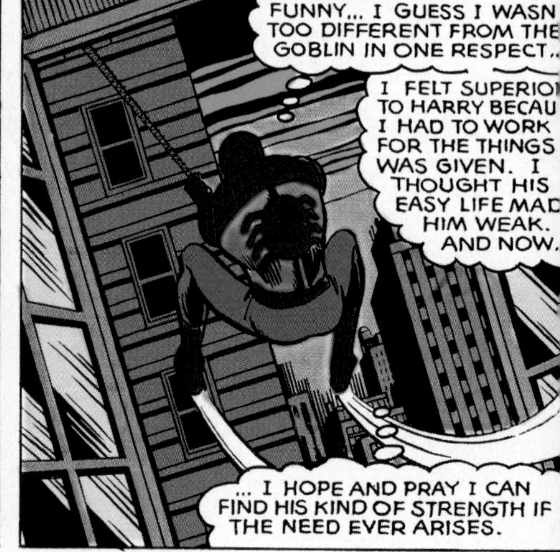
FUNNY... I GUESS I WASN TOO DIFFERENT FROM THE GOBLIN IN ONE RESPECT..
I FELT SUPERIO TO HARRY BECAU I HAD TO WORK FOR THE THINGS WAS GIVEN. I THOUGHT HIS EASY LIFE MAD HIM WEAK. AND NOW.
... I HOPE AND PRAY I CAN FIND HIS KIND OF STRENGTH IF THE NEED EVER ARISES.

SO MAYBE IT ISN'T MY DECISION, BUT I'M MAKING IT ANYWAY! THE OSBORNS HAVE SUFFERED ENOUGH...
THEY DESERVE A CHANCE TO GET IT TOGETHER!
KRUPP
CE IT, WEB-SLINGER--
--YOU'RE A SUCKER FOR HAPPY ENDINGS!
AND A SHORT TIME LATER...
I'M HOME, DEAR.
PETER!

I'VE BEEN YOUR BASIC NERVOUS WRECK SINCE YOU SWUNG OFF AFTER THE GOBLIN!
WERE YOU ABLE TO STOP HIM WITHOUT--

ELAX, HONEY. THE GREEN GOBLIN ILL NEVER HURT ANYBODY EVER GAIN--
--AND NORMAN OSBORN IS JUST FINE, TOO!
HEN THERE ISN'T NYTHING TO REVENT US FROM ETTING MARRIED, IS THERE, r. PARKER?
NOW THAT YOU MENTION IT, LOVE OF MY LIFE, THERE IS ONE MORE DANGEROUS JOB WE HAVE TO HANDLE FIRST...

"...AND I DON'T MIND TELLING YOU...
"...JUST THINKING ABOUT IT HAS ME SCARED RIGHT DOWN TO MY SOCKS!"

Uh... AUNT MAY? THERE'S SOMETHING I'D LIKE TO... I MEAN... THERE'S SOMETHING WE'D LIKE TO...
LOOK AT THE POOR DEAR TREMBLING! I HOPE HE DOESN'T TAKE TOO LONG TO TELL ME WHAT'S SO OBVIOUSLY ON HIS AND GWENDOLYN'S MINDS...
WE HAVE A WEDDING TO PLAN!

AND, WITH A VITALITY THAT BELIES HER YEARS, MAY PARKER PROCEEDS TO DO JUST THAT...
WHY SO GLUM, PARKER?
DON'T TELL ME THAT THE BLUSHING GROOM-TO-BE HAS A CASE OF THE DREADED "WEDDING-DAY JITTERS"?

IT'S THIS TELEGRAM, FLASH. I GUESS I'M JUST DOWN BECAUSE HARRY AND MARY JANE CAN'T BE HERE TODAY.
YEAH... HARRY CALLED ME YESTERDAY FROM THAT CLINIC THEY TOOK HIS DAD TO.
THEY WANTED TO BE HERE, PETE.

BUT HARRY'S FATHER NEEDS HIM-- AND MJ FIGURED BOTH OF THEM COULD USE A FRIEND NEARBY.
MAYBE GWEN AND I SHOULD HAVE WAITED...

AND MAYBE I SHOULD TAKE O MORE SHOT AT CONVINCING A CERTAIN GORGEOUS BLONDE THAT JOCKS MAKE BETTER HUSBANDS THAN PUNY BIO-CHEM MAJORS...
HEY! I WAS ONLY KIDDING-

-- UNLESS, OF COURSE, YOU DON'T GET YOUR TUXEDOED BUTT DOWN TO THAT CHAPEL IN ABOUT FIVE MINUTES!
I'M WARNING YOU NOW, THOMPSON!

AFTER THE CEREMONY, I'M GONNA HAVE MY WIFE DUSTED FOR FINGERPRINTS!

SECONDS LATER...
I SHOULD HEAD DOW STAIRS, BUT I HAVE T TALK TO GWEN ONE MORE TIME BEFORE THE CEREMONY.
SHE SHOULD BE ALONE NOW.

TER! DON'T YOU KNOW IT'S BAD
CK FOR THE GROOM TO SEE THE
IDE BEFORE THE CEREMONY?
ITS EVEN WORSE LUCK TO LEAVE HIM HANGING OUTSIDE A WINDOW WHERE SOME TRIGGER-HAPPY COP MIGHT SPOT HIM!
I SEE... THIS IS WHERE YOU GIVE ME A CHANCE TO BACK OUT BECAUSE IT WON'T BE EASY BEING MARRIED TO SPIDER-MAN.
I...

STEN TO ME,
TER PARKER:
HEN WE GO DOWNSTAIRS IN A
W MINUTES, THAT'S FOR EVERY-
ODY ELSE. THIS IS FOR US:

I LOVE YOU VERY MUCH...
...AND I'M GOING TO MAKE YOU VERY HAPPY FOR A VERY LONG TIME.
GWEN...
HUSH NOW, MAN OF MINE, AND GET OUT OF HERE. I'VE GOT A WEDDING TO GET READY FOR!

ND SO...
IN A WORD, FRIEND: WOW.
OU KNOW
, Mr. T.
LOOK AT JOE ROBERTSON BEAM! IT'S AS IF IT WERE HIS OWN DAUGHTER HE WAS GIVING AWAY TODAY!

COB - AREN'T THEY THE MOST
EAUTIFUL COUPLE YOU EVER SAW?
ONLY BEN COULD BE HERE...
NED... HAVE YOU SEEN Mr. JAMESON?
DON'T WORRY ABOUT JONAH, BETTY.
THE OLD SKINFLINT IS PROBABLY OUT LOOKING FOR THE CHEAPEST PRESENT HE CAN FIND.

AND THEN... WITH WORDS THAT HAVE EVER EXPRESSED, FAITHFULLY IF NOT ADEQUATELY, THE SANCTITY OF THIS MOMENT...
... THEY ARE JOINED IN HOLY WEDLOCK.
THEY HAVE SHARED MUCH OF THE HARDSHIP TO WHICH MANKIND HAS ALWAYS BEEN HEIR.
NOW THEY SHARE A HAPPINESS THAT REDUC ANY AND ALL SUCH SORROWS TO INSIGNIFICANCE...
... A HAPPINESS THAT IS AS TOTAL...
... AS IT IS TRAGICALLY SHORT-LIVED!
THAT'S HIM, MEN! THAT'S PETER PARKER!
ALSO KNOWN AS SPIDER-MAN!
OKAY, MEN -- YOU HEARD JAMESON. BE READY.
YOU'VE GONE BANANAS, JONAH! WHERE DO YOU GET OFF BUSTING UP MY WEDDING THIS WAY?
YOU CAN CUT THE CUTE ACT, PARKER! IT WON'T WORK ANYMORE!
THIS PACKAGE THE GOBLIN SENT ME CONTAINS ALL THE PROOF I NEED-- AND ON THE BASIS OF THAT PROOF--
--THESE OFFICERS HAVE A WARRANT FO YOUR ARREST!

PETER? AT AWFUL DER- AN?
UUNNHH...
CAN'T BE! IT ST CAN'T B--

SHE'S FAINTED! GIVE HER SOME ROOM!
I THINK IT'S WORSE THAN THAT, SON!
HOLY -- SOMEBODY GET A DOCTOR!

AUNT MAY!
LOOK OUT, SARGE! HE'S GONNA--
WHOOF
HE IS SPIDER-MAN!
SHEESH! HE TOSSED THEM ASIDE LIKE THEY WERE PAPER DOLLS!

RAW YOUR WEAPON, INGERSOL! HIS GUY IS AS DANGEROUS S JAMESON CLAIMED!
HEY--COME ON! EASY ON THE TRIGGER FINGERS!
GIVE THE MAN A CHANCE TO EXPLAIN!

PETE-- YOU CAN'T LET THOSE GUN-HAPPY CLOWNS START SHOOTING IN HERE! SOME-BODY'LL GET KILLED!
YOU'VE GOT TO GIVE YOURSELF UP!

GIVE MYSELF UP?!

NOT ON YOUR LIFE, BOYS!
AW, PETE!
SARGE?
SHOOT THAT SUCKE DOWN, ROOKIE

TAKE GOOD CARE OF MY LADIES, Mr. T.
HAD TO GET OUT OF THERE SO THAT AUNT MAY COULD GET THE MEDICA ATTENTION SHE NEEDS...
NO MATTE WHAT HAPPENS T ME, SHE HAS TO PULL THROUGH.
SH HA TO
KRASH

STOP SHOOTING, YOU MINDLESS FOOLS! CAN'T YOU SEE THAT HE'S GONE?
HOW MANY DECENT PEOPLE DO YOU HAVE TO HURT BEFORE YOU CALL IT A DAY?
BAM

DIDJA SEE THE WAY THAT WALL-CRAWLING COWARD TOOK OFF? THIS IS THE GREATEST DAY OF MY LIFE!
HOW COULD YOU DO SUCH A THING, JONAH
DON'T GO SHEDDING ANY TEARS OVER PARKER, ROBBIE THAT LITTLE CREEP'S BEEN PLAYING US ALL FOR SUCKERS

EVERY TIME I HANDED HIM A CHECK, HE MUST'VE FELT LIKE LAUGHING IN MY FACE!
IT WAS NEVER THAT WAY MAN! YOU WEREN'T JUST A BOSS TO PETER AND YOU KNOW IT!
WELL, NOW IT'S MY TURN TO LAUGH!
AS SPIDER-MAN, HE'S SAVED YOUR SKIN A DOZEN TIMES OR MORE

I WAS AFRAID YOU'D GO SOFT ON ME, ROBBIE. THAT'S WHY I WAITED UNTIL YOU LEFT TO PUT THIS ON THE PRESSES.
Daily BUGLE
BUGLE PUBLISHER
POSES SPIDER-MAN
JOHN GORDON LECTURES ON ART
DON'T YOU REALIZE WHAT THIS MEANS, JONAH? EVERY VILLAIN HE EVER DEFEATED WILL BE GOING AFTER PETER NOW.
HE'LL NEVER KNOW A MOMENT'S PEACE AGAIN!

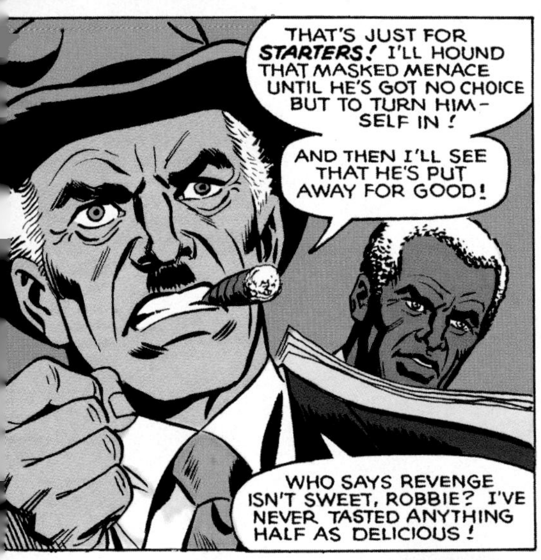
THAT'S JUST FOR STARTERS! I'LL HOUND THAT MASKED MENACE UNTIL HE'S GOT NO CHOICE BUT TO TURN HIM-SELF IN!
AND THEN I'LL SEE THAT HE'S PUT AWAY FOR GOOD!
WHO SAYS REVENGE ISN'T SWEET, ROBBIE? I'VE NEVER TASTED ANYTHING HALF AS DELICIOUS!

REVENGE ALWAYS HAS A PRICE, JONAH--
HUH?
--AND IN THIS CASE, IT'S ONE CITY EDITOR!
I CAN'T CONTINUE WORKING FOR SOMEONE CAPABLE OF THE HEART-LESS THING YOU'VE DONE HERE TODAY.

WE'RE IN THIS TOGETHER, GWEN. FIRST, WE'LL SEE WHAT WE CAN DO FOR MAY PARKER--
--THEN WE'LL FIND SOME WAY TO HELP PETER.
COME ON, LADY-- IT'S TIME TO BE STRONG.
TH--THANKS, Mr. ROBERTSON.

WE'LL GO TO THE OTHER PAPERS-- LET THEM KNOW THE WHOLE STORY-- WHAT KIND OF MAN PETER PARKER IS--
--AND BY THE TIME WE'RE THROUGH, THEY WON'T EVEN BE USING THE DAILY BUGLE TO WRAP FISH IN!

Epilogue

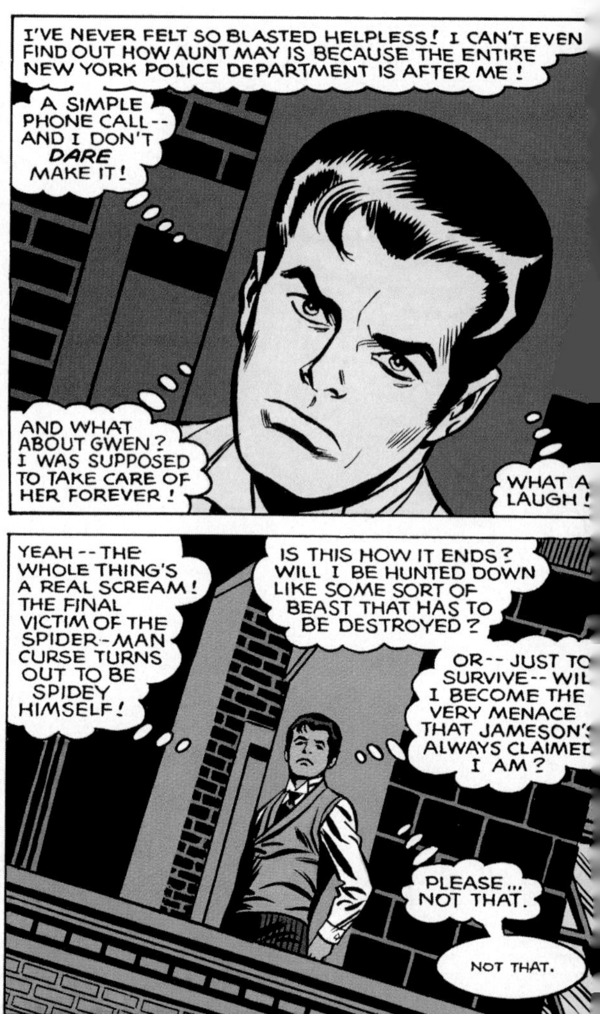

AND SO, A TROUBLED MAN STANDS AND BROODS, WITH THE FATE OF SOCIETY AT STAKE. WHAT WILL HIS DECISION BE?

ONLY TIME WILL TELL.

TIME... AND THE WATCHER.

END

TWO-GUN KID
IN
JUST DESERTS
AMBUSH!
RODE INTO DEVIL'S CAULDRON TRACKING JOHN BAKER...
...AND LOOKS LIKE I GOT ALL OF THE UNLUCKY THIRTEEN GANG IN THE BARGAIN.
TAKE OUT KREBBS FIRST--
--HE'S TOO GOOD A RIFLEMAN TO LET LIVE.
THUNDER, BLESS HER, KEEPS AHEAD OF EVERY BULLET--
--SAVE ONE.
ZPANG
ZPANG

SHE BUCKS HARD.
KPOOM
KPOOM
JUST RIDE IT, MATT.
AND ABOVE ALL...
...KEEP SHOOTING,
KPOOM
KPOOM
GUNFIRE AND A SCREAMIN' MARE --
--ALL IT TAKES TO SEND THE PROVISIONS AND TRANSPORT STAMPEDING BACK TOWARDS TOMBSTONE.

HEY SAY A DAY IN EVIL'S CAULDRON LONE CAN KILL A MAN.
KPOOM
KPOOM
NO TIME TO THINK ABOUT THAT.
'CAUSE A BULLET'LL KILL YOU...
...FAR QUICKER THAN HEAT AND THE SU--
YAHHHH!

BAKER!
HE MUSTIVE BEEN THROWN FROM HIS HORSE DURING THE RUSH.
DON'T EVEN THINK ABOUT IT.
GIVE ME A REASON NOT TO.
YOU'RE JUST GONNA SHOOT ME ANYWAYS, AREN'T YA, KID?
I TOLD THE LAW IN TOMBSTONE THAT I'D BRING YOU IN ALIVE.
BUT I RECKON I COULD DO IT THE OTHER WAY, IF'N I HAD TO.

FOURTEEN OF US CAME INTO THE CAULDRON.
TWO LEAVE.
AS WE START OUR TREK BACK TO TOWN I SCOPE THE BARREN PLANE IN FRONT OF US.
CHURCH SPIRE'S THE ONLY THING IN TOMBSTONE OVER TWO STORIES. ABOUT FOUR HOURS AGO, ON THE WAY OUT, I SAW IT SINK INTO THE HORIZON.
AND THAT WAS ON HORSEBACK.

IT HAS TO BE NOON. SUN'S RIGHT OVER-HEAD.
COULD REALLY USE THE SHADE OF MY HAT'S BRIM... BUT I DON'T DARE LOWER A PISTOL, EVEN FOR A SECOND.
AS THE HOURS GO BY, BAKER STARTS PLAYING A GAME WITH ME.
KEEPS CHANGIN' THE PACE.
GETTING FAR AHEAD.
OR DANGEROUSLY CLOSE.
THE DANCE HE'S MAKING ME DO IS TAKING ITS TOLL ON MY BUM LEG.
LOST LOTS OF BLOOD.
GETTING DIZZY.
CAN'T GO ANY FURTHER.
I USE THE PISTOL TO MOTION HIM ONWARDS.
THEY FEEL LIKE A HUNDRED POUNDS EACH.
GET UP.
I CAN'T AFFORD TO STOP, NOT WITH THIS LEG. MIGHT NOT BE ABLE TO START AGAIN.

KAFF
HANDFUL OF SAND, HE WAS FAK--
AAAGH!
WHAT NOW, MASKED MAN?
SEE, I GOT THE GUNS NOW!
KAKRAK

IT'S TWO MORE LEAGUES TILL WE HIT THE EDGE OF TOMBSTONE.
WE'LL MAKE IT BY SUNSET.
HOTEL
SALOON
JAIL
WELL, I'LL BE...!
SAID YOU'D BRING IN BAKER, KID, AND YA STUCK T'YOUR WORD!

SO WHERE'S THE REST OF THE UNLUCKY THIRTEEN?
KID BLEW 'EM ALL TO BLAZES.

AND THEN YOU MARCHED HIM CLEAR 'CROSS THE DESERT?
YUP.

HAHAHA
HAHAH
WHAT'S SO DANG FUNNY?

BOY, THAT THERE'S THE TWO-GUN KID.
HE'S ONLY GOT TWELVE BULLETS!
CLICK
CLICK
THE END.

ing the 1970s, Gil Kane became Marvel Comics' premier cover artist, penciling dreds of covers. Kane most enjoyed his work on Marvel's western line, where he had greatest freedom to experiment and the often-rare opportunity to ink his own work.

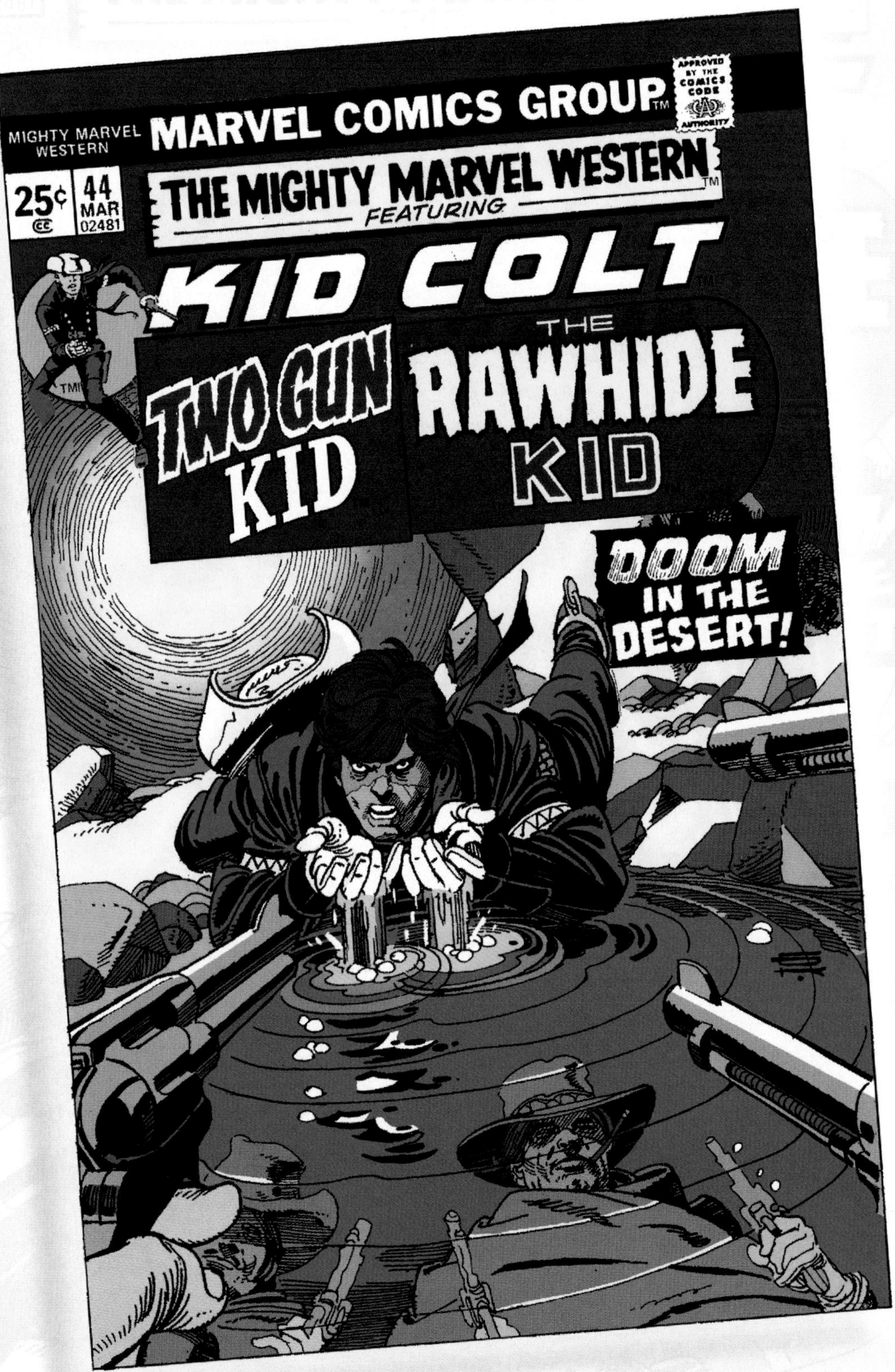

Of them all, *Mighty Marvel Western #44* was Kane's personal career favorite.

WESTERN GUNFIGHTERS
MARVEL COMICS GROUP
APPROVED BY THE COMICS CODE AUTHORITY
25¢
31 SEPT
02495
WESTERN GUNFIGHTERS FEATURING
KID COLT
GUN-SLINGER
APACHE KID
BACK OFF, SMITTY! I CAN'T FIGHT AN UNARMED MAN!
BUT I'M NOT UNARMED, KID!
MY FISTS AND MY HAMMER ARE THE ONLY WEAPONS I NEED!
WITHOUT HIS SIX-GUNS, CAN EVEN KID COLT SURVIVE
HAVOK HAND-TO-HAND!

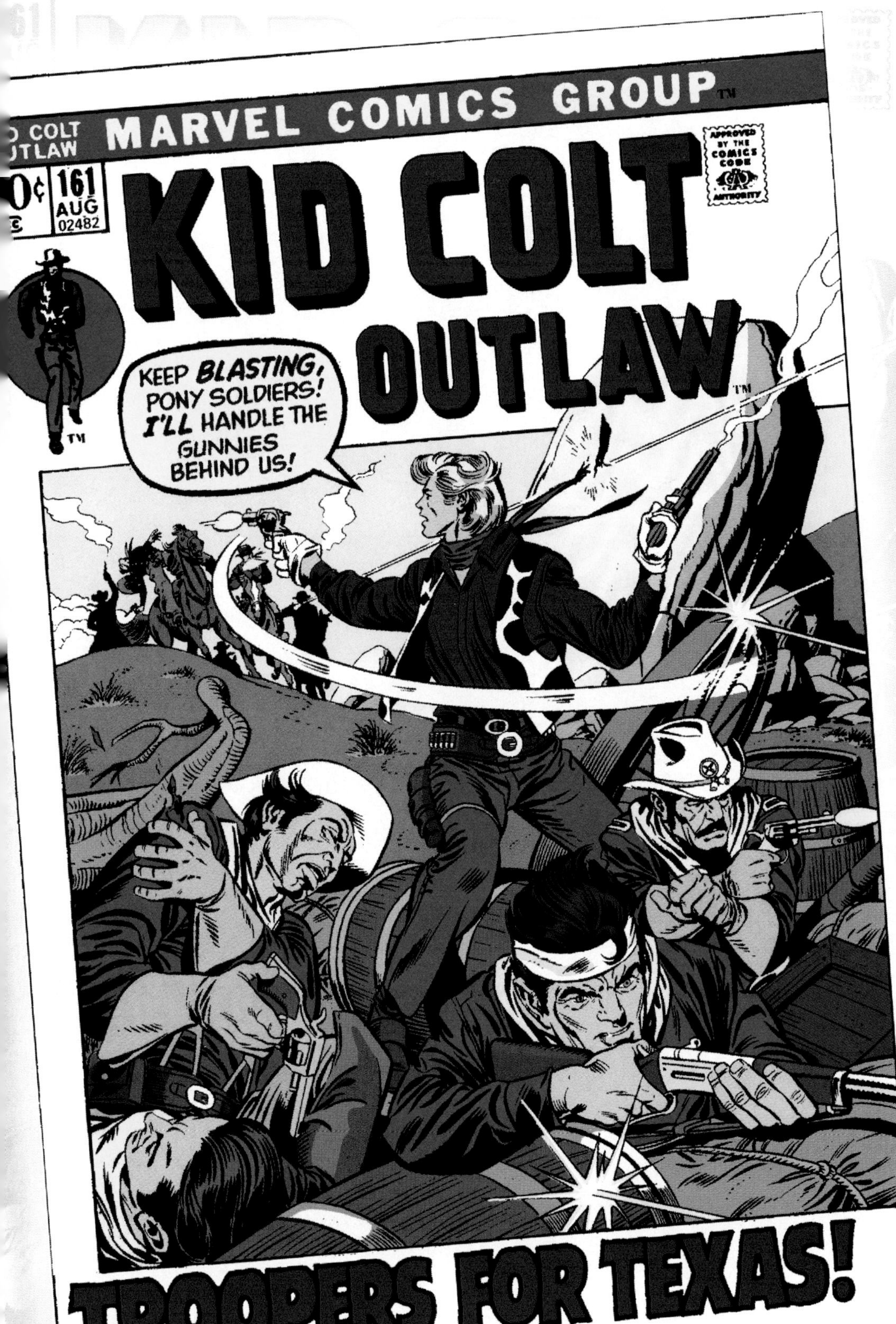

MARVEL COMICS GROUP

TROOPERS FOR TEXAS!

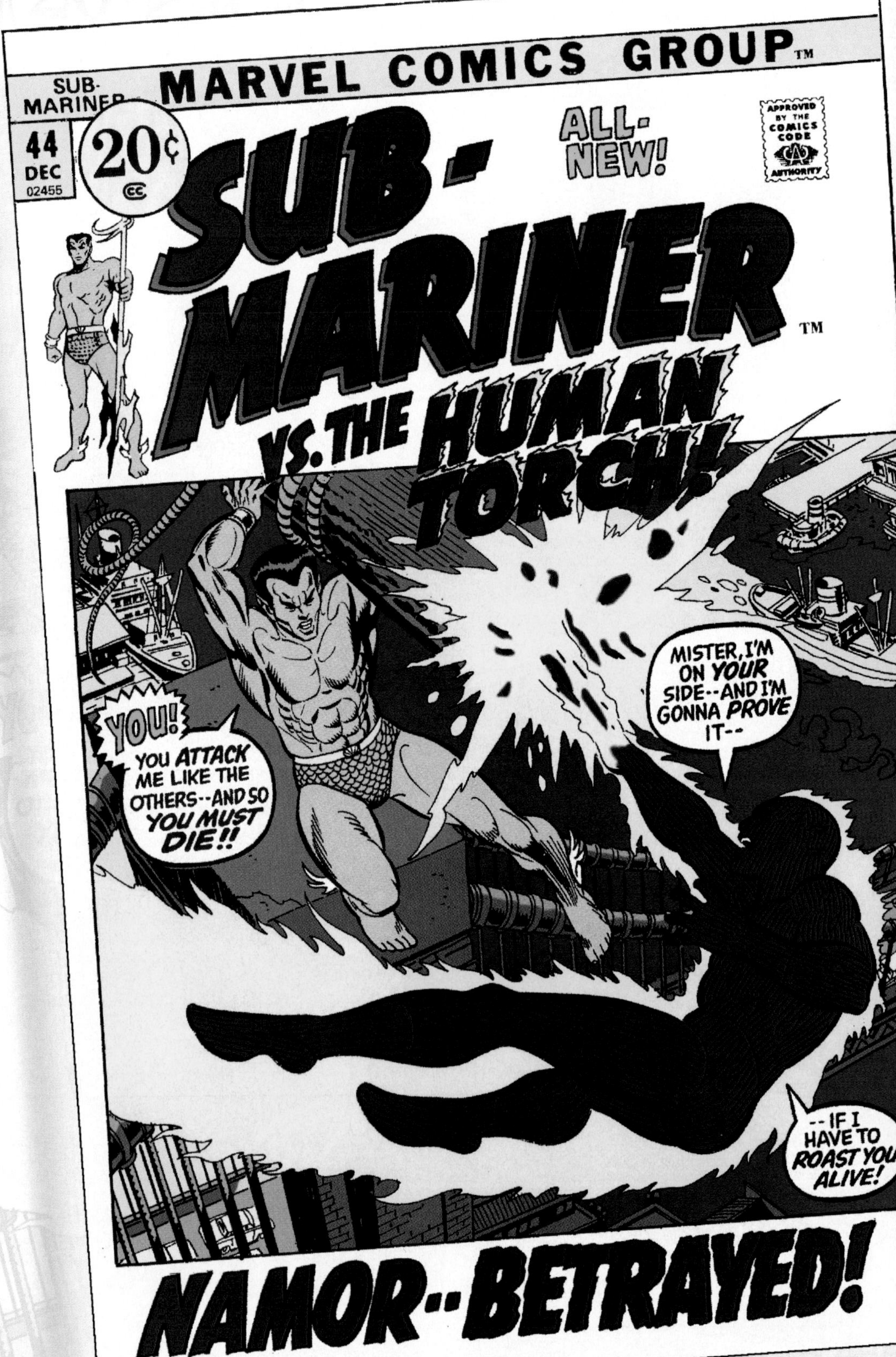

MARVEL COMICS GROUP™
SUB-MARINER
44
DEC
02455
20¢
CC
ALL-NEW!
APPROVED BY THE COMICS CODE AUTHORITY
SUB-MARINER™
VS. THE HUMAN TORCH!
YOU! YOU ATTACK ME LIKE THE OTHERS--AND SO YOU MUST DIE!!
MISTER, I'M ON YOUR SIDE--AND I'M GONNA PROVE IT--
--IF I HAVE TO ROAST YOU ALIVE!
NAMOR--BETRAYED!

MARVEL COMICS GROUP™

APPROVED BY THE COMICS CODE AUTHORITY

CAPTAIN MARVEL

23 NOV 02460

CAPTAIN MARVEL

RICK! WAKE UP! YOU MUST FREE ME TO FIGHT-- BEFORE IT'S TOO LATE!

IT-- IT'S ALREADY TOO LATE!

MEGATON IS HERE!!

BEWARE THE LIVING H-BOMB!

Gil Kane's definitive contribution as a comic artist and storyteller lay in challenging camera angles and fluid depiction of movement. The following layouts f *What If? #3* and *Marvel Premiere #2* present an inside look at Ka creative process as he designed and laid out the comic-art page.

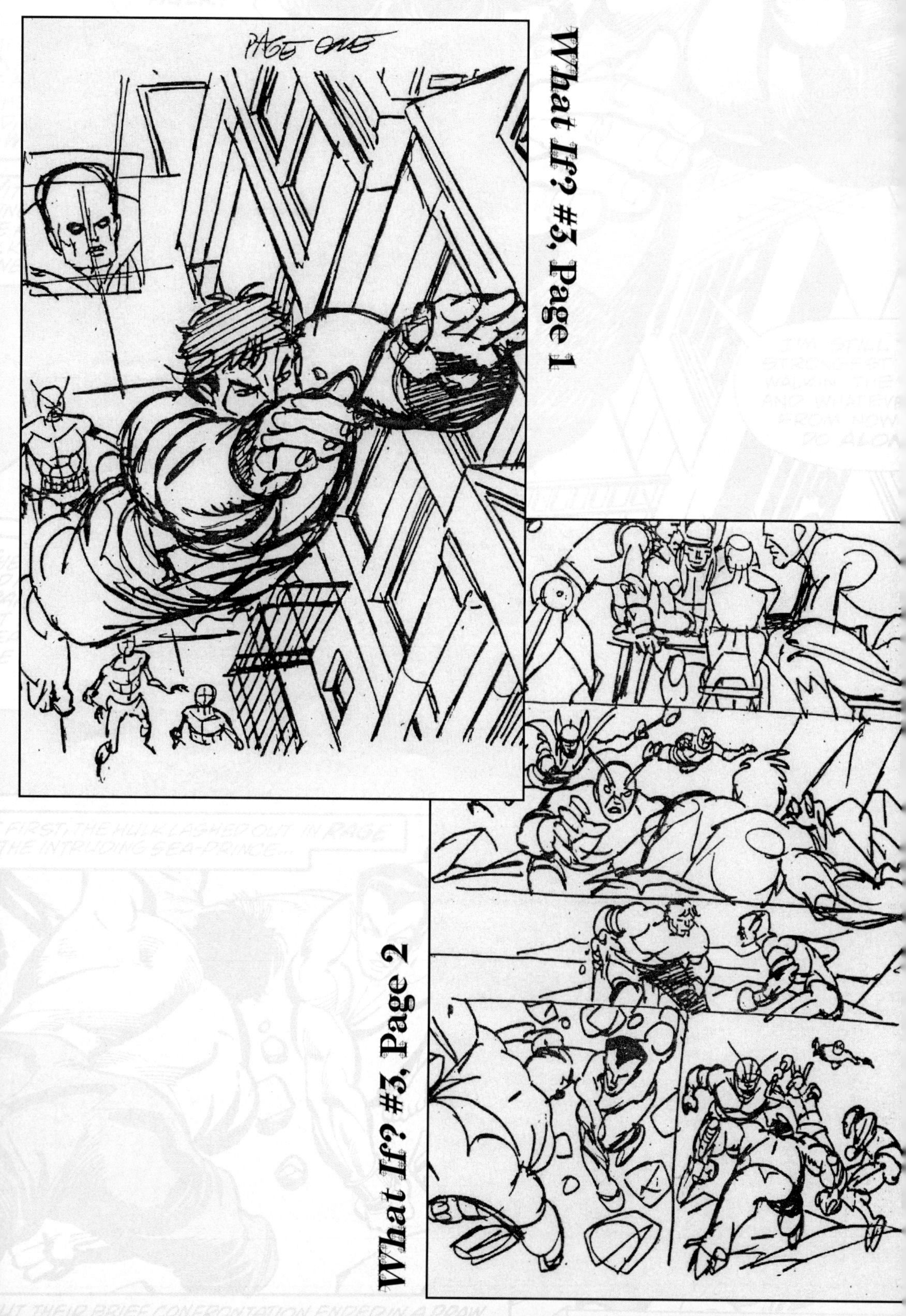

What If? #3, Page 1

What If? #3, Page 2

What If? #3, Page 7

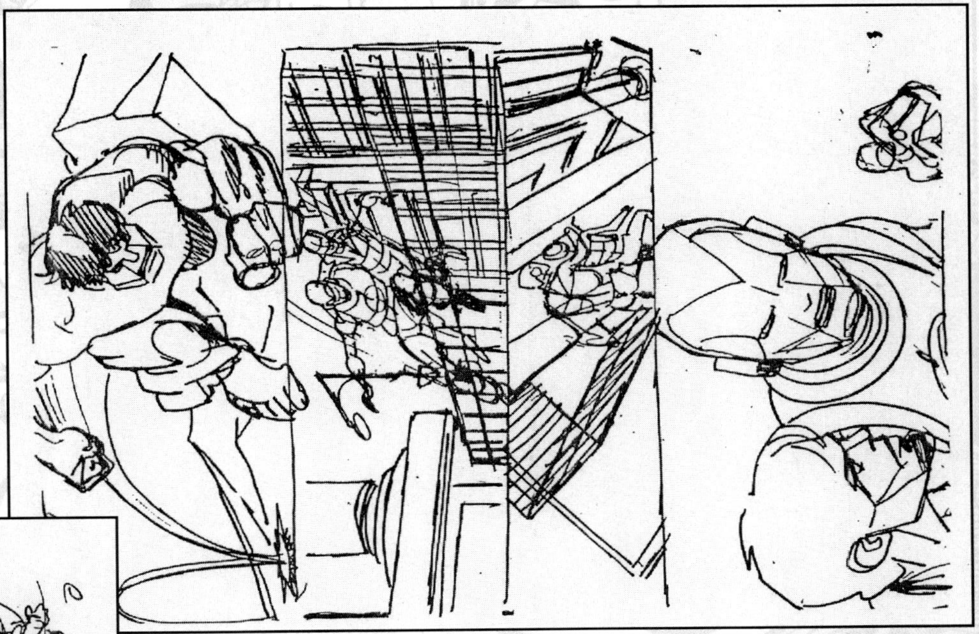

What If? #3, Page 8

What If? #3, Page 15

What If? #3, Page 16

What If? #3, Page 23

What If? #3, Page 24

Marvel Premiere #2, Page 3

Marvel Premiere #2, Page 4

Amazing Spider-Man #123, Page Five

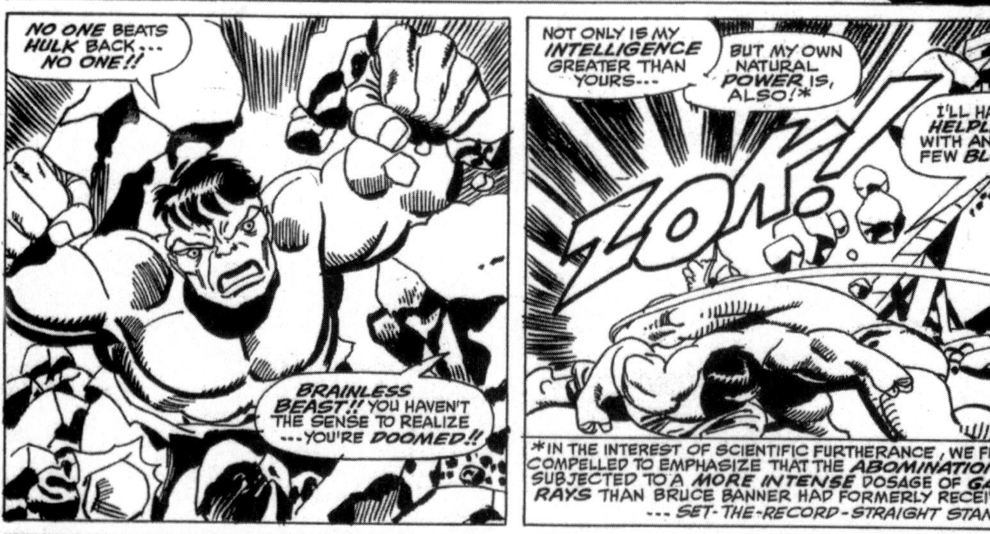

Tales to Astonish #80, Page Eigh

Marvel Comics Presents #116, Page Three

Marvel Comics Presents #116, Page S

Marvel Comics Presents #116, Page Seven

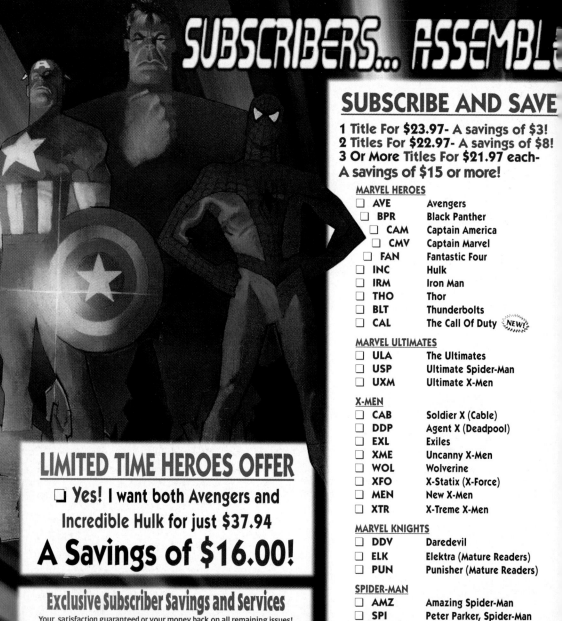